LAW, CRIME AND LAW ENFORCEMENT

CONSPIRATORIAL CRIMES AND RELATED FEDERAL CRIMINAL LAW

Law, Crime and Law Enforcement

Additional books in this series can be found on Nova's website under the Series tab.

Additional E-books in this series can be found on Nova's website under the E-book tab.

Criminal Justice, Law Enforcement and Corrections

Additional books in this series can be found on Nova's website under the Series tab.

Additional E-books in this series can be found on Nova's website under the E-book tab.

LAW, CRIME AND LAW ENFORCEMENT

CONSPIRATORIAL CRIMES AND RELATED FEDERAL CRIMINAL LAW

LESTER C. WRIGHT
AND
JOSEPH C. MILLER
EDITORS

nova publishers
New York

For permission to use material from this book please contact us:
Telephone 631-231-7269; Fax 631-231-8175
Web Site: http://www.novapublishers.com

Additional color graphics may be available in the e-book version of this book.

Library of Congress Cataloging-in-Publication Data

ISBN: 978-1-62618-426-8

Published by Nova Science Publishers, Inc. † New York

Contents

PREFACE

Terrorists, drug traffickers, mafia members, and corrupt corporate executives have one thing in common: most are conspirators subject to federal prosecution. Federal conspiracy laws rest on the belief that criminal schemes are equally or more reprehensible than are the substantive offenses to which they are devoted. The essence of conspiracy is an agreement of two or more persons to engage in some form of prohibited misconduct. The crime is complete upon agreement, although some statutes require prosecutors to show that at least one of the conspirators has taken some concrete steps or committed some overt act in furtherance of the scheme. There are dozens of federal conspiracy statutes. This book examines conspiratorial crimes and related federal criminal law with a focus on the federal Racketeer Influenced and Corrupt Organization (RICO) provision of the Organized Crime Control Act of 1970; money laundering and the 18 U.S.C. 1956 statute; mail and wire fraud; and an overview of federal criminal law.

Chapter 1 - Zacarias Moussaoui, members of the Colombian drug cartels, members of organized crime, and some of the former Enron executives have at least one thing in common: they all have federal conspiracy convictions. The essence of conspiracy is an agreement of two or more persons to engage in some form of prohibited misconduct. The crime is complete upon agreement, although some statutes require prosecutors to show that at least one of the conspirators has taken some concrete step or committed some overt act in furtherance of the scheme. There are dozens of federal conspiracy statutes. One, 18 U.S.C. 371, outlaws conspiracy to commit some other federal crime. The others outlaw conspiracy to engage in various specific forms of proscribed conduct. General Section 371 conspiracies are punishable by imprisonment for not more than five years; drug trafficking, terrorist, and racketeering conspiracies all carry the same penalties as their underlying substantive offenses, and thus are punished more severely than are Section 371 conspiracies. All are subject to fines of not more than $250,000 (not more than $500,000 for organizations), most may serve as the basis for a restitution order, and some for a forfeiture order.

The law makes several exceptions for conspiracy because of its unusual nature. Because many united in crime pose a greater danger than the isolated offender, conspirators may be punished for the conspiracy, any completed substantive offense which is the object of the plot, and any foreseeable other offenses which one of the conspirators commits in furtherance of the scheme. Since conspiracy is an omnipresent crime, it may be prosecuted wherever an overt act is committed in its furtherance. Because conspiracy is a continuing crime, its statute of limitations does not begin to run until the last overt act committed for its benefit. Since conspiracy is a separate crime, it may be prosecuted following conviction for the underlying substantive offense, without offending constitutional double jeopardy principles; because conspiracy is a continuing offense, it may be punished when it straddles enactment of the prohibiting statute, without offending constitutional ex post facto principles. Accused conspirators are likely to be tried together, and the statements of one may often be admitted in evidence against all.

In some respects, conspiracy is similar to attempt, to solicitation, and to aiding and abetting. Unlike aiding and abetting, however, it does not require commission of the underlying offense. Unlike attempt and solicitation, conspiracy does not merge with the substantive offense; a conspirator may be punished for both.

Chapter 2 - Congress enacted the federal Racketeer Influenced and Corrupt Organization (RICO) provisions as part of the Organized Crime Control Act of 1970. In spite of its name and origin, RICO is not limited to "mobsters" or members of "organized crime" as those terms are popularly understood. Rather, it covers those activities which Congress felt characterized the conduct of organized crime, no matter who actually engages in them.

RICO proscribes no conduct that is not otherwise prohibited. Instead it enlarges the civil and criminal consequences, under some circumstances, of a list of state and federal crimes.

In simple terms, RICO condemns:

(1) any person
(2) who
  (a) invests in, or

(b) acquires or maintains an interest in, or
(c) conducts or participates in the affairs of, or
(d) conspires to invest in, acquire, or conduct the affairs of
(3) an enterprise
(4) which
(a) engages in, or
(b) whose activities affect, interstate or foreign commerce
(5) through
(a) the collection of an unlawful debt, or
(b) the patterned commission of various state and federal crimes.

Violations are punishable by (a) the forfeiture of any property acquired through a RICO violation and of any property interest in the enterprise involved in the violation, and (b) imprisonment for not more than 20 years, or for life if one of the predicate offenses carries such a penalty, and/or a fine of not more than the greater of twice the amount of gain or loss associated with the offense or $250,000 for individuals and $500,000 for organizations. RICO has generally survived constitutional challenges, although its forfeiture provisions are subject to an excessive fines clause analysis and perhaps to cruel and unusual punishment disproportionality analysis.

RICO violations also subject the offender to civil liability. The courts may award anyone injured in their business or property by a RICO violation treble damages, costs and attorneys' fees, and may enjoin RICO violations, order divestiture, dissolution or reorganization, or restrict an offender's future professional or investment activities. Civil RICO has been controversial. At one time commentators urged Congress to amend its provisions. Congress found little consensus on the questions raised by proposed revisions, however, and the issue seems to have been put aside at least for the time being.

The text of the RICO sections, citations to state RICO statutes, and a selected bibliography are appended.

Chapter 3 - This is an overview of the elements of federal criminal money laundering statutes and the sanctions imposed for their violation. The most prominent is 18 U.S.C. 1956. Section 1956 outlaws four kinds of money laundering—promotional, concealment, structuring, and tax evasion laundering of the proceeds generated by designated federal, state, and foreign underlying crimes (predicate offenses)—committed or attempted under one or more of three jurisdictional conditions (i.e., laundering involving certain financial transactions, laundering involving international transfers, and stings). Its companion, 18 U.S.C. 1957, prohibits depositing or spending more than

$10,000 of the proceeds from a Section 1956 predicate offense. Violations of Section 1956 are punishable by imprisonment for not more than 20 years; Section 1957 carries a maximum penalty of imprisonment for 10 years. Property involved in either case is subject to confiscation. Misconduct which implicates Sections 1956 and 1957 may implicate other federal criminal statutes as well. Federal racketeer influenced and corrupt organization (RICO) provisions outlaw acquiring or conducting the affairs of an enterprise (whose activities affect interstate or foreign commerce) through the patterned commission of a series of underlying federal or state crimes. RICO violations are also 20-year felonies. Every RICO predicate offense, including each "federal crime of terrorism," is automatically a Section 1956 money laundering predicate offense. A second related statute, the Travel Act (18 U.S.C. 1952), punishes interstate or foreign travel, or the use of interstate or foreign facilities, conducted with the intent to distribute the proceeds of a more modest list of predicate offenses or to promote or carry on such offenses when an overt act is committed in furtherance of that intent. Such misconduct is punishable by imprisonment for not more than five years. Other federal statutes proscribe, with varying sanctions, bulk cash smuggling, layering bank deposits to avoid reporting requirements, failure to comply with federal anti-money laundering provisions, or conducting an unlawful money transmission business.

The Supreme Court has held that the Section 1956 ban on attempted international transportation of tainted proceeds for the purpose of concealing their ownership, source, nature, or ultimate location is limited to instances where concealment is a purpose rather than an attribute of the transportation (simple smuggling is not proscribed as such), United States v. Cuellar, 553 U.S. 550 (2008). In a second case, the Court indicated that for purposes of Section 1956 the "proceeds" of a predicate offense often referred to the profits rather than the gross receipts realized from the offense, United States v. Santos, 553 U.S. 507 (2008). Congress responded by defining "proceeds" for purposes of Sections 1956 and 1957 as the property obtained or retained as a consequence of a predicate offense, including gross receipts, P.L. 111-21, 123 Stat. 1618 (2009)(S. 386)(111th Cong.).

Chapter 4 - It is a federal crime to devise a scheme to defraud another of property, when either mail or wire communications are used in furtherance of the scheme, 18 U.S.C. 1341, 1343. Mail or wire fraud includes schemes to defraud another of honest services, when the scheme involves bribery or a kick back, 18 U.S.C. 1346; *Skilling v. United States*, 130 S.Ct. 2896 (2010). In order to convict, the government must prove beyond a reasonable doubt that the defendant (1) used either mail or wire communications in the foreseeable furtherance, (2) of a scheme to defraud, (3) involving a material deception, (4) with the intent to deprive another of, (5) either property or honest services.

Offenders face the prospect of imprisonment for not more than 20 years, a fine of not more than $250,000 (not more than $500,000 for organizations), an order to pay victim restitution, and the confiscation of any property realized from the offense.

Misconduct that constitutes mail or wire fraud may also constitute a violation of one or more other federal crimes. Principal among these are predicate offense crimes, frauds based on jurisdictional factors other than use of mail or wire communications, and other honest services frauds in the form of bribery or kickbacks. The other federal bribery and kickback offenses include bribery of public officials, federal program bribery, extortion under color of official right, and Medicare/Medicaid kickbacks. Mail and wire fraud are money laundering and racketeering predicate offenses. Numbered among the fraud offenses based on other jurisdiction grounds are the false claims and false statement offenses, bank fraud, health care fraud, securities fraud, and foreign labor contracting fraud.

Chapter 5 - It is not a crime to attempt to commit most federal offenses. Unlike state law, federal law has no generally applicable crime of contempt. Congress, however, has outlawed the attempt to commit a substantial number of federal crimes on an individual basis. In doing so, it has proscribed the attempt, set its punishment, and left to the federal courts the task of further developing the law in the area.

The courts have identified two elements in the crime of attempt: an intent to commit the underlying substantive offense and some substantial step towards that end.

The point at which a step may be substantial is not easily discerned; but it seems that the more serious and reprehensible the substantive offense, the less substantial the step need be. Ordinarily, the federal courts accept neither impossibility nor abandonment as an effective defense to a charge of attempt. Attempt and the substantive offense carry the same penalties in most instances.

A defendant may not be convicted of both the substantive offense and the attempt to commit it. Commission of the substantive offense, however, is neither a prerequisite for, nor a defense against, an attempt conviction.

Whether a defendant may be guilty of an attempt to attempt to commit a federal offense is often a matter of statutory construction. Attempts to conspire and attempts to aid and abet generally present less perplexing questions.

In: Conspiratorial Crimes ... ISBN: 978-1-62618-426-8
Editors: L. C. Wright and J. C. Miller

Chapter 1

FEDERAL CONSPIRACY LAW: A BRIEF OVERVIEW*

Charles Doyle

SUMMARY

Zacarias Moussaoui, members of the Colombian drug cartels, members of organized crime, and some of the former Enron executives have at least one thing in common: they all have federal conspiracy convictions. The essence of conspiracy is an agreement of two or more persons to engage in some form of prohibited misconduct. The crime is complete upon agreement, although some statutes require prosecutors to show that at least one of the conspirators has taken some concrete step or committed some overt act in furtherance of the scheme. There are dozens of federal conspiracy statutes. One, 18 U.S.C. 371, outlaws conspiracy to commit some other federal crime. The others outlaw conspiracy to engage in various specific forms of proscribed conduct. General Section 371 conspiracies are punishable by imprisonment for not more than five years; drug trafficking, terrorist, and racketeering conspiracies all carry the same penalties as their underlying substantive offenses, and thus are punished more severely than are Section 371 conspiracies. All are subject to fines of not more than $250,000 (not more than $500,000 for

* This is an edited, reformatted and augmented version of a Congressional Research Service publication, CRS Report for Congress R41223, from www.crs.gov, prepared for Members and Committees of Congress, dated June 25, 2012.

organizations), most may serve as the basis for a restitution order, and some for a forfeiture order.

The law makes several exceptions for conspiracy because of its unusual nature. Because many united in crime pose a greater danger than the isolated offender, conspirators may be punished for the conspiracy, any completed substantive offense which is the object of the plot, and any foreseeable other offenses which one of the conspirators commits in furtherance of the scheme. Since conspiracy is an omnipresent crime, it may be prosecuted wherever an overt act is committed in its furtherance. Because conspiracy is a continuing crime, its statute of limitations does not begin to run until the last overt act committed for its benefit. Since conspiracy is a separate crime, it may be prosecuted following conviction for the underlying substantive offense, without offending constitutional double jeopardy principles; because conspiracy is a continuing offense, it may be punished when it straddles enactment of the prohibiting statute, without offending constitutional ex post facto principles. Accused conspirators are likely to be tried together, and the statements of one may often be admitted in evidence against all.

In some respects, conspiracy is similar to attempt, to solicitation, and to aiding and abetting. Unlike aiding and abetting, however, it does not require commission of the underlying offense. Unlike attempt and solicitation, conspiracy does not merge with the substantive offense; a conspirator may be punished for both.

INTRODUCTION

Terrorists, drug traffickers, mafia members, and corrupt corporate executives have one thing in common: most are conspirators subject to federal prosecution.[1] Federal conspiracy laws rest on the belief that criminal schemes are equally or more reprehensible than are the substantive offenses to which they are devoted. The Supreme Court has explained that a "collective criminal agreement—[a] partnership in crime—presents a greater potential threat to the public than individual delicts. Concerted action both increases the likelihood that the criminal object will be successfully attained and decreases the probability that the individuals involved will depart from their path of criminality."[2] Moreover, observed the Court, "[g]roup association for criminal purposes often, if not normally, makes possible the attainment of ends more complex than those which one criminal could accomplish. Nor is the danger of a conspiratorial group limited to the particular end toward which it has embarked."[3] Finally, "[c]ombination in crime makes more likely the commission of crimes unrelated to the original purpose for which the group was formed."[4] In sum, "the danger which a conspiracy generates is not confined to the substantive offense which is the immediate aim of the enterprise."[5] Congress and the courts have fashioned federal conspiracy law accordingly.[6]

The *United States Code* contains dozens of criminal conspiracy statutes. One, 18 U.S.C. 371, outlaws conspiracy to commit any other federal crime. The others outlaw conspiracy to commit some specific form of misconduct, ranging from civil rights violations to drug trafficking.[7] Conspiracy is a separate offense under most of these statutes,[8] regardless of whether conspiracy accomplishes its objective.[9] The various conspiracy statutes, however, differ in several other respects. A few, including Section 371, require at least one conspirator to take some affirmative step in furtherance of the scheme. Most have no such overt act requirement.[10]

Section 371 has two prongs. One outlaws conspiracy to commit a federal offense; a second, conspiracy to defraud the United States. Conspiracy to commit a federal crime under Section 371 requires that the underlying misconduct be a federal crime. Conspiracy to defraud the United States under Section 371 and in several other instances has no such prerequisite.[11] Section 371 conspiracies are punishable by imprisonment for not more than five years. Elsewhere, conspirators often face more severe penalties.[12]

These differences aside, federal conspiracy statutes share much common ground because Congress decided they should. As the Court observed in *Salinas*, "When Congress uses well-settled terminology of criminal law, its words are presumed to have their ordinary meaning and definition. [When] [t]he relevant statutory phrase is 'to conspire,' [w]e presume Congress intended to use the term in its conventional sense, and certain well-established principles follow."[13]

These principles include the fact that regardless of its statutory setting, every conspiracy has at least two elements: (1) an agreement (2) between two or more persons.[14] Members of the conspiracy are also liable for the foreseeable crimes of their fellows committed in furtherance of the common plot.[15] Moreover, statements by one conspirator are admissible evidence against all.[16] Conspiracies are considered continuing offenses for purposes of the statute of limitations and venue.[17] They are also considered separate offenses for purposes of sentencing and of challenges under the Constitution's ex post facto and double jeopardy clauses.[18] This is a brief discussion of the common features of federal conspiracy law that evolved over the years, with passing references to some of the distinctive features of some of the statutory provisions.

BACKGROUND

Although it is not without common law antecedents, federal conspiracy law is largely of Congress's making. It is what Congress provided, and what the courts understood Congress intended. This is not to say that conspiracy was unknown in pre-colonial and colonial England,[19] but simply that it was a faint shadow of the crime we now know. Then, it was essentially a narrow form of malicious prosecution, subject to both a civil remedy and prosecution.[20] In the late 18th and early 19th centuries, state courts and legislatures recognized a rapidly expanding accumulation of narrowly described wrongs as "conspiracy." The patchwork reached a point where one commentator explained that there were "few things left so doubtful in the criminal law, as the point at which a combination of several persons in a common object becomes illegal."[21] Congress enacted few conspiracy statutes prior to the Civil War. It did pass a provision in 1790 that outlawed confining the master of a ship or endeavoring revolt on board.[22] This, Justice Story, sitting as a circuit judge, interpreted to include any conspiracy to confine the prerogatives of the master of ship to navigate, maintain, or police his ship.[23] The same year, 1825, Congress outlawed conspiracies to engage in maritime insurance fraud.[24] Otherwise, there were no federal conspiracy statutes until well after the mid-century mark. During the War Between the States, however, Congress enacted four sweeping conspiracy provisions, creating federal crimes that have come down to us with little substantive change. The first, perhaps thought more pressing at the beginning of the war, was a seditious conspiracy statute.[25] Shortly thereafter, Congress outlawed conspiracies to defraud the United States through the submission of false claim,[26] and followed that four years later with a prohibition on conspiracies to violate federal law or to defraud the United States.[27] Subsequent conspiracy statutes, though perhaps no less significant, were more topically focused. The Reconstruction civil rights conspiracy provisions,[28] the Sherman Act anti-trust provisions,[29] and the drug and racketeering statutes[30] may be the best known of these. All of them begin the same way—with an agreement by two or more persons.

TWO OR MORE PERSONS

There are no one-man conspiracies.[31] At common law where husband and wife were considered one, this meant that the two could not be guilty of conspiracy without the participation of some third person.[32] This is no longer the case.[33] In like manner at common law, corporations could not be charged with a crime.[34] This too is no longer the case. A corporation is criminally liable for the crimes, including conspiracy, committed at least in part for its benefit, by its employees and agents.[35] Moreover, a corporation may be criminally liable for intra-corporate conspiracies, as long as at least two of its officers, employees, or agents are parties to the plot.[36]

Notwithstanding the two-party requirement, no co-conspirator need have been tried or even identified, as long as the government produces evidence from which the conspiracy might be inferred.[37] Even the acquittal of a co-conspirator is no defense,[38] although no conviction is possible if all but one alleged conspirator are acquitted.[39] Moreover, a person may conspire for the commission of a crime by a third person though he himself is legally incapable of committing the underlying offense.[40]

On the other hand, two people may not always be enough. The so-called Wharton's Rule placed a limitation on conspiracy prosecutions when the number of conspirators equaled the number of individuals necessary for the commission of the underlying offense.[41] Under federal law, the rule "stands as an exception to the general principle that a conspiracy and the substantive offense that is its immediate end do not merge upon proof of the latter."[42] And under federal law, the rule reaches no further than to the types of offenses that gave birth to its recognition—duelling, adultery, bigamy, and incest.[43]

AGREEMENT

It is not enough, however, to show that the defendant agreed only with an undercover officer to commit the underlying offense, for there is no agreement on a common purpose in such cases.[44] As has been said, the essence of conspiracy is an agreement, an agreement to commit some act condemned by law either as a separate federal offense or for purposes of the conspiracy statute.[45] The agreement may be evidenced by word or action; that is, the government may prove the existence of the agreement either by direct evidence or by circumstantial evidence from which the agreement may be inferred.[46] "Relevant circumstantial evidence [may] include: the joint appearance of defendants at transactions and negotiations in furtherance of the conspiracy; the relationship among codefendants; mutual representation of defendants to third parties; and other evidence suggesting unity of purpose or common design and understanding among conspirators to accomplish the objects of the conspiracy."[47]

The lower federal appellate courts have acknowledged that evidence of a mere buyer-seller relationship is insufficient to support a drug trafficking conspiracy charge. Some do so under the rationale that there is no singularity of purpose, no necessary agreement, in such cases: "the buyer's purpose is to buy; the seller's purpose is to sell."[48] Others do so to avoid sweeping mere customers into a large-scale trafficking operation.[49] Still others do so lest traffickers and their addicted customers face the same severe penalties.[50] All agree, however, that purchasers may be liable as conspirators when they are part of a large scheme.[51]

Again, in most cases the essence of conspiracy is agreement. "Nevertheless, mere association, standing alone, is inadequate; an individual does not become a member of a conspiracy merely associating with conspirators known to be involved in crime."[52]

One or Many Overlapping Conspiracies

The task of sifting agreement from mere association becomes more difficult and more important with the suggestion of overlapping conspiracies. Criminal enterprises may involve one or many conspiracies. Some time ago, the Supreme Court noted that "[t]hieves who dispose of their loot to a single receiver—a single 'fence'—do not by that fact alone become confederates: They may, but it takes more than knowledge that he is a 'fence' to make them such."[53] Whether it is a fence, or a drug dealer, or a money launderer, when several seemingly independent criminal groups share a common point of contact, the question becomes whether they present one overarching conspiracy or several separate conspiracies with a coincidental overlap. In the analogy suggested by the Court, when separate spokes meet at the common hub they can only function as a wheel if the spokes and hub are enclosed within a rim.[54] When several criminal enterprises overlap, they are one overarching conspiracy or several overlapping conspiracies depending upon whether they share a single unifying purpose and understanding—one common agreement.[55]

In determining whether they are faced with a single conspiracy or a rimless collection of overlapping schemes, the courts will look for "the existence of a common purpose ... (2) interdependence of various elements of the overall play; and (3) overlap among the participants."[56] "Interdependence is present if the activities of a defendant charged with conspiracy facilitated the endeavors of other alleged co-conspirators or facilitated the venture as a whole."[57]

If this common agreement exists, it is of no consequence that a particular conspirator joined the plot after its inception as long as he joined it knowingly and voluntarily.[58] Nor does it matter that a defendant does not know all of the details of a scheme or all of its participants, or that his role is relatively minor.[59]

Overt Acts

Conviction under 18 U.S.C. 371 for conspiracy to commit a substantive offense requires proof that one of the conspirators committed an overt act in furtherance of the conspiracy.[60] In the case of prosecution under other federal conspiracy statutes that have no such requirement, the existence of an overt act may be important for evidentiary and procedural reasons. The overt act need not be the substantive crime which is the object of the conspiracy, an element of that offense, or even a crime in its own right.[61] Moreover, a single overt act by any of the conspirators in furtherance of plot will suffice.[62]

Conspiracy to Defraud the United States

Federal law contains several statutes that outlaw defrauding the United States. Two of the most commonly prosecuted are 18 U.S.C. 286, which outlaws conspiracy to defraud the United States through the submission of a false claim, and 18 U.S.C. 371, which in addition to conspiracies to violate federal law, outlaws conspiracies to defraud the United States of property or by obstructing the performance of its agencies. Section 371 has an overt act requirement;[63] Section 286 does not.[64] The general principles of federal conspiracy law apply to both.[65]

The elements of conspiracy to defraud the United States under 18 U.S.C. 371 are (1) an agreement of two or more persons; (2) to defraud the United States; and (3) an overt act in furtherance of the conspiracy committed by one of the conspirators.[66] The "fraud covered by the statute reaches any conspiracy for the purpose of impairing, obstructing or defeating the lawful functions of any department of the Government"[67] by "deceit, craft or trickery, or at least by means that are dishonest."[68]

The plot must be directed against the United States or some federal entity; a scheme to defraud the recipient of federal funds is not sufficient.[69] The scheme may be designed to deprive the United States of money or property, but it need not be so; a plot calculated to frustrate the functions of an entity of the United States will suffice.[70]

In contrast, a second federal statute, 18 U.S.C. 286, condemns conspiracies to defraud the United States of money or property through submission of a false claim.[71]

The elements of a Section 286 violation are that "the defendant entered into a conspiracy to obtain payment or allowance of a claim against a department or agency of the United States; (2) the claim was false, fictitious, or fraudulent; (3) the defendant knew or was deliberately ignorant of the claim's falsity, fictitiousness, or fraudulence; (4) the defendant knew of the conspiracy and intended to join it; and (5) the defendant voluntarily participated in the conspiracy."[72] Conviction does not require proof of an overt act in furtherance of the conspiracy.[73]

When Does It End?

Conspiracy is a crime which begins with a scheme and may continue on until its objective is achieved or abandoned.[74] The liability of individual conspirators continues on from the time they joined the plot until it ends or until they withdraw.[75] The want of an individual's continued active participation is no defense as long as the underlying conspiracy lives and he has not withdrawn.[76] An individual who claims to have withdrawn must show either that he took some action to make his departure clear to his co-conspirators or that he disclosed the scheme to the authorities.[77] Having done so, there is some difference of opinion over whether the government must overcome, beyond a reasonable doubt, the defendant's assertion or whether the defendant must carry his point before the jury by a preponderance of the evidence.[78]

As a general rule, overt acts of concealment do not extend the life of the conspiracy beyond the date of the accomplishment of its main objectives.[79] On the other hand, the rule does not apply when concealment is one of the main objectives of the conspiracy.[80]

SANCTIONS

Imprisonment and Fines

Section 371 felony conspiracies are punishable by imprisonment for not more than five years and a fine of not more than $250,000 (not more than $500,000 for organizations).[81] Most drug trafficking, terrorism, racketeering, and many white collar conspirators face the same penalties as those who committed the underlying substantive offense, e.g., 21 U.S.C. 846 ("Any person who ... conspires to commit any offense defined in [the Controlled Substances Act] shall be subject to the same penalties as those prescribed for the offense, the commission of which was the object of the ... conspiracy"); 18 U.S.C. 2339B ("Whoever knowingly provides material support or resources to a foreign terrorist organization.... or conspires to do so, shall be fined under this title, or imprisoned not more than 15 years, or both"); 18 U.S.C. 1962(d), 1963(a)("(d) It shall be unlawful for any person to conspire to violate any of the [racketeering] provisions of subsection (a), (b), or (c) of this section.... (a) Whoever violates any provision of section 1962 ... shall be fined under this title, or imprisoned for not more than 20 years ... or both"); 18 U.S.C. 1349 ("Any person who ... conspires to commit any offense under this chapter [relating to mail fraud, wire fraud, etc.] shall be subject to the same penalties as those prescribed for the offense, the commission of which was the object of ... the conspiracy").

The United States Sentencing Guidelines greatly influence the sentences for federal crimes. Federal courts are bound to impose a sentence within the statutory maximums and minimums. Their decision of what sentence to impose within those boundaries, however, must begin with a determination of the sentencing recommendation under the guidelines.[82] Reasonableness standards govern review of their sentencing decisions,[83] and a sentence within the Sentencing Guidelines range is presumed reasonable.[84]

The Sentencing Guidelines system is essentially a scoring system. Federal crimes are each assigned a numerical base offense level and levels are added and subtracted to account for the various aggravating and mitigating factors in a particular case. Thus, for example, providing material support to a terrorist organization, 18 U.S.C. 2339B, has a base offense level of 26, which may be increased by 2 levels if the support comes in the form of explosives, U.S.S.G. Section 2M5.3(a), (b) and may be increased or decreased still further for other factors. The guidelines designate six sentencing ranges of each total offense level; the appropriate range within the six is determined by extent of the offender's criminal record. For instance, the sentencing range for a first-time offender with a total offense level of 28 would be imprisonment for between 78 and 97 months (Category I); while the range for an offender in the highest criminal history category (Category VI) would be imprisonment for between 140 and 175 months.[85]

The base offense level for conspiracy is generally the same as that for the underlying offense, either by operation of an individual guideline, for example, U.S.C. Section 2D1.1 (drug trafficking), or by operation of the general conspiracy guideline, U.S.S.C. Section 2X1.1. In any event, conspirators who play a leadership role in an enterprise are subject to an increase of from 2 to 4 levels, U.S.S.G. Section 3B1.1, and those who play a more subservient role may be entitled to reduction of from 2 to 4 levels, U.S.S.G. Section 3B1.2. In the case of terrorism offenses, conspirators may also be subject to a special enhancement which sets the minimum total offense level at 32 and the criminal history category at VI (regardless of the extent of the offender's criminal record), U.S.S.G. Section 3A1.4.[86]

The Sentencing Guidelines also address the imposition of fines below the statutory maximum. The total offense level dictates the recommended fine range for individual and organizational defendants. For instance, the fine range for an individual with a total offense level of 28 is $12,500 to $125,000, U.S.C. Section 5E1.2. The recommended fine range for an organization with a total offense level of 28 is $6,300,000 (assuming the loss or gain associated with the organization offense exceeds the usual $500,000 ceiling), U.S.S.G. Section 8C2.4.

Restitution

A conspirator's liability for restitution is a matter of circumstance. Most conspiracy statutes do not expressly provide for restitution, but in most instances restitution may be required or permitted under any number of grounds. As a general rule, federal law requires restitution for certain offenses and permits it for others. A sentencing court is generally required to order a defendant to make restitution following conviction for a crime of violence or for a crime against property (including fraud), 18 U.S.C. 366A(a), (c). Those entitled to restitution under Section 3663A include those "directly and proximately harmed" by the crime of conviction and "in the case of an offense that involves as an element a scheme, conspiracy, or pattern of criminal activity, any person directly harmed by the defendant's criminal conduct in the course of the scheme, conspiracy or pattern," 18 U.S.C. 3663A(b).[87]

Otherwise, a court is permitted to order restitution (a) following conviction for an offense proscribed under Title 18 of the *United States Code* or for drug trafficking, 18 U.S.C. 3663;[88] (b) as a condition of probation or supervised release, 18 U.S.C. 3563(b)(2), 3583(d); or (c) pursuant to a plea agreement, 18 U.S.C. 3663(a)(3), 3663A(c)(2).[89]

Forfeiture

The treatment of forfeiture in conspiracy cases is perhaps even more individualistic than restitution in conspiracy cases. The general criminal forfeiture statute, 18 U.S.C. 982, authorizes confiscation for several classes of property as a consequence of a particular conspiracy conviction, for example, 18 U.S.C. 982(a)(2)(calling for the confiscation of proceeds realized from "a violation of, or a conspiracy to—(A) section ... 1341, 1343, 1344 of this title [relating to mail, wire and bank fraud], affecting a financial institution"); 18 U.S.C. 982(a)(8)(calling for the confiscation of proceeds from, and property used to facilitate or promote, "an offense under section ... 1341, or 1343, or of a conspiracy to commit such an offense, if the offense involves telemarketing").

In the case of drug trafficking, forfeiture turns on the fact that it is authorized for any Controlled Substances Act violation, 21 U.S.C. 853,[90] of which conspiracy is one, 21 U.S.C. 846. The same can be said of racketeering conspiracy provisions of 18 U.S.C. 1962(d).[91]

Relation of Conspiracy to Other Crimes

Conspiracy is a completed crime upon agreement, or upon agreement and the commission of an overt act under statutes with an overt act requirement. Conviction does not require commission of the crime that is the object of the conspiracy.[92] On the other hand, conspirators may be prosecuted for conspiracy, for any completed offense which is the object of the conspiracy, as well as for any foreseeable offense committed in furtherance of the conspiracy.[93]

Aid and Abet

Anyone who "aids, abets, counsels, commands, induces, or procures" the commission of a federal crime by another is punishable as a principal, that is, as though he had committed the offense himself, 18 U.S.C. 2. If the other agrees and an overt act is committed, they are conspirators, each liable for conspiracy and any criminal act committed to accomplish it. If the other commits the offense, they are equally punishable for the basic offense. "Typically, the same evidence will support both a conspiracy and an aiding and abetting conviction."[94] The two are clearly distinct, however, as the Ninth Circuit has noted:

> The difference between the classic common law elements of aiding and abetting and a criminal conspiracy underscores this material distinction, although at first blush the two appear similar. Aiding and abetting the commission of a specific crime, we have held, includes four elements: (1) that the accused had the specific intent to facilitate the commission of a crime by another, (2) that the accused had the requisite intent to commit the underlying substantive offense, (3) that the accused assisted or participated in the commission of the underlying substantive offense, and (4) that the principal committed the underlying offense. As Lopez emphasized, the accused generally must associate] himself with the venture ... participate[ ] in it as something he wish[es] to bring about, and [sought by] his action to make it succeed.
>
> By contrast, a classic criminal conspiracy as charged in 18 U.S.C. § 371 is broader. The government need only prove (1) an agreement to engage in criminal activity, (2) one or more overt acts taken to implement the agreement, and (3) the requisite intent to commit the substantive crime. Indeed, a drug conspiracy does not even require commission of an overt act in furtherance of the conspiracy.
>
> Two distinctions become readily apparent after a more careful comparison. First, the substantive offense which may be the object in a § 371 conspiracy need not be completed. Second, the emphasis in a § 371 conspiracy is on whether one or more overt acts was undertaken. This language necessarily is couched in passive voice for it matters only that a co-conspirator commit the overt act, not necessarily that the accused herself does so. In an aiding and abetting case, not only must the underlying substantive offense actually be completed by someone, but the accused must take some action, a substantial step, toward associating herself with the criminal venture.[95]

Attempt

Conspiracy and attempt are both inchoate offenses, unfinished crimes in a sense. They are forms of introductory misconduct that the law condemns lest they result in some completed form of misconduct.[96] Federal law has no general attempt statute.[97] Congress, however, has outlawed attempt to commit a number of specific federal offenses.[98] Like conspiracy, a conviction for attempt does not require the commission of the underlying offense.[99] Both require an intent to commit the contemplated substantive offense.[100] Like conspiracy, the fact that it may be impossible to commit the target offense is no defense to a charge of attempt to commit it.[101] Unlike conspiracy, attempt can be committed by a single individual.[102] Attempt only becomes a crime when it closely approaches a substantive offense. Conspiracy becomes a crime far sooner. Mere acts of preparation will satisfy the most demanding conspiracy statute, not so with attempt.[103] Conspiracy requires no more than an overt act in furtherance; attempt, a substantial step to completion.[104] Moreover, unlike a conspirator, an accused may not be convicted of both attempt and the underlying substantive offense.[105]

An individual may be guilty of both conspiring with others to commit an offense and of attempting to commit the same offense, either himself or through his confederates.[106] In some circumstances, he may be guilty of attempted conspiracy. Congress has outlawed at least one example of an attempt to conspire in the statute which prohibits certain invitations to conspire, that is, solicitation to commit a federal crime of violence, 18 U.S.C. 373.

Solicitation

Section 373 prohibits efforts to induce another to commit a crime of violence "under circumstances strongly corroborative" of intent to see the crime committed, 18 U.S.C. 373(a). Section 373's crimes of violence are federal "felon[ies] that [have] as an element the use, attempted use, or threatened use of physical force against property or against the person of another," id.[107] Examples of "strongly corroborative" circumstances include "the defendant offering or promising payment or another benefit in exchange for committing the offense; threatening harm or other detriment for refusing to commit the offense; repeatedly soliciting or discussing at length in soliciting the commission of the offense, or making explicit that the solicitation is serious; believing or knowing that the persons solicited had previously committed similar offenses; and acquiring weapons, tools, or information or use in committing the offense, or making other apparent preparations for its commission."[108]

As is the case of attempt, "[a]n individual cannot be guilty of both the solicitation of a crime and the substantive crime."[109] Although the crime of solicitation is complete upon communication with the requisite intent, renunciation prior to commission of the substantive offense is a defense.[110] The offender's legal incapacity to commit the solicited offense himself, however, is not a defense.[111]

PROCEDURAL ATTRIBUTES

Statute of Limitations

The statute of limitations for most federal crimes is five years, 18 U.S.C. 3282.[112] The five-year limitation applies to the general conspiracy statute, 18 U.S.C. 371, and to the false claims conspiracy statute, 18 U.S.C. 286. Section 371 requires proof of an overt act;[113] Section 286 does not.[114] For conspiracy offenses with an overt act requirement like those under Section 371, the statute of limitations begins with completion of the last overt act in furtherance of the conspiracy.[115]

For conspiracy offenses with no such requirement like those under Section 286, the statute of limitations begins with the abandonment of the conspiracy or the accomplishment of its objectives.[116]

Venue

The presence or absence of an overt act requirement makes a difference for statute of limitations purposes. For venue purposes, it does not. The Supreme Court has observed in passing that "this Court has long held that venue is proper in any district in which an overt act in furtherance of the conspiracy was committed, even where an overt act is not a required element of the conspiracy offense."[117] The lower federal appellate courts are seemingly of the same view, for they have found venue proper for a conspiracy prosecution wherever an overt act occurs—under overt act statutes and non-overt act statutes alike.[118]

Joinder and Severance (One Conspiracy, One Trial)

Three rules of the Federal Rules of Criminal Procedure govern joinder and severance for federal criminal trials. Rule 8 permits the joinder of common criminal charges and defendants.[119] Rule 12 insists that a motion for severance be filed prior to trial.[120] Rule 14 authorizes the court to grant severance for separate trials as a remedy for prejudicial joinder.[121]

The Supreme Court has pointed out that "[t]here is a preference in the federal system for joint trials of defendants who are indicted together. Joint trials play a vital role in the criminal justice system. They promote efficiency and serve the interests of justice by avoiding the scandal and inequity of inconsistent verdicts."[122] In conspiracy cases, a "conspiracy charge combined with substantive counts arising out of that conspiracy is a proper basis for joinder under Rule 8(b)."[123]

Moreover, "the preference in a conspiracy trial is that persons charged together should be tried together."[124] In fact, "it will be the rare case, if ever, where a district court should sever the trial of alleged co-conspirators."[125] The Supreme Court has reminded the lower courts that "a district court should grant a severance under Rule 14 only if there is a serious risk that a joint trial would compromise a specific trial right of one of the defendants, or prevent the jury from making a reliable judgment about guilt or innocence."[126] The Court noted that the risk may be more substantial in complex cases with multiple defendants, but that "less drastic measures, such as limiting instructions, often will suffice to cure any risk of prejudice."[127] Subsequently lower federal appellate court opinions have emphasized the curative effect of appropriate jury instructions.[128]

Double Jeopardy and Ex Post Facto

Because conspiracy is a continuing offense, it stands as an exception to the usual ex post facto principles. Because it is a separate crime, it also stands as an exception to the usual double jeopardy principles.

The ex post facto clauses of the Constitution forbid the application of criminal laws which punish conduct that was innocent when it was committed or punish more severely criminal conduct than when it was committed.[129] Increasing the penalty for an ongoing conspiracy, however, does not offend ex post facto constraints as long as the conspiracy straddles the date of the legislative penalty enhancement.[130]

The double jeopardy clause of the Fifth Amendment declares that no person shall "be subject for the same offence to be twice put in jeopardy of life or limb."[131] This prohibition condemns successive prosecutions, successive punishments, and successive use of charges rejected in acquittal.[132]

For successive prosecution or punishment, the critical factor is the presence or absence of the same offense. Offenses may overlap, but they are not the same crime as long as each requires proof of an element that the other does not.[133] Since conspiracy and its attendant substantive offense are ordinarily separate crimes—one alone requiring agreement and the other alone requiring completion of the substantive offense—the double jeopardy clause poses no impediment to successive prosecution or to successive punishment of the two.[134] Double jeopardy issues arise most often in a conspiracy context when a case presents the question of whether the activities of the accused conspirators constitute a single conspiracy or several sequential, overlapping conspiracies. Multiple conspiracies may be prosecuted sequentially and punished with multiple sanctions; single conspiracies must be tried and punished once. Asked to determine whether they are faced with one or more than one conspiracy, the courts have said they inquire whether:

- the *locus criminis* [place] of the two alleged conspiracies is the same;
- there is a significant degree of *temporal overlap* between the two conspiracies charged;
- there is an overlap of personnel between the two conspiracies (including unindicted as well as indicted co-conspirators);
- the overt acts charged [are related];
- the *role played* by the defendant [relates to both];
- there was a common goal among the conspirators;
- whether the agreement contemplated bringing to pass a continuous result that will not continue without the continuous cooperation of the conspirators; and
- the extent to which the participants overlap[ped] in [their] various dealings.[135]

Co-Conspirator Declarations

At trial, the law favors the testimony of live witnesses—under oath, subject to cross examination, and in the presence of the accused and the jury—

over the presentation of their evidence in writing or through the mouths of others. The hearsay rule is a product of this preference. Exceptions and definitions narrow the rule's reach. For example, hearsay is usually defined to include only those out-of-court statements which are offered in evidence "to prove the truth of the matter asserted."[136]

Although often referred to as the exception for co-conspirator declarations, the Federal Rules of Evidence treats the matter within its definition of hearsay. Thus, Rule 801(d)(2)(E) of the Federal Rules provides that an out-of-court "statement is not hearsay if ... (2) The statement is offered against a party and is ... (E) a statement by a coconspirator of a party during the course and in furtherance of the conspiracy."

To admit a co-conspirator declaration into evidence under the Rule, a "court must find: (1) the conspiracy existed; (2) the defendant was a member of the conspiracy; and (3) the co-conspirator made the proffered statements in furtherance of the conspiracy."[137] The court, however, may receive the statement preliminarily subject to the prosecution's subsequent demonstration of its admissibility by a preponderance of the evidence.[138] As to the first two elements, a coconspirator's statement without more is insufficient; there must be "some extrinsic evidence sufficient to delineate the conspiracy and corroborate the declarant's and the defendant's roles in it."[139] As to the third element, "[a] statement is in furtherance of a conspiracy if it is intended to promote the objectives of the conspiracy."[140] A statement is in furtherance, for instance, if it describes for the benefit of a co-conspirator the status of the scheme, its participants, or its methods.[141] Bragging, or "mere idle chatter or casual conversation about past events," however, are not considered statements in furtherance of a conspiracy.[142]

Under some circumstances, evidence admissible under the hearsay rule may nevertheless be inadmissible because of Sixth Amendment restrictions. The Sixth Amendment provides, among other things, that "[i]n all criminal prosecutions, the accused shall enjoy the right ... to be confronted with the witnesses against him." The provision was inspired in part by reactions to the trial of Sir Walter Raleigh, who argued in vain that he should be allowed to confront the alleged co-conspirator who had accused him of treason.[143] Given its broadest possible construction, the confrontation clause would eliminate any hearsay exceptions or limitations.[144] The Supreme Court in *Crawford v. Washington* explained, however, that the clause has a more precise reach. The clause uses the word "witnesses" to bring within its scope only those who testify or whose accusations are made in a testimonial context. In a testimonial context, the confrontation clause permits use at trial of prior testimonial accusations only if the witness is unavailable and only if the accused had the opportunity to cross examine him when the testimony was taken.[145] The Court elected to "leave for another day any effort to spell out a comprehensive definition of 'testimonial,'"[146] but has suggested that the term includes "affidavits, depositions, prior testimony, or confessions [,and other] statements that were made under circumstances which would lead an objective witness reasonably to believe that the statement would be available for use at a later trial."[147]

Since *Crawford*, the lower federal courts have generally held that the confrontation clause poses no obstacle to the admissibility of the co-conspirator statements at issue in the cases before them, either because the statements were not testimonial;[148] were not offered to establish the truth of the asserted statement;[149] or because the clause does not bar co-conspirator declarations generally.[150]

End Notes

[1] Zacarias Moussaoui was convicted of conspiring to commit the terrorist attacks that occurred on September 11, 2001, United States v. Moussaoui, 591 F.3d 263, 266 (4th Cir. 2010); Wadih El-Hage was convicted of conspiring to bomb the U.S. embassies in Kenya and Tanzania, In re Terrorist Bombings, 552 F.3d 93, 107 (2d Cir. 2008).

Members of an Atlanta street gang were convicted of conspiring to engage in drug trafficking, among other offenses, United States v. Flores, 572 F.3d 1254, 1258 (11th Cir. 2009); motorcycle gang members were convicted of conspiracy to traffic in drugs, United States v. Deitz, 577 F.3d 672, 675-76 (6th Cir. 2009).

Dominick Pizzponia was convicted on racketeering conspiracy charges in connection with the activities of the "Gambino organized crime family of La Cosa Nostra," United States v. Pizzonia, 577 F.3d 455, 459 (2d Cir. 2009); Michael Yannotti was also convicted on racketeering conspiracy in connection with activities of the "Gambino Crime Family," United States v. Yannotti, 541 F.3d 112, 115-16 (2d Cir. 2008).

Jeffrey Skilling, a former Enron Corporation executive, was convicted of conspiracy to commit securities fraud and mail fraud, United States v. Skilling, 554 F.3d 529, 534 (5th Cir. 2009); Bernard Ebbers, a former WorldCom, Inc. executive, was likewise convicted of conspiracy to commit securities fraud, United States v. Ebbers, 458 F.3d 110, 112 (2d Cir. 2006).

[2] Iannelli v. United States, 420 U.S. 770, 778 (1975), quoting Callanan v. United States, 364 U.S. 587, 593-94 (1961).

[3] Id.

[4] Id.

[5] Id.

There have long been contrary views, e.g., Sayre, Criminal Conspiracy, 35 HARVARD LAW REVIEW 393, 393 (1922)("A doctrine so vague in its outlines and uncertain in its fundamental nature as criminal conspiracy lends no strength or glory to the law; it is a veritable quicksand of shifting opinion and ill-considered thought"); Hyde v. United States, 222 U.S. 347, 387 (1912)(Holmes, J, with Lurton, Hughes 7 Lamarr, JJ.)(dissenting)("And as wherever two or more have united for the commission of a crime there is a conspiracy, the opening to oppression thus made is very wide indeed. It is even wider if success should be held not to merge the conspiracy in the crime intended and achieved"), both quoted in substantial part in Katyal, Conspiracy Theory, 112 YALE LAW JOURNAL 1307, 1310 n. 6 (2003).

[6] Federal prosecutors have used, and been encouraged to use, the law available to them, Harrison v. United States, 7 F.2d 259, 263 (2d Cir. 1925)("[C]onspiracy, that darling of the modern prosecutor's nursery"); United States v. Reynolds, 919 F.2d 435, 439 (7th Cir. 1990)("[P]rosecutors seem to have conspiracy on their word processors as Count I"); Chesney, Terrorism, Criminal Prosecution, and the Preventive Detention Debate, 50 SOUTH TEXAS LAW REVIEW 669, 684 (2009)("What options do prosecutors have in the terrorism-prevention scenario when [other charges] are unavailable for lack of evidence linking the suspect to a designated foreign terrorist organization? One possibility is conspiracy liability").

[7] 18 U.S.C. 241 (civil rights conspiracies); 21 U.S.C. 846 (drug trafficking conspiracies).

[8] Iannelli v. United States, 420 U.S. 770, 777 (1975).

[9] United States v. Crippen, 627 F.3d 1056, 1065 (8th Cir. 2010); United States v. Scaffer, 586 F.3d 414, 423 (6th Cir. 2009); United States v. Wittig, 575 F.3d 1085, 1104 (10th Cir. 2009).

[10] Whitfield v. United States, 543 U.S. 209, 219 (2005)(18 U.S.C. 1956(h) – conspiracy to commit money laundering – has no overt act requirement); United States v. Shabani, 513 U.S. 10, 13-4 (1994)(21 U.S.C. 846 – conspiracy to violate the Controlled Substances Act – has no overt act requirement).

[11] E.g., 18 U.S.C. 956 (conspiracy in the U.S. to commit certain violent acts overseas, acts which ordinarily are crimes under the laws of the place where they occur but which need not be separate federal crimes for purposes of a prosecution under §956). Although it is generally known for its proscription against conspiracies to violate other federal laws, §371 also outlaws conspiracies to defraud the United States. Conviction under the defraud portion of §371 does not require that the underlying misconduct be a separate federal crime.

[12] The 20-year maximum penalties of Section 1956 apply to conspiracies to launder and to the underlying laundering offense alike, 18 U.S.C. 1956(h). The penalties that apply to drug trafficking under 21 U.S.C. 841 (up to life imprisonment) apply with equal force to conspiracies to traffic, 21 U.S.C. 846.

[13] Salinas v. United States, 522 U.S. 52, 63 (1997).

[14] United States v. Jimenez Recio, 537 U.S.270, 274 (2003).

[15] Pinkerton v. United States, 328 U.S. 640, 647 (1946).

[16] F.R.Evid. 801(d)(2)(E).

[17] Toussie v. United States, 397 U.S. 112, 122 (1970)(statute of limitations begins to run with the last overt act in furtherance of the conspiracy); Whitfield v. United States, 543 U.S. 209, 218 (2005)(venue is proper in any district in which an overt act in furtherance of the conspiracy was committed).

[18] Salinas v. United States, 522 U.S. 52, 65 (1997)("conspiracy is a distinct evil, dangerous to the public, and so punishable in itself"); United States v. Felix, 503 U.S. 378, 390 (1992)("[T]he commission of the substantive offense and a conspiracy to commit it are separate and distinct offenses ... [a]nd the plea of double jeopardy is no defense to a conviction for both offenses"); United States v. Munoz-Franco, 487 F.3d 25, 55 (1st Cir.

2007)("For 'continuing offenses' such as the bank fraud and conspiracy charges at issue here, however, the critical question is when the conduct ended. As we have explained, where a 'continuing offense' straddles the old and new law ... applying the new is recognized as constitutionally sound. In other words, a conviction for a continuing offense straddling enactment of a statute will not run afoul of the Ex Post Facto clause unless it was possible for the jury, following the court's instructions, to convict 'exclusively' on pre-enactment conduct")(here and hereafter internal citations and quotation marks have been omitted unless otherwise indicated).

[19] See generally, Bryan, THE DEVELOPMENT OF THE ENGLISH LAW OF CONSPIRACY (1909); Winfield, The History of Conspiracy and Abuse of Legal Process, CAMBRIDGE STUDIES IN ENGLISH LEGAL HISTORY (1921); Sayre, Criminal Conspiracy, 35 HARVARD LAW REVIEW 393 (1922).

[20] IV BLACKSTONE, COMMENTARIES ON THE LAWS OF ENGLAND 136 (1769)(transliteration supplied)("A conspiracy also to indict an innocent man of felony falsely and maliciously, who is accordingly indicted and acquitted, is a farther abuse and perversion of public justice; for which the party injured may either have a civil action by writ of the conspirators ... or the conspirators, for there must be at least two to form a conspiracy, may be indicted at the suit of the king").

[21] III CHITTY, A PRACTICAL TREATISE ON THE CRIMINAL LAW 1138 (3d Am. ed. 1839) noting that conspiracy included combinations "to commence suits against a person with a view to extorting money from him" or "to manufacture a base material in the form and color of genuine indigo, with the intent to sell it as indigo" or to cheat a man "by making him drunk and playing falsely at cards with him, but did not include combinations "to obtain money from a bank by drawing their checks on the bank when they have no funds there" or "to cheat and defraud a man by selling him an unsound horse." Of course, this is not a situation limited to the law of conspiracy.

[22] Act of April 30, 1790, ch. IX, §12, 1 Stat. 114 (1790).

[23] United States v. Hamilton, 26 Fed.Cas. 259, 260 (C.C.D.Mass. 1825)(No. 15,346).

[24] Act of March 3, 1825, ch.65, §23, 4 Stat. 122 (1825)(conspiracy "to cast away, burn, or otherwise destroy, ship or vessel ... with intent to injure any person ... that hath underwritten ... any policy of insurance thereon.").

[25] Act of July 31, 1861, c. 33, 12 Stat. 284 (1861), as amended 18 U.S.C. 2384.

[26] Act of March 2, 1863, c.67, §§1, 3, 12 Stat. 696, 698 (1863), as amended, 18 U.S.C. 286.

[27] Act of March 2, 1867, c.169, §30, 14 Stat. 484 (1867)("that if two or more persons conspire either to commit any offence against the laws of the United States, or to defraud the United States in any manner whatever, and one or more of said parties to said conspiracy shall do any act to effect the object thereof, the parties to said conspiracy shall be deemed guilty of a misdemeanor, and on conviction thereof shall be liable to a penalty of not less than one thousand dollars and not more than ten thousand dollars, and to imprisonment not exceeding two years. And when any offence shall be begun in one judicial district of the United State and completed in another, every such offence shall be deemed to be committed in either of the said districts, and may be dealt with, inquired of, tried, determined and punished in either of the said district, in the same manner as if it had been actually and wholly committed therein"), as amended 18 U.S.C. 371.

[28] Act of April 20, 1871, c. 22, §2, 17 Stat. 13, 14 (1871), as amended, 18 U.S.C. 241.

[29] Act of July 2, 1890, c. 647, §§1, 2, 3, 26 Stat. 209 (1890), as amended, 15 U.S.C. 1, 2, 3.

[30] P.L. 91-513, Tit. II, §406, 84 Stat. 1265 (1970), as amended, 21 U.S.C. 846, and P.L. 91-452, Tit. IX, §901(a), 84 Stat. 942 (1970), as amended, 18 U.S.C. 1962(d), respectively.

[31] Rogers v. United States, 340 U.S. 367, 375 (1951)("at least two persons are required to constitute a conspiracy"); United States v. Dumeisi, 424 F.3d 566, 580 (7th Cir. 2005)("the elements of the crime of conspiracy are not satisfied unless one conspires with at least one true co-conspirator").

[32] Dawson v. United States, 10 F.2d 106, 107 (9th Cir. 1926).

[33] United States v. Dege, 364 U.S. 51, 54-5 (1960).

[34] I BLACKSTONE, COMMENTARIES ON THE LAWS OF ENGLAND 464 (1765)(transliteration supplied)(punctuation in the original)("a corporation cannot commit treason, or felony, or other crime, in it's corporate capacity: though it's members, may, in their distinct individual capacities").

[35] United States v. Agosto-Vega, 617 F.3d 541, 552-53 (1st Cir. 2010); United States v. Singh, 518 F.3d 236, 249-51 (4th Cir. 2008); United States v. Hughes Aircraft Co., 20 F.3d 974, 978-80 (9th Cir. 1994).

[36] United States v. Sain, 141 F.3d 463, 474-75 (3d Cir. 1998); United States v. Stevens, 909 F.2d 431, 432-35 (6th Cir. 1990).

[37] United States v. Vasquez, 677 F.3d 685, 693-94 (5th Cir. 2012); United States v. Sanchez-Garcia, 461 F.3d 939, 946 (8th Cir. 2006); United States v. Price, 258 F.3d 539, 545 (6th Cir. 2001); United States v. Contreras, 249 F.3d 595, 598 (7th Cir. 2001).

[38] United States v. Lo, 447 F.3d 1212, 1226 (9th Cir. 2006); United States v. Johnson, 440 F.3d 1286, 1294-295 (11th Cir. 2006); United States v. Morton, 412 F.3d 901, 904 (8th Cir. 2005).

[39] United States v. Tyson, 653 F.3d 192, 207 (3d Cir. 2011).

[40] Salinas v. United States, 522 U.S. 52, 64 (1997); United States v. Moussaoui, 591 F.3d 263, 297 (4th Cir. 2010); United States v. Zichettello, 208 F.3d 72, 99 (2d Cir. 2000).

[41] United States v. Wright, 506 F.3d 1293, 1298 n.4 (10th Cir. 2007)("Wharton's Rule is that an agreement by two persons to commit a particular crime cannot be prosecuted as conspiracy when the crime is of such a nature as to necessarily require the participation of two persons for its commission").

[42] Iannelli v. United States, 420 U.S. 770, 781-82 (1975); United States v. Bornman, 559 F.3d 150, 156 (3d Cir. 2009).

[43] United States v. Bornman, 559 F.3d at 156 ("In the classic Wharton's Rule offenses – adultery, bigamy, incest, and duelling – the harms attendant upon the commission of the substantive offense are restricted to the parties in the agreement. Hence, Wharton's Rule has no applicability here [to bribery]"); United States v. Hines, 541 F.3d 833, 838 (8th Cir. 2008)("Wharton's Rule ... applies when there is a general congruence of the conspiracy agreement and the completed substantive offense. This general congruence exists when the parties to the agreement are the only persons who participate in commission of the substantive offense, ... the immediate consequences of the crime rest on the parties themselves rather than on society at large, and when the agreement that attends the substantive offense does not appear like to pose the distinct kinds of threats to society that the law of conspiracy seeks to avert").

[44] United States v. Edmonds, 679 F.3d 169, 175 (4th Cir. 2012); United States v. Spagnola, 632 F.3d 981, 986 (7th Cir. 2011); United States v. Paret-Ruiz, 567 F.3d 1, 6 (1st Cir. 2009); United States v. Williams, 547 F.3d 1187, 1195 n.7 (9th Cir. 2008).

[45] United States v. Jimenez Recio, 537 U.S.270, 274 (2003), citing, Iannelli v. United States, 420 U.S. 770, 777 (1975); United States v. Edmonds, 679 F.3d at 173; United States v. Corson, 579 F.3d 804, 810 (7th Cir. 2009); United States v. Chavez, 549 F.3d 119, 125 (2d Cir. 2008).

[46] United States v. Ruiz-Zarate, 678 F.3d 683, 689 (8th Cir. 2012); United States v. Whiteford, 676 F.3d 348, 357 (3d Cir. 2012); United States v. Rodriguez-Velez, 597 F.3d 32, 39 (1st Cir. 2010); United States v. Johnson, 592 F.3d 749, 754-55 (7th Cir. 2010); United States v. Wardell, 591 F.3d 1279, 1287 (10th Cir. 2009).

[47] United States v. Wardell, 591 F.3d at 1287-288.

[48] United States v. Donnell, 596 F.3d 913, 924-25 (8th Cir. 2010)("Mere proof of a buyer-seller agreement without any prior or contemporaneous understanding does not support a conspiracy conviction because there is no common illegal purpose: In such circumstances, the buyer's purpose is to buy; and the seller's purpose is to sell"); United States v. Bacon, 598 F.3d 772, 777 (11th Cir. 2010)(" ... the joint objective necessary for a conspiracy conviction is missing where the conspiracy is based simply on an agreement between a buyer and a seller for the sale of drugs").

[49] United States v. Johnson, 592 F.3d 749, 754 (7th Cir. 2010)("When the alleged coconspirators are in a buyer-seller relationship, however, we have cautioned against conflating the underlying buy-sell agreement with the drug-distribution agreement that is alleged to form the basis of the charge conspiracy. To support a conspiracy conviction there must be sufficient evidence of an agreement to commit a crime other than the crime that consists of the sale itself"); United States v. Deitz, 577 F.3d 672, 680 (6th Cir. 2009)("Generally, a buyer-seller relationship alone is insufficient to tie a buyer to a [larger] conspiracy because mere sales do not prove the existence of the agreement that must exist for there to be a conspiracy").

[50] United States v. Parker, 554 F.3d 230, 234-35 (2d Cir. 2009)("As a literal matter, when a buyer purchases illegal drugs from a seller, two persons have agreed to a concerted effort to achieve the unlawful transfer of the drugs from the seller to the buyer. According to the customary definition, that would constitute a conspiracy with the alleged objective of a transfer of drugs. Our case law, however, has carved out a narrow exception to the general conspiracy rule for such transactions.... [If] an addicted purchaser, who acquired drugs for his own use and without intent to distribute it to others, were deemed to have joined a conspiracy with his seller for the illegal transfer of the drugs from the seller to himself, the purchaser would be guilty of substantially the same crime, and liable for the same punishment, as the seller. The policy to distinguish between transfer of an illegal drug and the acquisition of possession of the drug would be frustrated. The buyer-seller exception thus protects a buyer or transferee from the severe liabilities intended only for transferors"); see also, United States v. Delgado, 672 F.3d 320, 333 (5th Cir. 2012).

[51] United States v. Bacon, 598 F.3d. at 777 ("Jamison was highly involved in the drug operation.... Jamison's drug transactions were larger than those that an ordinary buyer would make.... From this evidence, the jurors could reasonably infer that Jamison was a distributor"); United States v. Johnson, 592 F.3d at 754 ("Articulating this principle is somewhat easier than applying it; it is often difficult to determine what proof is sufficient to establish that individuals in a buyer-seller relationship also agreed to distribute drugs. Certain characteristics inherent in any ongoing buyer-seller relationships will also generally suggest the existence of a conspiracy. For example, sales of large quantities or drugs, repeated and/or standardized transactions, and a prolonged relationship between the parties constitute circumstantial evidence of a conspiracy"); United States v. Parker, 554 F.3d at 235 ("While providing that the unlawful transfer from seller to buyer cannot serve as the basis for a charge that the seller and buyer conspired with one another to make the illegal transfer from seller to buyer, the rule does not protect either the seller or buyer from a charge they conspired together to transfer drugs if the evidence supports a finding that they

shared a conspiratorial purpose to advance other transfers, whether by the seller or by the buyer").

[52] United States v. Wardell, 591 F.3d at 1288; see also United States v. Ruiz-Zarate, 678 F.3d 683, 690 (8th Cir. 2012)("But a defendant's mere presence, coupled with the knowledge that someone else who is present intends to sell drugs, is insufficient to establish membership in a conspiracy"); United States v. Tran, 568 F.3d 1156, 1165 9th Cir. 2009).

[53] Kotteakos v. United States, 328 U.S. 750, 755 (1946).

[54] Id. at 754-55("As the Circuit Court of Appeals said, there were at least eight, and perhaps more, separate and independent groups, none of which had any connection with any other, though all dealt independently with Brown as their agent. As the Government puts it, the pattern was that of separate spokes meeting at a common center, though, we may add, without the rim of the wheel to enclose the spokes").

[55] United States v. Brown, 587 F.3d 1082, 1089 (11th Cir. 2009)("Separate transactions are not necessarily separate conspiracies, so long as the conspirators act in concert to further a common goal. If a defendant's actions facilitated the endeavors of other co-conspirators, or facilitated the venture as a whole, a single conspiracy is established"); United States v. Baldridge, 559 F.3d 1126, 1136 (10th Cir. 2009)(emphasis in the original) ("A single conspiracy does not exist solely because many individuals deal with a common central player. What is required is a shared single criminal objective, not just similar or parallel objectives between similarly situated people").

[56] United States v. Calderon, 578 F.3d 78, 89 (1st Cir. 2009); see also United States v. Franklin, 561 F.3d 632, 402 (5th Cir. 2009); United States v. Brown, 587 F.3d 1082, 1089 (11th Cir. 2009).

[57] United States v. Wardell, 591 F.3d 1279, 1291 (10th Cir. 2009); see also, United States v. Acosta-Gallardo, 656 F.3d 1109, 1124 (10th Cir. 2011).

[58] United States v. Johnson, 592 F.3d 749, 754 (7th Cir. 2010)("To convict a defendant of conspiracy, the government must prove that (1) two or more people agreed to commit an unlawful act, and (2) the defendant knowingly and intentionally joined in the agreement"); United States v. Boria, 592 F.3d 476, 481 (3d Cir. 2010); United States v. Franklin, 561 F.3d at 402.

[59] United States v. Reed, 575 F.3d 900, 924 (9th Cir. 2009)("Once a conspiracy is established, only a slight connection to the conspiracy is necessary to support conviction. The term slight connection means that a defendant need not have known all the conspirators, participated in the conspiracy from its beginning, participated in all its enterprises, or known all its details"); United States v. Brown, 587 F.3d at 1089; United States v. Robinson, 547 F.3d 632, 642 (6th Cir. 2009); United States v. Eppolito, 543 F.3d 25, 47-8 (2d Cir. 2008).

[60] 18 U.S.C. 371 ("and one or more of such persons do any act to effect the object of the conspiracy"); United States v. Wardell, 591 F.3d 1279, 1287 (10th Cir. 2009); United States v. Schaffer, 586 F.3d 414, 422 (6th Cir. 2009); United States v. Kingrea, 573 F.3d 186, 195 (4th Cir. 2009).

[61] Braverman v. United States, 317 U.S. 49, 53 (1942); United States v. Kozeny, 667 F.3d 122, 132 (2d Cir. 2011); United States v. Rehak, 589 F.3d 965, 971 (8th Cir. 2009); United States v. Soy, 454 F.3d 766, 768 (7th Cir. 2006); United States v. Lukens, 114 F.3d 1220, 1222 (D.C.Cir. 1997).

[62] United States v. LaSpina, 299 F.3d 165, 176 (2d Cir. 2002); United States v. Schlei, 122 F.3d 944, 975 (11th Cir. 1997); United States v. Nelson, 66 F.3d 1036, 1044 (9th Cir. 1995).

[63] See Overt Acts, supra.

[64] United States v. Saybolt, 577 F.3d 195, 202 (3d Cir. 2009); United States v. Dedman, 527 F.3d 577, 594 n.7 (6th Cir. 2008); United States v. Lanier, 920 F.2d 887, 892 (11th Cir. 1991).

[65] See generally Goldstein, Conspiracy to Defraud the United States, 68 YALE LAW JOURNAL 405 (1958).

[66] United States v.Mubayyid, 658 F.3d 35, 52 (1st Cir. 2011); United States v. Root, 585 F.3d 145, 157 (3d Cir. 2009); United States v. World Wide Moving, N.V., 411 F.3d 502, 516 (4th Cir. 2005).

[67] Tanner v. United States, 483 U.S. 107, 128 (1987), citing, Dennis v. United States, 384 U.S. 855, 861 (1966); Glasser v. United States, 315 U.S. 60, 66 (1942); Hammerschmidt v. United States, 265 U.S. 182, 188 (1924); and Haas v. Henkel, 216 U.S. 462, 479 (1910); see also, United States v. Whiteford, 676 F.3d 348, 356 (3d Cir. 2012).

[68] Glasser v. United States, 315 U.S. at 66; Hammerschmidt v. United States, 265 U.S. at 188; United States v. Stewart, 590 F.3d 93, 109 (2d Cir. 2009)("In order to establish a conspiracy-to-defraud offense under 18 U.S.C. §371 ... a reasonable jury must have been able to conclude beyond a reasonable doubt (1) that the defendants entered into an agreement (2) to obstruct a lawful function of the government in this case, the administration and enforcement of the SAMs (3) by deceitful or dishonest means and (4) at least one overt act in furtherance of the conspiracy").

[69] Tanner v. United States, 483 U.S. 107, 128-32 (1987); United States v. Mendez, 528 F.3d. 811, 814-15 (11th Cir. 2008).

[70] Hammerschmidt v. United States, 265 U.S. at 188 ("It is not necessary that the government shall be subjected to property or pecuniary loss by the fraud, but only that its legitimate official action and purpose shall be defeated by misrepresentation"); United States v. Ballistrea, 101 F.3d 827, 832 (2d Cir. 1996)(This provision not only reaches schemes which deprive the government of money or property, but also is designed to protect the integrity of the United States and its agencies"); United States v. Dean, 55 F.3d 640, 647 (D.C. Cir. 1995)("If the government's evidence showed that Dean conspired to impair the functioning of the Department of Housing and Urban Development, no other form of injury to the Federal Government need be established for the conspiracy to fall under §371").

[71] "Whoever enters into any agreement, combination, or conspiracy to defraud the United States, or any department or agency thereof, by obtaining or aiding to obtain the payment or allowance of any false, fictitious, or fraudulent claim, shall be fined under this title or imprisoned not more than ten years, or both," 18 U.S.C. 286.

[72] United States v. Dedman, 527 F.3d 577, 593-94 (6th Cir. 2008). At least one other circuit also includes a materiality requirement, that is, the false, fictitious, or fraudulent assertion must be one which naturally has a material effect on the government's decision to pay or deny the claim, United States v. Saybolt, 577 F.3d 195, 201-204 (3d Cir. 2009).

[73] United States v. Saybolt, 577 F.3d 195, 202 (3d Cir. 2009); United States v. Dedman, 527 F.3d 577, 594 n.7 (6th Cir. 2008); United States v. Lanier, 920 F.2d 887, 892 (11th Cir. 1991).

[74] United States v. Payne, 591 F.3d 46, 69 (2d Cir. 2010)("Conspiracy is a continuing offense ... one that involves a prolonged course of conduct; its commission is not complete until the conduct has run its course"); United States v. Caldwell, 589 F.3d 1323, 1330 (10th Cir. 2009).

[75] United States v. Hodge, 594 F.3d 614, 619 (8th Cir. 2010); United States v. Caldwell, 589 F.3d at 1330; United States v. Egbert, 562 F.3d 1092, 1098 (10th Cir. 2009).

[76] United States v. Hodge, 594 F.3d at 619; United States v. Mangual-Santiago, 562 F.3d 411, 423 (1st Cir. 2009); United States v. Eppolito, 543 F.3d 25, 49 (2d Cir. 2008).

[77] United States v. Gonzalez, 596 F.3d 1228, 1234 (10th Cir. 2010)("The defense of termination by withdrawal requires that the defendant show that he or she has done some act to disavow or defeat the purpose of the conspiracy. Affirmative acts inconsistent with the object of the conspiracy and communicated in a manner reasonably calculated to reach co-conspirators have generally been regarded as sufficient to establish withdrawal"); United States v. Spotted Elk, 548 F.3d 641, 673 (8th Cir. 2008)("To withdraw from a conspiracy at common law, a conspirator must show not only that he ceased activities in furtherance of the conspiracy, but also that he either made a 'clean breast' to the government or else communicated the fact of withdrawal to his co-conspirators in a manner reasonably calculated to reach them"); United States v. Eppolito, 543 F.3d at 49.

[78] United States v. Lothian, 976 F.3d 1257, 1261 (9th Cir. 1992)("[B]ecause due process requires that the government prove each element of the offense beyond a reasonable doubt, once the defendant introduces sufficient evidence to make a prima facie case of withdrawal, the burden shifts to the government to prove beyond a reasonable doubt that the defendant did not withdraw"); accord, United States v. West, 877 F.2d 281, 289 (4th Cir. 1989); contra, United States v. Moore, 651 F.3d 30, 89-90 (D.C. Cir. 2011); United States v. Brown, 332 F.3d 363, 374 (6th Cir. 2003). The Supreme Court has agreed to review the issue, Smith v. United States, (Doc. No. 11-8976), cert. granted, ___ S.Ct. ___ (June 18, 2012).

[79] United States v. Bornman, 559 F.3d 150, 153 (3d Cir. 2009), citing Grunewald v. United States, 353 U.S. 391, 413 (1957); United States v. Turner, 548 F.3d 1094, 1097 (D.C. Cir. 2008).

[80] United States v. Upton, 559 F.3d 3, 10 (1st Cir. 2009); United States v. Weaver, 507 F.3d 178, 185-86 (3d Cir. 2007).

[81] 18 U.S.C. 371, 3571. An offender may fined twice of the amount of the gain or loss associated with the offense, even when such a fine would exceed the otherwise applicable $250,000/$500,000 maximums, 18 U.S.C. 3571(b)(2), (d).

[82] Gall v. United States, 552 U.S. 38, 49 (2007).

[83] Gall v. United States, 552 U.S. at 46, citing United States v. Booker, 543 U.S. 220, 260-62 (2005).

[84] Rita v. United States, 551 U.S. 338, 347 (2007).

[85] U.S.S.G. Sentencing Table.

[86] E.g., United States v. Stewart, 590 F.3d 93, 136 (2d Cir. 2009)("The district court initially calculated Yousry's Guidelines range based on a total offense level of 28 criminal history category of I, for a range of 78 to 97 months. According to the government, Yousry's applicable Guidelines range should have been enhanced in accordance with the terrorism enhancement provided by the Guidelines, U.S.S.G. §3A1.4. The district court concluded to the contrary that the terrorism enhancement did not apply to Yousry because he did not act with the requisite state of mind.).

[87] United States v. Farish, 535 F.3d 815, 826 (8th Cir. 2008)("If the jury had clearly convicted Farish of conspiracy to commit arson at the Diamond Lake Road West home, then the district court's entire restitution order would have been appropriate"); United States v. Brock-Davis, 504 F.3d 991, 999 (9th Cir. 2007)("Even were the law of restitution not more expansive for convictions for conspiracy than for other crimes, the district would not have committed error [in ordering restitution pursuant to a conspiracy conviction].... Finally, [omission] in the indictment is immaterial ... United States v. Boyd, 222 F.3d 47, 50 (2d Cir. 2000)(finding restitution payable under the MVRA [18 U.S.C. 3663A] 'by all convicted co-conspirators in respect of damage suffered by all victims of a conspiracy, regardless of the facts underlying courts of conviction in individual prosecutions')").

[88] United States v. Gutierrez-Avascal, 542 F.3d 495, 498 (5th Cir. 2008)("The language of [21 U.S.C. 846] is clear: those convicted of a conspiracy are subject to the same punishment as the target of that conspiracy. It is undisputed that a district court, in its discretion, has authority under [18 U.S.C. 3663] to order a defendant convicted under § 841 to pay restitution. The same authority exists, under the express terms of §846, against those who conspire to commit that crime"); United States v. Lanzotti, 205 F.3d 951, 958 (7th Cir. 2000)("In other words, the burden is on the defendant to show why restitution [under 18 U.S.C. 3663] is not warranted.... Lanzotti, as a member of the conspiracy, is liable for the actions of his co-conspirators, which includes restitution where appropriate. United States v. Brewer, 983 F.2d 181, 185 (10th Cir. 1993); United States v. Chaney, 964 F.2d 437, 452-53 (5th Cir. 1992)").

[89] United States v. Elson, 577 F.3d 713, 724-25 (6th Cir. 2009)("Elson's plea agreement explicitly provides that Elson will 'pay restitution to victims of the conspiracy to defraud orchestrated by Richard D. Schultz (J.A. 209), which is an offense different from his offense conviction – conspiracy to obstruct a grand jury investigation.... Accordingly, the district court properly ordered Elson to pay restitution to the victims of the conspiracy to defraud Schultz's creditors")

[90] 21 U.S.C. 853(a)("Any person convicted of a violation of this subchapter [the Controlled Substances Act] ... shall forfeit ... (1) any property constituting ... any proceeds.... the result of such violation; (2) any ... property used ... to commit, or to facilitate the commission of, such violation ... ").

[91] 18 U.S.C. 1963(a)("Whoever violates any provision of section 1962 ... shall forfeit to the United States ... (3) any property constituting ... any proceeds ... obtained ... from racketeering activity ... in violation of section 1962").

[92] United States v. Jimenez Recio, 537 U.S. 270, 274 (2003)(the conspiratorial "agreement is a distinct evil, which may exist and be punished whether or not the substantive offense ensues"); United States v. Mincoff, 574 F.3d 1186, 1198 (9th Cir. 2009); United States v. Eppolito, 543 F.3d 25, 47 (2d Cir. 2008).

[93] Pinkerton v. United States, 328 U.S. 640, 646-47 (1946); Callanan v. United States, 364 U.S. 587, 593 (1961); United States v. Wardell, 591 F.3d 1279, 1291 (10th Cir. 2009); United States v. Simmons, 581 F.3d 582, 587 (7th Cir. 2009).

[94] United States v. Rodriguez, 553 F.3d 380, 391 (5th Cir. 2008).

[95] United States v. Hernandez-Orellana, 539 F.3d 994, 1006-1007 (9th Cir. 2008)(emphasis in the original).

[96] United States v. Rehak, 589 F.3d 965, 971 (8th Cir. 2009); United States v. Iribe, 564 F.3d 1155, 1160 (9th Cir. 2009).

[97] United States v. Douglas, 525 F.3d 225, 251 (2d Cir. 2008).

[98] E.g., 18 U.S.C.32(b)(4)(attempts to sabotage commercial aircraft), 33 (attempts to sabotage commercial motor vehicles); 37(a) (attempted violation at international airports), 43(a)(2)(C)(attempted violence directed at animal enterprises), 81 (attempted arson within the special maritime or territorial jurisdiction of the United States), 175 (attempt use of biological weapons), 351(c)(attempted murder or kidnapping of a Member of Congress), 1512 (attempted obstruction of justice), 1956 (attempted money laundering). There are dozens of other attempt statutes in Title 18 of the United States Code and many others scattered throughout the other titles.

[99] United States v. Macias-Valencia, 510 F.3d 1012, 1014 (9th Cir. 2007)("conspiracy and attempt are inchoate crimes that do not require completion of the criminal objective"); United States v. Vigil, 523 F.3d 1258, 1267 (10th Cir. 2008)(attempt)("We do not require

that a defendant be on the verge of committing the specific act, rather the law allows criminal liability to attach at some point prior to the last proximate act"); United States v. Edmonds, 679 F.3d 169, 173 (4th Cir. 2012)("[T]he crime of conspiracy may exist and be punished whether or not the substantive crime ensues").

[100] United States v. Engle, 676 F.3d 405, 419-20 (4th Cir. 2012)(attempt); United States v. Wahlstrom, 588 F.3d 538, 543 (8th Cir. 2009)(attempt); United States v. Bristol-Martir, 570 F.3d 29, 39 (1st Cir. 2009)(attempt); United States v. Boria, 592 F.3d 476, 481 (3d Cir. 2010)("To establish a charge of conspiracy, the Government must show ... (2) an intent to achieve a common illegal goal").

[101] United States v. Williams, 553 U.S. 285, 300 (2008)("As with other inchoate crimes – attempt and conspiracy, for example – impossibility of completing the crime because the facts wee not as the defendant believed is not a defense"); United States v. Rehak, 589 F.3d at 971 ("Factual impossibility is not a defense to an inchoate offense such as conspiracy or attempt"); United States v. Engle, 676 F.3d 405, 420 (4th Cir. 2012)(attempt); United States v. Williams, 547 F.3d 1187, 1197 (9th Cir. 2008)(conspiracy).

[102] United States v. Iribe, 564 F.3d at 1160 ("Each of those crimes contains an element that the other does not: Conspiracy does not require a 'substantial step,' while attempt does not require an 'agreement'").

[103] United States v. Irving, 665 F.3d 1184, 1198 n.14 (10th Cir. 2011)(internal citations omitted)("In conspiracy law, given the existence of an unlawful agreement, virtually any act will satisfy the overt act requirement. In other words, the overt act need not necessarily be substantial. Attempt must include proof of a substantial step directed toward actual consummation of the crime, while conspiracy need not"); United States v. DeMarce, 564 F.3d 989, 998 (8th Cir. 2009)("The requisite elements of attempt are: 1) an intent ... and 2) conduct constituting a substantial step toward the commission of the substantive offense which strongly corroborates the actor's criminal intent. A substantial step goes beyond 'mere preparation' ... "); United States v. Barrow, 568 F.3d 215, 219 ("We have defined a 'substantial step' as 'conduct which strongly corroborates the firmness of [the] defendant's criminal attempt.' 'Mere preparation' is not enough"); United States v. Morris, 549 F.3d 548, 550 (7th Cir. 2008)("The 'substantial step' [required for conviction of attempt] toward completion is the demonstration of dangerousness, and has been usefully described as 'some overt act adapted to, approximating, and which in the ordinary and likely course of things will result in, the commission of the particular crime'").

[104] United States v. Engle, 676 F.3d 405, 491-20 (4th Cir. 2012); United States v. Fleming, 667 F.3d 1098, 1007 (10th Cir. 2011); United States v. Villegas, 655 F.3d 662, 1669 (7th Cir. 2011).

[105] United States v. Rivera-Relle, 333 F.3d 914, 921 n.11 (9th Cir. 2003)("Unlike conspiracy, the prosecution may not obtain convictions for both the completed offense and the attempt if the attempt has in fact been completed. The attempt is an offense included in the completed crime, and, therefore, cannot support a separate conviction and sentence").

[106] United States v. Iribe, 564 F.3d at 1161 ("Here, Defendant conspired to commit an actual kidnapping. He also committed a substantial step toward kidnapping. Thus, he was properly convicted of both conspiring to kidnap and attempting to kidnap").

[107] United States v. Korab, 893 F.2d 212, 215 (9th Cir. 1989)("Section 373(a) encompasses only solicitations of federal felonies").

[108] United States v. Hale, 448 F.3d 971, 983 (7th Cir. 2006), citing United States v. McNeil, 887 F.2d 448, 450 (3d Cir. 1989).

[109] United States v. Korab, 893 F.3d 212, 213 (9th Cir. 1989).

[110] 18 U.S.C. 373(b)("It is an affirmative defense to a prosecution under this section that, under circumstances manifesting a voluntary and complete renunciation of his criminal intent, the defendant prevented the commission of the crime solicited. A renunciation is not "voluntary and complete" if it is motivated in whole or in part by a decision to postpone the commission of the crime until another time or to substitute another victim or another but similar objective. If the defendant raises the affirmative defense at trial, the defendant has the burden of proving the defense by a preponderance of the evidence").

[111] 18 U.S.C. 373(c)("It is not a defense to a prosecution under this section that the person solicited could not be convicted of the crime because he lacked the state of mind required for its commission, because he was incompetent or irresponsible, or because he is immune from prosecution or is not subject to prosecution").

[112] A few crimes, such as certain terrorism and child abuse offenses have special longer statute of limitations, e.g., 18 U.S.C. 3283, 3286. Capital offenses may be tried at any time, 18 U.S.C. 3281.

[113] 18 U.S.C. 371 (" ... and one or more of such persons do any act to effect the object of the conspiracy ... "); United States v. Wardell, 591 F.3d 1279, 1287 (10th Cir. 2009); United States v. Schaffer, 586 F.3d 414, 422 (6th Cir. 2009); United States v. Kingrea, 573 F.3d 186, 195 (4th Cir. 2009).

[114] United States v. Saybolt, 577 F.3d 195, 202 (3d Cir. 2009); United States v. Dedman, 527 F.3d 577, 594 n.7 (6th Cir. 2008); United States v. Lanier, 920 F.2d 887, 892 (11th Cir. 1991).

[115] United States v. Bornman, 559 F.3d 150, 153 (3d Cir. 2009)(prosecution under §371)("For a conspiracy indictment to fall within the statute of limitations, it is incumbent on the Government to prove that at least one overt act in furtherance of the conspiracy was performed within five years of the date the Indictment was returned"); see also, United States v. Amirnazmi, 645 F.3d 564, 592 (3d Cir. 2011); United States v. Wilbur, 674 F.3d 1160, 1171 (9th Cir. 2012).

[116] United States v. Seher, 562 F.3d 1344, 1364 (11th Cir. 2009)(prosecution under 18 U.S.C. 1956(h) which has no overt act requirement)("The government satisfies the requirements of the statute of limitations for a non-overt act conspiracy if it alleges and proves that the conspiracy continued into the limitations period. A conspiracy is deemed to continue as long as its purposes have neither been abandoned nor accomplished, and no affirmative showing has been made that it has terminated"); United States v. Yannotti, 541 F.3d 112, 123 (2d Cir. 2008) (prosecution under 18 U.S.C. 1962(d) a non-overt act statute); United States v. Saadey, 393 F.3d 669, 677 (6th Cir. 2005)(same).

[117] Whitfield v. United States, 543 U.S. 209, 218 (2005).

[118] United States v. Bradley, 644 F.3d 1213, 1255 (11th Cir. 2011); United States v. Tzolov, 642 F.2d 314, 319-20 (2d Cir. 2011); United States v. Brodie, 534 F.3d 259, 273 (D.C. Cir. 2008); (each of these cases involves conspiracy under 18 U.S.C. 371 which carries an overt act requirement); United States v. Zamora, 661 F.3d 200, 208-209 (5th Cir. 2011); United States v. Acosta-Gallardo, 656 F.3d 1109, 1118 (10th Cir. 2011); United States v. Morales, 445 F.3d 1081, 1084 (8th Cir. 2006) (each of these cases involves conspiracy under 21 U.S.C. 846 which does not include an overt act requirement).

[119] "(a) Joinder of Offenses. The indictment or information may charge a defendant in separate counts with 2 or more offenses if the offenses charged – whether felonies or misdemeanors or both – are of the same or similar character, or are based on the same act or transaction, or are connected with or constitute parts of a common scheme or plan.

"(b) Joinder of Defendants. The indictment or information may charge 2 or more defendants if they are alleged to have participated in the same act or transaction, or in the same series of acts or transactions, constituting an offense or offenses. The defendants may be charged in one or more counts together or separately. All defendants need not be charged in each count," F.R.Crim.P 8.

[120] "The following must be raised before trial: ... (D) a Rule 14 motion to sever charges or defendants," F.R.Crim.P. 12(b)(3)(D). If the motion is denied, the courts will require that the motion be renewed at the close of the presentation of evidence or it will be considered waived, United States v. Williams, 553 F.3d 1073, 1079 (7th Cir. 2009); United States v. Sullivan, 522 F.3d 967, 981 (9th Cir. 2008).

[121] "(a) Relief. If the joinder of offenses or defendants in an indictment, an information, or a consolidation for trial appears to prejudice a defendant or the government, the court may order separate trials of counts, sever the defendants' trials, or provide any other relief that justice requires.

"(b) Defendant's Statements. Before ruling on a defendant's motion to sever, the court may order an attorney for the government to deliver to the court for in camera inspection any defendant's statement that the government intends to use as evidence," F.R.Crim.P. 14.

[122] Zafiro v. United States, 506 U.S. 534, 537 (1993).

[123] United States v. Williams, 553 F.3d 1073, 78-79 (7th Cir. 2009).

[124] United States v. Zapata, 546 F.3d 1179, 1191 (10th Cir. 2008); United States v. Lewis, 557 F.3d 601, 609 (8th Cir. 2009); United States v. Saunders, 553 F.3d 81, 85 (1st Cir. 2009); United States v. Wilson, 481 F.3d 475,482 (7th Cir. 2007).

[125] United States v. Spotted Elk, 548 F.3d 641, 658 (8th Cir. 2008).

[126] Zafiro v. United States, 506 U.S. at 539; see also, United States v. Mueller, 661 F.3d 338, 347(8th Cir. 2011) ("Generally, persons charged in a conspiracy should be tried together, especially when proof of the charges against the defendants is based upon the same evidence and acts. Nonetheless, a defendant can demonstrate real prejudice to his right to a fair trial by showing (a) his defense is irreconcilable with that of his co-defendant or (2) the jury will be unable to compartmentalize the evidence as it relates to the separate defendants"); United States v. Lewis, 557 F.3d at 609 ("To demonstrate the severe and compelling prejudice necessary to show that the court abused its discretion in denying severance, a defendant must show that his defense was irreconcilable with that of the codefendant or that the jury was unable to compartmentalize the evidence").

[127] Zafiro v. United States, 506 U.S. at 539.

[128] United States v. Moore, 651 F.3d 30, 95, 96 (D.C. Cir. 2011)("[E]ven when the risk of prejudice is high ... less drastic measures, such as limiting instructions, often will suffice to cure any risk of prejudice.... [T]he district court's jury instructions, by explaining that each defendant's guilt should be considered individually based upon the evidence that pertained to him, were sufficient to cure any such prejudice"); United States v. Williams, 553 F.3d 1073, 1079 (7th Cir. 2009)("[T]he district court gave a limiting instruction both before the presentation of the evidence and again at closing arguments that the jury should consider the evidence regarding each defendant separately. Such instructions are normally sufficient to cure any possibility of prejudice"); United States v. Spotted Elk, 548 F.3d at 658 ("As a practical matter, disparity among the defendants in extent of involvement and culpability is commonplace in conspiracy cases and does not alone show the kind of prejudice that would require a district court to sever, rather than to respond with some less drastic measure such as a curative instruction"); United States v. Reyeros, 537 F.3d 270, 286 (3d Cir.

2008)("Even if there were some risk of prejudice, here it is of the type that can be cured with proper instructions, and juries are presumed to follow their instructions").

[129] U.S. Const. Art.I, §§9, 10; Stogner v. California, 539 U.S. 607, 612 (2003).

[130] United States v. Julian, 427 F.3d. 471, 482 (7th Cir. 2005)("It is well established that a statute increasing a penalty with respect to a criminal conspiracy which commenced prior to, but was continued beyond the effective date of the statute, is not ex post facto as to that crime"); United States v. Valladares, 544 F.3d 1257, 1270-271 (11th Cir. 2008).

[131] U.S. Const. Amend. V.

[132] United States v. Dixon, 509 U.S. 688, 696 (1993)("The prohibition applies both to successive punishments and to successive prosecutions for the same offense"); Yeager v. United States, 557 U.S. 110, 119 (2009)("[T]he Double Jeopardy Clause precludes [as collateral estoppel] the Government from relitigating any issue that was necessarily decided by a jury's acquittal in a prior trial"); United States v. Wittig, 575 F.3d 1085, 1100-101 (10th Cir. 2009) ("[W]hen the only way the government can prove one of the elements of a conspiracy offense is to prove the same facts decided against it in a prior trial on a substantive offense, collateral estoppel bars the attempt").

[133] Rutledge v. United States, 517 U.S. 292, 297 (1996).

[134] United States v. Felix, 503 U.S. 378, 391 (1992); United States v. Yearwood, 518 F.3d 220, 223 (4th Cir. 2008); United States v. Gerhard, 615 F.3d 7, 23 (1st Cir. 2010).

[135] United States v. Rigas, 584 F.3d 594, 610 (3d Cir. 2009)(emphasis in the original); see also, United States v. Wheeler, 535 F.3d 446, 449 (6th Cir. 2008)(citing factors [1] through [4] in addition to the statutory offenses charged in the indictments); United States v. el-Mezain, 664 F.3d 467, 546 (5th Cir. 2011)("To determine whether the alleged conspirators entered into more than one agreement, we evaluate five factors: 1) time; 2) persons acting as co-conspirators; 3) the statutory offenses charge in the indictments; 4) the overt acts charged by the government or any other description of the offense charged that indicates the nature and scope of the activity that the government sought to punish in each case; and 5) places where the events alleged as part of the conspiracy took place").

[136] F.R.Evid. 801(c).

[137] United States v. Warman, 578 F.3d 320, 335 (6th Cir. 2009); United States v. Flores, 572 F.3d 1254, 1264 (11th Cir. 2009); United States v. Harris, 585 F.3d 394, 398 (7th Cir. 2009); United States v. Mitchell, 596 F.3d 18, 23 (1st Cir. 2010); United States v. Farhane, 634 F.3d 127, 161 (2d Cir. 2011).

[138] United States v. Warman, 578 F.3d at 335; United States v. Dowdell, 595 F.3d 50, 74 (1st Cir. 2010).

[139] United States v. Mitchell, 596 F.3d at 23; United States v. Liera, 585 F.3d 1237, 1245-246 (9th Cir. 2009); United States v. Benson, 591 F.3d 491, 502 (6th Cir. 2010).

[140] United States v. Warman, 578 F.3d at 338; United States v. Flores, 572 F.3d at 1264.

[141] United States v. Warman, 578 F.3d at 338; United States v. Alviar, 573 F.3d 526, 545(7th Cir. 2009)("In conspiracy cases statements that are part of the information flow between conspirators intended to help each perform his role satisfy the 'in furtherance' requirement of Rule 801(d)(2)(E)"); United States v. Flores, 572 F.3d at 1264.

[142] United States v. Warman, 578 F.3d at 338.

[143] Crawford v. Washington, 541 U.S. 36, 44, 52 (2004)("One of Raleigh's trial judges later lamented that the justice of England has never been so degraded and injured as by the condemnation of Sir Walter Raleigh. Through a series of statutory and judicial reforms, English law developed a right of confrontation that limited these abuses.... Raleigh's trial has long been thought as a paradigmatic confrontation violation").

[144] "If taken literally, the Clause would bar all hearsay, or at least all hearsay uttered by a declarant unavailable for examination at trial," Trachtenberg, Coconspirator, "Coventurers," and the Exception Swallowing the Hearsay Rule, 61 HASTINGS LAW JOURNAL 581, 637 (2010).

[145] Crawford v. Washington, 541 U.S. at 68 ("Where nontestimonial hearsay is at issue, it is wholly consistent with the Framers' design to afford the States [and Congress] flexibility in their development of hearsay law ... as would an approach that exempted such statements from Confrontation Clause scrutiny altogether. Where testimonial evidence is at issue, however, the Sixth Amendment demands what the common law required: unavailability and a prior opportunity for cross-examination").

[146] Id.

[147] Melendez-Diaz v. Massachusetts, 557 U.S. 305, 321 (2009), quoting Crawford v. Washington, 541 U.S. at 51-2 (2004).

[148] United States v. Hyles, 521 F.3d 946, 960 (8th Cir. 2008)("Neither ... were ... formal statements, nor were [the] statements elicited in response to government interrogation. In other words, they did not bear testimony. Therefore, Crawford is inapplicable"); United States v. Spotted Elk, 548 F.3d 641, 662 (8th Cir. 2008)("Blue Bird's reported utterance was not a statement of fact, but a proposal of a future course of action (i.e., what to say in the future), uttered not to any official, but to a co-defendant. Blue Bird's reported words were not testimonial, and therefore Frogg's account of them could not have violated Spotted Elk's Sixth Amendment rights"); United States v. US Infrastructure, Inc., 576 F.3d 1195, 1209 (11th Cir. 2009)("Given that McNair's statement to Dawson was part of a private conversation, it is 'nontestimonial' within the meaning of Crawford, and Crawford's strict Confrontation Clause requirements do not apply"); United States v. Farhane, 634 F.3d 127, 163 (2d Cir. 2011).

[149] United States v. Cesareo-Ayala, 576 F.3d 1120, 1127-128 (10th Cir. 2009)("The government contends that Mendez' statements in the two conversations are not hearsay and do not implicate the Confrontation Clause because they were not offered in evidence to prove the truth of the matter asserted. We agree"); United States v. Brown, 560 F.3d 754, 765 (8th Cir. 2009)("Because Williams's statement was not admitted for the truth of the matter asserted, it does not implicate the confrontation clause").

[150] United States v. Hargrove, 508 F.3d 445, 449 (7th Cir. 2007)("Under Rule 801(d)(2)(E) the statements of coconspirators made during the course and in furtherance of the conspiracy are considered admissions by a party opponent and are not hearsay. The use of this sort of evidence does not implicate the Confrontation Clause"); United States v. Singh, 494 F.3d 653, 659 (8th Cir. 2007)("[C]o-conspirators' statements made in furtherance of a conspiracy and admitted under Rule 801(d)(2)(E) are generally non-testimonial and, therefore, do not violate the Confrontation Clause as interpreted by the Supreme Court"); but see United States v. Warman, 578 F.3d 320, 346 (6th Cir. 2009) ("[S]tatements of a confidential informant are testimonial in nature and therefore, may not be offered by the government to establish the guilt of an accused absent an opportunity for the accused to cross-examine the informant").

In: Conspiratorial Crimes … ISBN: 978-1-62618-426-8
Editors: L. C. Wright and J. C. Miller

Chapter 2

RICO: A BRIEF SKETCH*

Charles Doyle

SUMMARY

Congress enacted the federal Racketeer Influenced and Corrupt Organization (RICO) provisions as part of the Organized Crime Control Act of 1970. In spite of its name and origin, RICO is not limited to "mobsters" or members of "organized crime" as those terms are popularly understood. Rather, it covers those activities which Congress felt characterized the conduct of organized crime, no matter who actually engages in them.

RICO proscribes no conduct that is not otherwise prohibited. Instead it enlarges the civil and criminal consequences, under some circumstances, of a list of state and federal crimes.

In simple terms, RICO condemns:

(1) any person
(2) who
    (a) invests in, or
    (b) acquires or maintains an interest in, or
    (c) conducts or participates in the affairs of, or
    (d) conspires to invest in, acquire, or conduct the affairs of
(3) an enterprise
(4) which

---

* This is an edited, reformatted and augmented version of the Congressional Research Service Publication, CRS Report for Congress 96-950, dated December 7, 2012.

  (a) engages in, or
  (b) whose activities affect, interstate or foreign commerce
(5) through
  (a) the collection of an unlawful debt, or
  (b) the patterned commission of various state and federal crimes.

Violations are punishable by (a) the forfeiture of any property acquired through a RICO violation and of any property interest in the enterprise involved in the violation, and (b) imprisonment for not more than 20 years, or for life if one of the predicate offenses carries such a penalty, and/or a fine of not more than the greater of twice the amount of gain or loss associated with the offense or $250,000 for individuals and $500,000 for organizations. RICO has generally survived constitutional challenges, although its forfeiture provisions are subject to an excessive fines clause analysis and perhaps to cruel and unusual punishment disproportionality analysis.

RICO violations also subject the offender to civil liability. The courts may award anyone injured in their business or property by a RICO violation treble damages, costs and attorneys' fees, and may enjoin RICO violations, order divestiture, dissolution or reorganization, or restrict an offender's future professional or investment activities. Civil RICO has been controversial. At one time commentators urged Congress to amend its provisions. Congress found little consensus on the questions raised by proposed revisions, however, and the issue seems to have been put aside at least for the time being.

The text of the RICO sections, citations to state RICO statutes, and a selected bibliography are appended.

I. Introduction

Congress enacted the federal Racketeer Influenced and Corrupt Organization (RICO) provisions[1] as part of the Organized Crime Control Act of 1970.[2] In spite of its name and origin, RICO is not limited to "mobsters" or members of "organized crime," as those terms are popularly understood.[3] Rather, it covers those activities which Congress felt characterized the conduct of organized crime, no matter who actually engages in them.[4]

RICO proscribes no conduct that is not otherwise prohibited.[5] Instead it enlarges the civil and criminal consequences, under some circumstances, of a list of state and federal crimes.[6]

In simple terms, RICO condemns:

(1) any person
(2) who
  (a) invests in, or
  (b) acquires or maintains an interest in, or
  (c) conducts or participates in the affairs of, or
  (d) conspires to invest in, acquire, or conduct the affairs of
(3) an enterprise
(4) which
  (a) engages in, or
  (b) whose activities affect, interstate or foreign commerce
(5) through
  (a) the collection of an unlawful debt, or
  (b) the patterned commission of various state and federal crimes.[7]

Violations are punishable by (a) forfeiture of any property acquired through a RICO violation and of any property interest in the enterprise involved in the violation, and (b) imprisonment for not more than 20 years, or life if one of the predicate offenses carries such a penalty, and/or a fine of not more than the greater of twice of amount of gain or loss associated with the offense or $250,000 for individuals and $500,000 for organizations.[8]

RICO violations also subject the offender to civil liability. The courts may award anyone injured by a RICO violation treble damages, costs and attorneys' fees,[9] and may enjoin RICO violations, order divestiture, dissolution or reorganization, or restrict an offender's future professional or investment activities.[10]

RICO also makes provision (1) for venue and service of process in criminal and civil cases;[11] (2) for expedited judicial action in certain civil cases brought by the United States;[12] (3) for in camera proceedings in civil cases initiated by the United States;[13] and (4) for the Department of Justice's use of civil investigative demands.[14]

II. A Closer Look at the Elements

A. Any Person

Any person may violate RICO.[15] The "person" need not be a mobster or even a human being; "any individual or entity capable of holding a legal or beneficial interest in property" will do.[16]

Although the "person" and the "enterprise" must be distinct in the case of a subsection 1962(c) violation (conducting an enterprise's activities through racketeering activity),[17] a corporate entity and its sole shareholder are sufficiently distinct to satisfy the enterprise and person elements of a subsection (c) violation.[18] The "person" and "enterprise" need not be distinct for purposes of subsection 1962(a) (investing the racketeering activity proceeds in an enterprise) or subsection 1962(b) (acquiring or maintaining an enterprise through racketeering activity) violations.[19]

Even though governmental entities may constitute a corrupted RICO enterprise[20] or in some instances the victims of a RICO offense,[21] they are not considered "persons" capable of a RICO violation.[22]

B. Conduct

1. Invest

RICO addresses four forms of illicit activity reflected in the four subsections of section 1962: (a) acquiring or operating an enterprise using racketeering proceeds; (b) controlling an enterprise using racketeering activities; (c) conducting the affairs of an enterprise using racketeering activities; and (d) conspiring to so acquire, control, or conduct.

The first, 18 U.S.C. 1962(a), was designed as something of a money laundering provision.[23] "The essence of a violation of §1962(a) is not commission of predicate acts but investment of racketeering income."[24] It introduces several features of its own and has been described as the most difficult to prove.[25] Under its provisions, it is unlawful for

(1) any person
(2) who is liable as a principal
    (a) in the collection of an unlawful debt or
    (b) in a pattern of predicate offenses
(3) to use or invest
(4) the income from such misconduct
(5) to acquire, establish or operate
(6) an enterprise in or affecting commerce.[26]

The "person," the pattern of predicate offenses, and the enterprise elements are common to all of the subsections. For purposes of 1962(a), however, a legal entity that benefits from the offense may be both the "person" and the "enterprise."[27] The person must have committed usury or a pattern of predicate offenses or aided and abetted in their commission,[28] have received income that would not otherwise have been received as a result, and used those proceeds to acquire or operate an enterprise in or whose activities have an impact on interstate or foreign commerce.[29]

2. Acquire or Maintain

The second proscription, 18 U.S.C. 1962(b), is much the same, except that it forbids acquisition or control of an enterprise through the predicates themselves rather than through the income derived from the predicates. It makes it unlawful for

(1) any person
(2) to acquire or maintain an interest in or control of
(3) a commercial enterprise
(4) through
   (a) the collection of an unlawful debt or
   (b) a pattern of predicate offenses.[30]

As in the case of subsection 1962(a), the "person" and the "enterprise" may be one and the same.[31] There must be a nexus between the predicate offenses and the acquisition of control.[32] Exactly what constitutes "interest" or "control" is a case-by-case determination. The defendant must be shown to have played some significant role in the management of the enterprise, but a showing of complete control is unnecessary.[33]

3. Conduct of Affairs

Subsection 1962(c) makes it unlawful for

(1) any person,
(2) employed by or associated with,
(3) a commercial enterprise
(4) to conduct or participate in the conduct of the enterprise's affairs
(5) through
   (a) the collection of an unlawful debt or
   (b) a pattern of predicate offenses.[34]

Subsection 1962(c) is the most common substantive basis for RICO prosecution or civil action.[35] Although on its face subsection 1962(c) might appear to be less demanding than subsections 1962(a) and (b), the courts have not always read it broadly. Thus, in any charge of a breach of its provisions, the "person" and the "enterprise" must ordinarily be distinct.[36] The requirement cannot be avoided by charging a corporate entity as the "person" and the officers and employees through whom it must act as an "association in fact" enterprise.[37] A corporate entity and its sole shareholder, however, are sufficiently distinct for purposes of subsection 1962(c).[38]

The Supreme Court has identified an entrepreneurial stripe in the "conduct or participate in the conduct" element of subsection 1962(c) under which only those who direct the operation or management of the enterprise itself satisfy the "conduct" element.[39] Liability, however, is not limited to the "upper management" of an enterprise, but extends as well to those within the enterprise who exercise broad discretion in carrying out the instructions of upper management.[40] Moreover, conviction requires neither an economic predicate offense nor a predicate offense committed with an economic motive.[41]

C. Pattern of Racketeering Activity

1. Predicate Offenses

The heart of most RICO violations is a pattern of racketeering activities, i.e., the patterned commission of two or more designated state or federal crimes. The list of state and federal crimes upon which a RICO violation may be predicated includes:

(A) any act or threat involving—

murder	arson
kidnaping	bribery
gambling	extortion
robbery	

dealing in obscene material, or
dealing in controlled substances or listed chemicals
chargeable under state law and punishable by imprisonment for more than one year;

(B) violation of—

18 U.S.C. 201 (bribery of federal officials)
18 U.S.C. 224 (bribery in sporting contests)
18 U.S.C. 471, 472, 473 (counterfeiting)

18 U.S.C. 659 (theft from interstate shipments)(if felonious)
18 U.S.C. 664 (theft from employee benefit plan)
18 U.S.C. 891-894 (loansharking)
18 U.S.C. 1028 (fraudulent identification documents)(if for profit)
18 U.S.C. 1029 (computer fraud)
18 U.S.C. 1084 (transmission of gambling information)
18 U.S.C. 1341 (mail fraud)
18 U.S.C. 1343 (wire fraud)
18 U.S.C. 1344 (bank fraud)
18 U.S.C. 1425 (procuring nationalization unlawfully)
18 U.S.C. 1426 (reproduction of naturalization papers)
18 U.S.C. 1427 (sale of naturalization papers)
18 U.S.C. 1461-1465 (obscene matter)
18 U.S.C. 1503 (obstruction of justice)
18 U.S.C. 1510 (obstruction of criminal investigation)
18 U.S.C. 1511 (obstruction of state law enforcement)
18 U.S.C. 1512 (witness tampering)
18 U.S.C. 1513 (witness retaliation)
18 U.S.C. 1542, 1543, 1544, 1546 (passport or similar document fraud)
18 U.S.C. 1581-1592 (peonage & slavery)
18 U.S.C. 1951 (Hobbs Act (interference with commerce by threat or violence)
18 U.S.C. 1952 (Travel Act (interstate travel in aid of racketeering)
18 U.S.C. 1953 (transportation of gambling paraphernalia)
18 U.S.C. 1954 (bribery to influence employee benefit plan)
18 U.S.C. 1955 (illegal gambling business)
18 U.S.C. 1956, 1957 (money laundering)
18 U.S.C. 1958 (murder for hire)
18 U.S.C. 1960 (illegal money transmitters)
18 U.S.C. 2251, 2251A, 2252, 2260 (sexual exploitation of children)
18 U.S.C. 2312, 2313 (interstate transportation of stolen cars)
18 U.S.C. 2314, 2315 (interstate transportation of stolen property)
18 U.S.C. 2318-2320 (copyright infringement)
18 U.S.C. 2321 (trafficking in certain motor vehicles or motor vehicle parts)
18 U.S.C. 2341-2346 (contraband cigarettes)
18 U.S.C. 2421-2424 (Mann Act)

(C) indictable violations of—

29 U.S.C. 186 (payments and loans to labor organizations)
29 U.S.C. 501(c) (embezzlement of union funds)

(D) any offense involving—
fraud connected with a case under title 11 (bankruptcy)
fraud in the sale of securities
felonious violations of federal drug law

(E) violation of the Currency and Foreign Transactions Reporting Act [31 U.S.C. 5311-5332]

(F) violation (for profit) of the Immigration and Nationality Act, section 274 (bringing in and harboring aliens), section 277 (helping aliens enter the U.S. unlawfully), or section 278 (importing aliens for immoral purposes), and

(G) violation of [a statute identified as a federal crime of terrorism in 18 U.S.C.
2332b(g)(5)(B)]—
18 U.S.C. 32 (destruction of aircraft or aircraft facilities)
18 U.S.C. 37 (violence at international airports)
18 U.S.C. 81 (arson within special maritime and territorial jurisdiction)
18 U.S.C. 175 or 175b (biological weapons)
18 U.S.C. 175c (variola virus)
18 U.S.C. 229 (chemical weapons)
18 U.S.C. 351(a), (b), (c), or (d) (congressional, cabinet, and Supreme Court assassination and kidnaping)
18 U.S.C. 831 (nuclear materials)
18 U.S.C. 832 (participating in foreign nuclear program)
18 U.S.C. 842(m) or (n) (plastic explosives)
18 U.S.C. 844(f)(2) or (3) (arson and bombing of Government property risking or causing death)
18 U.S.C. 844(i) (arson and bombing of property used in interstate commerce)
18 U.S.C. 930(c) (killing or attempted killing during an attack on a Federal facility with a dangerous weapon)
18 U.S.C. 956(a)(1) (conspiracy to murder, kidnap, or maim persons abroad)
18 U.S.C. 1030(a)(1) (protection of computers)
18 U.S.C. 1030(a)(5)(A)(damage to protected computers under 1030(a)(4)(A)(i)(II) through (VI))

18 U.S.C. 1114 (killing or attempted killing of officers and employees of the United States)
18 U.S.C. 1116 (murder or manslaughter of foreign officials, official guests, or internationally protected persons)
18 U.S.C. 1203 (hostage taking)
18 U.S.C. 1361 (destruction of government property)
18 U.S.C. 1362 (destruction of communication lines, stations, or systems)
18 U.S.C. 1363 (injury to buildings or property within special maritime and territorial jurisdiction of the United States)
18 U.S.C. 1366(a) (destruction of an energy facility)
18 U.S.C. 1751(a), (b), (c), or (d) (presidential and presidential staff assassination and kidnaping)
18 U.S.C. 1992 (attacks on trains or mass transit)
18 U.S.C. 2155-2156 (destruction of national defense materials, premises, or utilities)
18 U.S.C. 2280 (violence against maritime navigation)
18 U.S.C. 2281 (violence against maritime fixed platforms)
18 U.S.C. 2332 (homicide and other violence against United States nationals occurring outside of the United States)
18 U.S.C. 2332a (use of weapons of mass destruction)
18 U.S.C. 2332b (acts of terrorism transcending national boundaries)
18 U.S.C. 2332f (bombing public places and facilities)
18 U.S.C. 2332g (anti-aircraft missiles)
18 U.S.C. 2332h (radiological dispersal devices)
18 U.S.C. 2339 (harboring terrorists)
18 U.S.C. 2339A (providing material support to terrorists)
18 U.S.C. 2339B (providing material support to terrorist organizations)
18 U.S.C. 2339C (financing terrorism)
18 U.S.C. 2339D (receipt of training from foreign terrorist organization)
18 U.S.C. 2340A (torture)
21 U.S.C. 960A (narco-terrorism)
42 U.S.C. 2122 (atomic weapons)
42 U.S.C. 2284 (sabotage of nuclear facilities or fuel)
49 U.S.C. 46502 (aircraft piracy)
49 U.S.C. 46504 (2d sentence) (assault on a flight crew with a dangerous weapon)

49 U.S.C. 46505(b)(3) or (c) (explosive or incendiary devices, or endangerment of human life by means of weapons, on aircraft)
49 U.S.C. 46506 (if homicide or attempted homicide is involved, application of certain criminal laws to acts on aircraft)
49 U.S.C. 60123(b) (destruction of interstate gas or hazardous liquid pipeline facility).[42]

To constitute "racketeering activity," the predicate offense need only be *committed*; there is no requirement that the defendant or anyone else have been convicted of a predicate offense before a RICO prosecution or action may be brought.[43] Conviction of a predicate offense, on the other hand, does not preclude a subsequent RICO prosecution, nor is either conviction or acquittal a bar to a subsequent RICO civil action.[44]

2. Pattern

The pattern of racketeering activities element of RICO requires (1) the commission of two or more predicate offenses, (2) that the predicate offenses be related and not simply isolated events, and (3) that they are committed under circumstances that suggest either a continuity of criminal activity or the threat of such continuity.

i. *Predicates*: The first element is explicit in section 1961(5): "'Pattern of racketeering activity' requires at least two acts of racketeering activity." The two remaining elements, relationship and continuity, flow from the legislative history of RICO. That history "shows that Congress indeed had a fairly flexible concept of a pattern in mind. A pattern is not formed by sporadic activity.... [A] person cannot be subjected to the sanctions [of RICO] simply for committing two widely separate and isolated criminal offenses. Instead, the term 'pattern' itself requires the showing of a relationship between the predicates and of the threat of continuing activity. It is this factor of *continuity plus relationship* which combines to produce a pattern."[45]
ii. *Related predicates*: The commission of predicate offenses forms the requisite related pattern if the "criminal acts ... have the same or similar purposes, results, participants, victims, or methods of commission, or otherwise are interrelated by distinguishing characteristics and are not isolated events."[46]
iii. *Continuity*: The law recognizes continuity in two forms, pre-existing ("closed-ended") and anticipated ("open-ended"). The first is

> characterized by "a series of related predicates, extending over a substantial period of time. Predicate acts extending over a few weeks or months and threatening no future criminal conduct do not satisfy this requirement."[47] The second exists when a series of related predicates has begun and, but for intervention, would be a threat to continue in the future.[48] The Supreme Court has characterized a pattern extending over a period of time but which posed no threat of reoccurrence as a pattern with "closed-ended" continuity; and a pattern marked by a threat of reoccurrence as a pattern with "open-ended continuity."[49]

In the case of a "closed-ended" pattern, the lower courts have been reluctant to find predicate activity extending over less than a year sufficient for the "substantial period[s] of time" required to demonstrate continuity.[50] Whether the threat of future predicate activity is sufficient to recognize an "open-ended" pattern of continuity depends upon the nature of the predicate offenses and the nature of the enterprise. "Though the number of related predicates involved may be small and they may occur close together in time, the racketeering acts themselves include a specific threat of repetition extending indefinitely into the future, and thus supply the requisite continuity. In other cases, the threat of continuity may be established by showing that the predicate acts or offenses are part of an ongoing entity's regular way of doing business."[51] Moreover, the threat "is generally presumed when the enterprise's business is primarily or inherently unlawful."[52]

D. Collection of an Unlawful Debt

Collection of an unlawful debt may be the only instance in which the commission of a single predicate offense will support a RICO prosecution or cause of action. No proof of pattern seems to be necessary.[53]

The predicate covers both usury and the collection of gambling debts:

> "[U]nlawful debt" means a debt (A) incurred or contracted in gambling activity which was in violation of the law of the United States, a State or political subdivision thereof, or which is unenforceable under State or Federal law in whole or in part as to principal or interest because of the laws relating to usury, and (B)

> which was incurred in connection with the business of gambling in violation of the law of the United States, a State or political subdivision thereof, or the business of lending money or a thing of value at a rate usurious under State or Federal law, where the usurious rate is at least twice the enforceable rate.[54]

E. Enterprise in or Affecting Interstate or Foreign Commerce

1. Enterprise

The statute defines "enterprise" to include "any individual, partnership, corporation, association, or other legal entity, and any union or group of individuals associated in fact although not a legal entity."[55] The enterprise may be devoted to entirely legitimate ends or to totally corrupt objectives.[56] It may be governmental as well as nongovernmental.[57] As noted earlier, an entity may not serve as both the "person" and the "enterprise" whose activities are conducted through a pattern of racketeering activity for a prosecution under subsection 1962(c).[58] No such distinction is required, however, for a prosecution under either subsection 1962(a)(investing the racketeering activity proceeds in an enterprise) or subsection 1962(b) (acquiring or maintaining an enterprise through racketeering activity) violations.[59] Even under subsection 1962(c), a corporate entity and its sole shareholder are sufficiently distinct to satisfy the "enterprise" and "person" elements of a subsection (c) violation.[60] As for "associated in fact" enterprises, the Supreme Court in *Boyle* rejected the suggestion that such enterprises must be "business-like" creatures, having discernible hierarchical structures, unique modus operandi, chains of command, internal rules and regulations, regular meetings regarding enterprise activities, or even a separate enterprise name or title.[61] The statute demands only "that an association-in-fact enterprise must have at least three structural features: a purpose, relationships among those associated with the enterprise, and longevity sufficient to permit these associates to pursue the enterprise's purpose."[62]

2. In or Affecting Interstate or Foreign Commerce

To satisfy RICO's jurisdictional element, the corrupt or corrupted enterprise must either engage in interstate or foreign commerce or engage in activities that affect interstate or foreign commerce.[63] An enterprise that orders supplies and transports its employees and products in interstate commerce is "engaged in interstate commerce" for purposes of RICO.[64] As a general rule, the impact of the enterprise on interstate or foreign commerce need only be minimal to satisfy RICO requirements.[65] Where the predicate offenses associated with an enterprise have an effect on interstate commerce, the enterprise is likely to have an effect on interstate commerce.[66] However, "where the enterprise itself [does] not engage in economic activity, a minimal effect on commerce will not do."[67]

III. CONSPIRACY

Conspiracy under subsection 1962(d) is

(1) the agreement of
(2) two or more
(3) to invest in, acquire, or conduct the affairs of
(4) a commercial enterprise
(5) in a manner which violates 18 U.S.C. 1962(a), (b), or (c).[68]

The heart of the crime lies in the agreement rather than any completed, concerted violation of the other three RICO subsections. In fact, unlike the general conspiracy statute, RICO conspiracy is complete upon the agreement, even if none of the conspirators ever commit an overt act towards the accomplishment of its criminal purpose.[69] Moreover, contrary to the view once held by some of the lower courts, there is no requirement that a defendant commit or agree to commit two or more predicate offenses himself.[70] Nor is necessary that the government prove the existence of RICO qualified enterprise.[71] It is enough that the defendant, in agreement with another, intended to further an endeavor which, if completed, would satisfy all of the elements of a RICO violation.[72]

A conspirator is liable not only for the conspiracy but for any foreseeable substantive offenses committed by any of the conspirators in furtherance of the common scheme, until the objectives of the plot are achieved, abandoned, or the conspirator withdraws.[73] "To withdraw from a conspiracy, an individual must take some affirmative action either by reporting to authorities or communicating his intentions to his coconspirators."[74]

IV. CONSEQUENCES

The commission of a RICO violation exposes offenders to a wide range of criminal and civil consequences: imprisonment, fines, restitution, forfeiture, treble damages, attorneys' fees, and a wide range of equitable restrictions.

A. Criminal Liability

RICO violations are punishable by fine *or* by imprisonment for life in cases where the predicate offense carries a life sentence, *or* by imprisonment for not more than 20 years in all other cases.[75] Although an offender may be sentenced to either a fine or a term of imprisonment under the strict terms of the statute, the operation of the applicable sentencing guidelines makes it highly likely that offenders will face *both* fine and imprisonment.[76] The maximum amount of the fine for a RICO violation is the greater of twice the amount of the gain or loss associated with the crime, or $250,000 for an individual, $500,000 for an organization.[77] Offenders sentenced to prison are also sentenced to a term of supervised release of not more than three years to be served following their release from incarceration.[78] Most RICO violations also trigger mandatory federal restitution provisions, that is, one of the RICO predicate offenses will be a crime of violence, drug trafficking, or a crime with respect to which a victim suffers physical injury or pecuniary loss.[79] Finally, property related to a RICO violation is subject to confiscation.[80]

Even without a completed RICO violation, committing any crime designated a RICO predicate offense opens the door to additional criminal liability. It is a 20-year felony to launder the proceeds from any predicate offense (including any RICO predicate offense) or to use them to finance further criminal activity.[81] Moreover, the proceeds of any RICO predicate offense are subject to civil forfeiture (confiscation without the necessity of a criminal conviction) by virtue of the RICO predicate's status as a money laundering predicate.[82]

B. Civil Liability

RICO violations may result in civil as well as criminal liability. "Any person injured in his business or property by reason" of a RICO violation has a cause of action for treble damages and attorneys' fees.[83] No prior criminal conviction is required, except in the case of certain security fraud based causes of action.[84]

Liability begins with a RICO violation under subsections 1962(a), (b), (c), or (d). If the underlying violation involves subsection 1962(a)(use of predicate offense tainted proceeds to acquire an interest in an enterprise), it is the use or investment of the income rather than the predicate offenses that must have caused the injury.[85] If the underlying violation involves subsection 1962(b)(use of predicate offenses to acquire an enterprise), it is the access or control of the RICO enterprise rather than the predicate offenses that must have caused the injury.[86] If the underlying violation involves subsection 1962(c) (use of predicate offenses to conduct the activities of an enterprise), it is the predicate offenses which must have caused the injury.[87] If the underlying violation involves subsection 1962(d) (conspiracy to violate subsections 1962(a), (b), or (c)), the injury must follow from the conspiracy. Moreover, while a criminal conspiracy prosecution under subsection 1962(d) requires no overt act, RICO plaintiffs whose claim is based on a conspiracy under subsection 1962(d) must prove an overt act that is a predicate offense or one of the substantive RICO offenses, since a mere agreement cannot be the direct or proximate cause of an injury.[88]

In order to recover, the plaintiff must establish an injury to his or her business or property directly or proximately caused by the defendant's RICO violation.[89] Downstream victims have no RICO cause of action. The presence of an intervening victim or cause of the harm is fatal.[90] The RICO-caused injury must involve a "concrete financial loss," a "mere injury to a valuable intangible property interest" such as a right to pursue employment will not do.[91] The courts agree generally that personal injuries may not form the basis for recovery, since they are not injuries to "business or property,"[92] but the courts sometimes disagree on what does constitute a qualified injury.[93]

"Fraud in the sale of securities" is a RICO predicate offense.[94] However, the Private Securities Litigation Reform Act amended the civil RICO cause of action to bar suits based on allegations of fraud in the purchase or sale of securities.[95]

Although the United States is apparently not a "person" that may sue for treble damages under RICO,[96] the term does include state and local governmental entities.[97] On the other hand, private parties have enjoyed scant success when they have sought to bring a RICO suit for damages against the United States or other governmental entities.[98] Nor in most instances have the courts been receptive to RICO claims based solely on allegations that the defendant aided and abetted commission of the underlying RICO violation.[99]

Notwithstanding the inability of the United States to sue for treble damages under RICO, the Attorney General may seek to prevent and restrain RICO violations under the broad equitable powers vested in the courts to order disgorgement, divestiture, restitution, or the creation of receiverships or trusteeships.[100] This authority has been invoked relatively infrequently, primarily to rid various unions of organized crime and other forms of corruption.[101] There is some question whether private plaintiffs, in addition to the Attorney General, may seek injunctive and other forms of equitable relief.[102]

On the procedural side, RICO's long-arm jurisdictional provisions authorize nationwide service of process.[103] In addition, the Supreme Court has held that (1) state trial courts of general jurisdiction have concurrent jurisdiction over federal civil RICO claims;[104] (2) under the appropriate circumstances parties may agree to make potential civil RICO claims subject to arbitration;[105] (3) the Clayton Act's four-year period of limitation applies to civil RICO claims as well,[106] and that the period begins when the victim discovers or should have discovered the injury;[107] and (4) in the absence of an impediment to state regulation, the McCarran-Ferguson Act does not bar civil RICO claims based on insurance fraud allegations.[108]

V. CONSTITUTIONAL QUESTIONS

Over the years, various aspects of RICO have been challenged on a number of constitutional grounds. Most either attack the RICO scheme generally or its forfeiture component. The general challenges have been based on vagueness, ex post facto, and double jeopardy. Attacks on the constitutionality of RICO forfeiture have been grounded in the right to counsel, excessive fines, cruel and unusual punishment, and forfeiture of estate. While the challenges have been unsuccessful by and large, some have helped to define RICO's outer reaches.

A. General

1. Legislative Authority under the Commerce Clause

The Constitution authorizes Congress to "regulate Commerce with foreign Nations, and among the several States, and with the Indian Tribes," and "to make all Laws which shall be necessary and proper for carrying to Execution" that authority, U.S. Const. Art. I, §8, cls.3, 18. The powers which the Constitution does not confer upon the federal government, it reserves to the states and the people, U.S. Const. Amend. X. Although RICO deals only with enterprises "engaged in, or the activities of which affect, interstate or foreign commerce," some have suggested that RICO has been applied beyond the scope of Congress' constitutional authority to legislate under the commerce clause.[109] The courts have yet to agree.[110]

2. Double Jeopardy

Even a general description of RICO evokes double jeopardy and ex post facto questions. RICO rests on a foundation of other crimes. At a glance, double jeopardy might appear to block any effort to base a RICO charge on a crime for which the accused had already been tried. By the same token, ex post facto might appear to bar a RICO charge built upon a predicate offense committed before RICO was enacted or before the crime was added to the list of RICO predicates. On closer examination, neither presents insurmountable obstacles in most instances.

The Constitution's double jeopardy clause commands that no person "be subject for the same offense to be twice put in jeopardy of life or limb."[111] In general terms, it condemns multiple prosecutions or multiple punishments for the same offense. The Supreme Court has long adhered to the so-called "*Blockburger*" test under which offenses are considered the same when they have the same elements, that is, unless each requires proof of an element not required of the other.[112]

RICO defendants have raised three double jeopardy arguments without much success. The courts have held that prosecution for a predicate offense does not bar prosecution for a RICO violation[113] nor does it bar prosecution for both a RICO conspiracy and the substantive RICO violation which is the object of the conspiracy,[114] nor successive RICO prosecutions of the same defendants on charges of involving different predicate offenses, enterprises, or patterns.[115]

The courts have been more receptive to double jeopardy concerns in the case of successive prosecutions of the same enterprise. There, they have invoked a totality of the circumstances test which asks: "(1) the time of the various activities charged as parts of [the] separate patterns; (2) the identity of the persons involved in the activities under each charge; (3) the statutory offenses charged as racketeering activities in each charge; (4) the nature and scope of the activity the government seeks to punish under each charge; and (5) the places where the activities took place under each charge."[116]

3. Ex Post Facto

The ex post facto clauses preclude (1) punishment of past conduct which was not a crime when it was committed, (2) increased punishment over that which attended a crime when it was committed, and (3) punishment made possible by elimination of a defense which was available when a crime was committed.[117] Yet because RICO offenses are thought to continue from the beginning of the first predicate offense to the commission of the last, a RICO prosecution survives ex post facto challenge even if grounded on pre-enactment predicate offenses as long as the pattern of predicate offenses straddles the date of legislative action.[118]

4. Vagueness

"[T]he void-for-vagueness doctrine requires that a penal statute define the criminal offense with sufficient definiteness that ordinary people can understand what conduct is prohibited and in a manner that does not encourage arbitrary and discriminatory enforcement."[119] Vagueness became a more common constitutional object to RICO, after Justice Scalia and three other justices implied its vulnerability to such an attack.[120] Subsequent lower courts appear to have uniformly rejected the suggestion that RICO is unconstitutionally vague either generally or as applied to the facts before them.[121]

B. Forfeiture

1. Eighth Amendment

RICO forfeitures can be severe. The Eighth Amendment supplies the constitutional bounds within which criminal sentences must be drawn. Under its directives, fines may not be excessive nor punishments cruel and unusual.[122] Any more precise definition becomes somewhat uncertain. When presented with the issue in *Harmelin*, a majority of the Supreme Court appeared to believe that the Eighth Amendment's cruel and unusual punishment clause forbids sentences which are "grossly disproportionate" to the seriousness of the crimes for which they are imposed.[123] Prior to *Harmelin*, the lower courts felt that at some point RICO forfeitures might be so disproportionate as to constitute cruel and unusual punishment.[124] Perhaps understandably, especially in light of developments under the excessive fines clause, the argument seems to have been rarely pressed since *Harmelin*.[125]

The Eighth Amendment's excessive fines clause is slightly more instructive. Historically, the clause was only infrequently invoked. The Supreme Court changed that when it identified the clause as one of the frontiers of permissible criminal forfeiture.[126] Forfeiture offends the excessive fines clause when it is "grossly disproportionate to the gravity of the offense."[127] Although the gravity of most RICO violations would seem to weigh heavily against most excessive fines clause challenges,[128] at least one circuit holds that the appropriate excessive fines analysis must include consideration of confiscation upon the property owner's livelihood.[129]

2. First Amendment

Forfeiture may raise First Amendment issues. The First Amendment guarantees the right of free speech and freedom of the press.[130] It generally precludes government prior restraint of expression.[131] In contrast to prior restraint, however, it generally permits punishment of the unlawful distribution of obscene material.[132] In the view of a majority of the Justices in *Alexander*, the application of RICO's provisions to confiscate the inventory of an adult entertainment business as punishment for a RICO conviction based upon obscenity predicates does not offend the First Amendment.[133]

3. Right to the Assistance of Counsel

In two cases decided under the criminal forfeiture provisions of the federal drug law, the Supreme Court held that a criminally accused's Sixth Amendment right to the assistance of counsel does not invalidate statutory provisions which call for the confiscation of forfeitable property paid as attorneys' fees or which permit the court, upon a probable cause showing, to freeze assets which the accused had intended to use to pay attorneys' fees.[134] The same can be said of the RICO forfeiture provisions.[135] Moreover, neither the Sixth Amendment nor the Fifth Amendment due process clause demands appointment of counsel to assist against government efforts to confiscate substitute assets.[136]

4. Right to Jury Trial

The Supreme Court concluded in *Libretti* that a property owner had no right to have a jury decide factual disputes in a forfeiture case, because forfeiture was a sentencing matter and the Sixth Amendment right to jury trial did not apply to sentencing questions.[137] After *Libretti* had been decided, the Court's announced view of the role of the jury as a fact finder changed somewhat, first in *Apprendi*, then in *Blakely*, and finally in *Booker*.[138] There the Court redefined the line between sentencing factors that the Constitution allows to be assigned to the court and factors that it insists be found by the jury as a matter of right. Henceforth, "any fact (other than a prior conviction) which is necessary to support a sentence exceeding the maximum authorized by the facts established by a plea of guilty or a jury verdict must be admitted by the defendant or proved to a jury beyond a reasonable doubt."[139] Dicta in *Booker* might be construed as an indication that property owners are still bound by the holding in *Libretti* – there is no constitutional right to have a jury decide factual questions in criminal forfeiture.[140] The lower courts appear to agree.[141]

5. Forfeiture of Estate

The "forfeiture of estate" argument was among the first constitutional challenges raised and dispatched. Article III, in its effort to protect against misuse of the law of treason, empowers Congress to set the punishment for treason but only with the understanding that "no attainder of treason shall work corruption of blood, or forfeiture."[142]

Article III speaks only of treason, but due process would likely preclude this type of forfeiture of estate as a penalty for lesser crimes as well. RICO forfeiture, however, is not properly classified as a forfeiture of estate. Forfeiture of estate occurs, when as a consequence of an offense, all of an offender's property is subject to confiscation, regardless of the absence of any nexus between the property and the crime which triggered the forfeiture. RICO forfeiture is, by contrast, a "statutory" forfeiture which turns on the relationship of the property to the crime and consequently is not forbidden by the due process corollary of Article III.[143]

Appendix A. Text of RICO Statutory Provisions

18 U.S.C. 1961

Definitions

As used in this chapter –

(1) "racketeering activity" means
   (A) any act or threat involving murder, kidnaping, gambling, arson, robbery, bribery, extortion, dealing in obscene matter, or dealing

in a controlled substance or listed chemical (as defined in section 102 of the Controlled Substances Act), which is chargeable under State law and punishable by imprisonment for more than one year;

(B) any act which is indictable under any of the following provisions of title 18, United States Code: Section 201 (relating to bribery), section 224 (relating to sports bribery), sections 471, 472, and 473 (relating to counterfeiting), section 659 (relating to theft from interstate shipment) if the act indictable under section 659 is felonious, section 664 (relating to embezzlement from pension and welfare funds), sections 891-894 (relating to extortionate credit transactions), section 1028 (relating to fraud and related activity in connection with identification documents), section 1029 (relating to fraud and related activity in connection with access devices), section 1084 (relating to the transmission of gambling information), section 1341 (relating to mail fraud), section 1343 (relating to wire fraud), section 1344 (relating to financial institution fraud), section 1425 (relating to the procurement of citizenship or nationalization unlawfully), section 1426 (relating to the reproduction of naturalization or citizenship papers), section 1427 (relating to the sale of naturalization or citizenship papers), sections 1461-1465 (relating to obscene matter), section 1503 (relating to obstruction of justice), section 1510 (relating to obstruction of criminal investigations), section 1511 (relating to the obstruction of State or local law enforcement), section 1512 (relating to tampering with a witness, victim, or an informant), section 1513 (relating to retaliating against a witness, victim, or an informant), section 1542 (relating to false statement in application and use of passport), section 1543 (relating to forgery or false use of passport), section 1544 (relating to misuse of passport), section 1546 (relating to fraud and misuse of visas, permits, and other documents), sections 1581-1592 (relating to peonage, slavery, and trafficking in persons), section 1951 (relating to interference with commerce, robbery, or extortion), section 1952 (relating to racketeering), section 1953 (relating to interstate transportation of wagering paraphernalia), section 1954 (relating to unlawful welfare fund payments), section 1955 (relating to the prohibition of illegal gambling businesses), section 1956 (relating to the laundering of monetary instruments), section 1957 (relating to engaging in monetary transactions in property derived from specified unlawful activity), section 1958 (relating to use of interstate commerce facilities in the commission of murder-for-hire), section 1960 (relating to illegal money transmitters), sections 2251, 2251A, 2252, and 2260 (relating to sexual exploitation of children), sections 2312 and 2313 (relating to interstate transportation of stolen motor vehicles), sections 2314 and 2315 (relating to interstate transportation of stolen property), section 2318 (relating to trafficking in counterfeit labels for phonorecords, computer programs or computer program documentation or packaging and copies of motion pictures or other audiovisual works), section 2319 (relating to criminal infringement of a copyright), section 2319A (relating to unauthorized fixation of and trafficking in sound recordings and music videos of live musical performances), section 2320 (relating to trafficking in goods or services bearing counterfeit marks), section 2321 (relating to trafficking in certain motor vehicles or motor vehicle parts), sections 2341-2346 (relating to trafficking in contraband cigarettes), sections 2421-24 (relating to white slave traffic), sections 175-178 (relating to biological weapons), sections 229-229F (relating to chemical weapons), section 831 (relating to nuclear materials),

(C) any act which is indictable under title 29, United States Code, section 186 (dealing with restrictions on payments and loans to labor organizations) or section 501(c) (relating to embezzlement from union funds),

(D) any offense involving fraud connected with a case under title 11 (except a case under section 157 of this title), fraud in the sale of securities, or the felonious manufacture, importation, receiving, concealment, buying, selling, or otherwise dealing in a controlled substance or listed chemical (as defined in section 102 of the Controlled Substances Act), punishable under any law of the United States,

(E) any act which is indictable under the Currency and Foreign Transactions Reporting Act,

(F) any act which is indictable under the Immigration and Nationality Act, section 274 (relating to bringing in and harboring certain aliens), section 277 (relating to aiding or assisting certain aliens to enter the United States), or section 278 (relating to importation of alien for immoral purpose) if the act indictable under such section of such Act was committed for the purpose of financial gain, or

(G) any act that is indictable under any provision listed in section 2332b(g)(5)(B);

(2) "State" means any State of the United States, the District of Columbia, the Commonwealth of Puerto Rico, any territory or possession of the United States, any political subdivision, or any department, agency, or instrumentality thereof;

(3) "person" includes any individual or entity capable of holding a legal or beneficial interest in property;

(4) "enterprise" includes any individual, partnership, corporation, association, or other legal entity, and any union or group of individuals associated in fact although not a legal entity;

(5) "pattern of racketeering activity" requires at least two acts of racketeering activity, one of which occurred after the effective date of this chapter and the last of which occurred within ten years (excluding any period of imprisonment) after the commission of a prior act of racketeering activity;

(6) "unlawful debt" means a debt

(A) incurred or contracted in gambling activity which was in violation of the law of the United States, a State or political subdivision thereof, or which is unenforceable under State or Federal law in whole or in part as to principal or interest because of the laws relating to usury, and

(B) which was incurred in connection with the business of gambling in violation of the law of the United States, a State or political subdivision thereof, or the business of lending money or a thing of value at a rate usurious under State or Federal law, where the usurious rate is at least twice the enforceable rate;

(7) "racketeering investigator" means any attorney or investigator so designated by the Attorney General and charged with the duty of enforcing or carrying into effect this chapter;

(8) "racketeering investigation" means any inquiry conducted by any racketeering investigator for the purpose of ascertaining whether any person has been involved in any violation of this chapter or of any final order, judgment, or decree of any court of the United States, duly entered in any case or proceeding arising under this chapter;

(9) "documentary material" includes any book, paper, document, record, recording, or other material; and

(10) "Attorney General" includes the Attorney General of the United States, the Deputy Attorney General of the United States, the Associate Attorney General of the United States, any Assistant Attorney General of the United States, or any employee of the Department of Justice or any employee of any department or agency of the United States so designated by the Attorney General to carry out the powers conferred on the Attorney General by this chapter. Any department or agency so designated may use in investigations authorized by this chapter either the investigative provisions of this chapter or the investigative power of such department or agency otherwise conferred by law.

18 U.S.C. 1962

Prohibited Activities

(a) It shall be unlawful for any person who has received any income derived, directly or indirectly, from a pattern of racketeering activity or through collection of an unlawful debt in which such person has participated as a principal within the meaning of section 2, title 18, United States Code, to use or invest, directly or indirectly, any part of such income, or the proceeds of such income, in acquisition of any interest in, or the establishment or operation of, any enterprise which is engaged in, or the activities of which affect, interstate or foreign commerce. A purchase of securities on the open market for purposes of investment, and without the intention of controlling or participating in the control of the issuer, or of assisting another to do so, shall not be unlawful under this subsection if the securities of the issuer held by the purchaser, the members of his immediate family, and his or their accomplices in any pattern or racketeering activity or the collection of an unlawful debt after such purchase do not amount in the aggregate to one percent of the outstanding securities of any one class, and do not confer, either in law or in fact, the power to elect one or more directors of the issuer.

(b) It shall be unlawful for any person through a pattern of racketeering activity or through collection of an unlawful debt to acquire or maintain, directly or indirectly, any interest in or control of any enterprise which is engaged in, or the activities of which affect, interstate or foreign commerce.

(c) It shall be unlawful for any person employed by or associated with any enterprise engaged in, or the activities of which affect, interstate or foreign commerce, to conduct or participate, directly or indirectly, in the conduct of such enterprise's affairs through a pattern of racketeering activity or collection of unlawful debt.

(d) It shall be unlawful for any person to conspire to violate any of the provisions of subsection (a), (b), or (c) of this section.

18 U.S.C. 1963

Criminal Penalties

(a) Whoever violates any provision of section 1962 of this chapter shall be fined under this title or imprisoned not more than 20 years (or for life if the violation is based on a racketeering activity for which the maximum penalty includes life imprisonment), or both, and shall forfeit to the United States, irrespective of any provision of State law –

  (1) any interest the person has acquired or maintained in violation of section 1962;

  (2) any –

    (A) interest in;

    (B) security of;

    (C) claim against; or

    (D) property or contractual right of any kind affording a source of influence over; any enterprise which the person has established, operated, controlled, conducted, or participated in the conduct of, in violation of section 1962; and

  (3) any property constituting, or derived from, any proceeds which the person obtained, directly or indirectly, from racketeering activity or unlawful debt collection in violation of section 1962. The court, in imposing sentence on such person shall order, in addition to any other sentence imposed pursuant to this section, that the person forfeit to the United States all property described in this subsection. In lieu of a fine otherwise authorized by this

section, a defendant who derives profits or other proceeds from an offense may be fined not more than twice the gross profits or other proceeds.

(b) Property subject to criminal forfeiture under this section includes –

(1) real property, including things growing on, affixed to, and found in land; and

(2) tangible and intangible personal property, including rights, privileges, interests, claims, and securities.

(c) All right, title, and interest in property described in subsection (a) vests in the United States upon the commission of the act giving rise to forfeiture under this section. Any such property that is subsequently transferred to a person other than the defendant may be the subject of a special verdict of forfeiture and thereafter shall be ordered forfeited to the United States, unless the transferee establishes in a hearing pursuant to subsection (l) that he is a bona fide purchaser for value of such property who at the time of purchase was reasonably without cause to believe that the property was subject to forfeiture under this section.

(d)

(1) Upon application of the United States, the court may enter a restraining order or injunction, require the execution of a satisfactory performance bond, or take any other action to preserve the availability of property described in subsection (a) for forfeiture under this section –

(A) upon the filing of an indictment or information charging a violation of section 1962 of this chapter and alleging that the property with respect to which the order is sought would, in the event of conviction, be subject to forfeiture under this section; or

(B) prior to the filing of such an indictment or information, if, after notice to persons appearing to have an interest in the property and opportunity for a hearing, the court determines that –

(i) there is a substantial probability that the United States will prevail on the issue of forfeiture and that failure to enter the order will result in the property being destroyed, removed from the jurisdiction of the court, or otherwise made unavailable for forfeiture; and

(ii) the need to preserve the availability of the property through the entry of the requested order outweighs the hardship on any party against whom the order is to be entered:

Provided, however, That an order entered pursuant to subparagraph (B) shall be effective for not more than ninety days, unless extended by the court for good cause shown or unless an indictment or information described in subparagraph (A) has been filed.

(2) A temporary restraining order under this subsection may be entered upon application of the United States without notice or opportunity for a hearing when an information or indictment has not yet been filed with respect to the property, if the United States demonstrates that there is probable cause to believe that the property with respect to which the order is sought would, in the event of conviction, be subject to forfeiture under this section and that provision of notice will jeopardize the availability of the property for forfeiture. Such a temporary order shall expire not more than ten days after the date on which it is entered, unless extended for good cause shown or unless the party against whom it is entered consents to an extension for a longer period. A hearing requested concerning an order entered under this paragraph shall be held at the earliest possible time, and prior to the expiration of the temporary order.

(3) The court may receive and consider, at a hearing held pursuant to this subsection, evidence and information that would be inadmissible under the Federal Rules of Evidence.

(e) Upon conviction of a person under this section, the court shall enter a judgment of forfeiture of the property to the United States and shall also authorize the Attorney General to seize all property ordered forfeited upon such terms and conditions as the court shall deem proper. Following the entry of an order declaring the property forfeited, the court may, upon application of the United States, enter such appropriate restraining orders or injunctions, require the execution of satisfactory performance bonds, appoint receivers, conservators, appraisers, accountants, or trustees, or take any other action to protect the interest of the United States in the property ordered forfeited. Any income accruing to, or derived from, an enterprise or an interest in an enterprise which has been ordered forfeited under this section may be used to offset ordinary and necessary expenses to the enterprise which are required by law, or which are necessary to protect the interests of the United States or third parties.

(f) Following the seizure of property ordered forfeited under this section, the Attorney General shall direct the disposition of the property by sale or any other commercially feasible means, making due provision for the rights of any innocent persons. Any property right or interest not exercisable by, or transferable for value to, the United States shall expire and shall not revert to the defendant, nor shall the defendant or any person acting in concert with or on behalf of the defendant be eligible to purchase forfeited property at any sale held by the United States. Upon application of a person, other than the defendant or a person acting in concert with or on behalf of the defendant, the court may restrain or stay the sale or disposition of the property pending the conclusion of any appeal of the criminal case giving rise to the forfeiture, if the applicant demonstrates that proceeding with the sale or disposition of the property will result in irreparable injury, harm or loss to him. Notwithstanding 31 U.S.C. 3302(b), the proceeds of any sale or other disposition of property forfeited under this section and any moneys forfeited shall be used to pay all proper expenses for the forfeiture and the sale, including expenses of seizure, maintenance and custody of the property pending its disposition, advertising and court costs. The Attorney General shall deposit in the Treasury any amounts of such proceeds or moneys remaining after the payment of such expenses.

(g) With respect to property ordered forfeited under this section, the Attorney General is authorized to –

  (1) grant petitions for mitigation or remission of forfeiture, restore forfeited property to victims of a violation of this chapter, or take any other action to protect the rights of innocent persons which is in the interest of justice and which is not inconsistent with the provisions of this chapter;

  (2) compromise claims arising under this section;

  (3) award compensation to persons providing information resulting in a forfeiture under this section;

  (4) direct the disposition by the United States of all property ordered forfeited under this section by public sale or any other commercially feasible means, making due provision for the rights of innocent persons; and

(5) take appropriate measures necessary to safeguard and maintain property ordered forfeited under this section pending its disposition.

(h) The Attorney General may promulgate regulations with respect to –

(1) making reasonable efforts to provide notice to persons who may have an interest in property ordered forfeited under this section;

(2) granting petitions for remission or mitigation of forfeiture;

(3) the restitution of property to victims of an offense petitioning for remission or mitigation of forfeiture under this chapter;

(4) the disposition by the United States of forfeited property by public sale or other commercially feasible means;

(5) the maintenance and safekeeping of any property forfeited under this section pending its disposition; and

(6) the compromise of claims arising under this chapter.

Pending the promulgation of such regulations, all provisions of law relating to the disposition of property, or the proceeds from the sale thereof, or the remission or mitigation of forfeitures for violation of the customs laws, and the compromise of claims and the award of compensation to informers in respect of such forfeitures shall apply to forfeitures incurred, or alleged to have been incurred, under the provisions of this section, insofar as applicable and not inconsistent with the provisions hereof. Such duties as are imposed upon the Customs Service or any person with respect to the disposition of property under the customs law shall be performed under this chapter by the Attorney General.

(i) Except as provided in subsection (l), no party claiming an interest in property subject to forfeiture under this section may –

(1) intervene in a trial or appeal of a criminal case involving the forfeiture of such property under this section; or

(2) commence an action at law or equity against the United States concerning the validity of his alleged interest in the property subsequent to the filing of an indictment or information alleging that the property is subject to forfeiture under this section.

(j) The district courts of the United States shall have jurisdiction to enter orders as provided in this section without regard to the location of any property which may be subject to forfeiture under this section or which has been ordered forfeited under this section.

(k) In order to facilitate the identification or location of property declared forfeited and to facilitate the disposition of petitions for remission or mitigation of forfeiture, after the entry of an order declaring property forfeited to the United States the court may, upon application of the United States, order that the testimony of any witness relating to the property forfeited be taken by deposition and that any designated book, paper, document, record, recording, or other material not privileged be produced at the same time and place, in the same manner as provided for the taking of depositions under Rule 15 of the Federal Rules of Criminal Procedure.

(l)

(1) Following the entry of an order of forfeiture under this section, the United States shall publish notice of the order and of its intent to dispose of the property in such manner as the Attorney General may direct. The Government may also, to the extent practicable, provide direct written notice to any person known to have alleged an interest in the property that is the subject of the order of forfeiture as a substitute for published notice as to those persons so notified.

(2) Any person, other than the defendant, asserting a legal interest in property which has been ordered forfeited to the United States pursuant to this section may, within thirty days of the final publication of notice or his receipt of notice under paragraph (1), whichever is earlier, petition the court for a hearing to adjudicate the validity of his alleged interest in the property. The hearing shall be held before the court alone, without a jury.

(3) The petition shall be signed by the petitioner under penalty of perjury and shall set forth the nature and extent of the petitioner's right, title, or interest in the property, the time and circumstances of the petitioner's acquisition of the right, title, or interest in the property, any additional facts supporting the petitioner's claim, and the relief sought.

(4) The hearing on the petition shall, to the extent practicable and consistent with the interests of justice, be held within thirty days of the filing of the petition. The court may consolidate the hearing on the petition with a hearing on any other petition filed by a person other than the defendant under this subsection.

(5) At the hearing, the petitioner may testify and present evidence and witnesses on his own behalf, and cross-examine witnesses who appear at the hearing. The United States may present evidence and witnesses in rebuttal and in defense of its claim to

the property and cross-examine witnesses who appear at the hearing. In addition to testimony and evidence presented at the hearing, the court shall consider the relevant portions of the record of the criminal case which resulted in the order of forfeiture.

(6) If, after the hearing, the court determines that the petitioner has established by a preponderance of the evidence that –

(A) the petitioner has a legal right, title, or interest in the property, and such right, title, or interest renders the order of forfeiture invalid in whole or in part because the right, title, or interest was vested in the petitioner rather than the defendant or was superior to any right, title, or interest of the defendant at the time of the commission of the acts which gave rise to the forfeiture of the property under this section; or

(B) the petitioner is a bona fide purchaser for value of the right, title, or interest in the property and was at the time of purchase reasonably without cause to believe that the property was subject to forfeiture under this section;

the court shall amend the order of forfeiture in accordance with its determination.

(7) Following the court's disposition of all petitions filed under this subsection, or if no such petitions are filed following the expiration of the period provided in paragraph (2) for the filing of such petitions, the United States shall have clear title to property that is the subject of the order of forfeiture and may warrant good title to any subsequent purchaser or transferee.

(m) If any of the property described in subsection (a), as a result of any act or omission of the defendant –

(1) cannot be located upon the exercise of due diligence;

(2) has been transferred or sold to, or deposited with, a third party;

(3) has been placed beyond the jurisdiction of the court;

(4) has been substantially diminished in value; or

(5) has been commingled with other property which cannot be divided without difficulty; the court shall order the forfeiture of any other property of the defendant up to the value of any property described in paragraphs (1) through (5).

18 U.S.C. 1964

Civil Remedies

(a) The district courts of the United States shall have jurisdiction to prevent and restrain violations of section 1962 of this chapter by issuing appropriate orders, including, but not limited to: ordering any person to divest himself of any interest, direct or indirect, in any enterprise; imposing reasonable restrictions on the future activities or investments of any person, including, but not limited to, prohibiting any person from engaging in the same type of endeavor as the enterprise engaged in, the activities of which affect interstate or foreign commerce; or ordering dissolution or reorganization of any enterprise, making due provision for the rights of innocent persons.

(b) The Attorney General may institute proceedings under this section. Pending final determination thereof, the court may at any time enter such restraining orders or prohibitions, or take such other actions, including the acceptance of satisfactory performance bonds, as it shall deem proper.

(c) Any person injured in his business or property by reason of a violation of section 1962 of this chapter may sue therefor in any appropriate United States district court and shall recover threefold the damages he sustains and the cost of the suit, including a reasonable attorney's fee, except that no person may rely upon any conduct that would have been actionable as fraud in the purchase or sale of securities to establish a violation of section 1962. The exception contained in the preceding sentence does not apply to an action against any person that is criminally convicted in connection with the fraud, in which case the statute of limitations shall start to run on the date on which the conviction becomes final.

(d) A final judgment or decree rendered in favor of the United States in any criminal proceeding brought by the United States under this chapter shall estop the defendant from denying the essential allegations of the criminal offense in any subsequent civil proceeding brought by the United States.

18 U.S.C. 1965

Venue and Process

(a) Any civil action or proceeding under this chapter against any person may be instituted in the district court of the United States for any district in which such person resides, is found, has an agent, or transacts his affairs.
(b) In any action under section 1964 of this chapter in any district court of the United States in which it is shown that the ends of justice require that other parties residing in any other district be brought before the court, the court may cause such parties to be summoned, and process for that purpose may be served in any judicial district of the United States by the marshal thereof.
(c) In any civil or criminal action or proceeding instituted by the United States under this chapter in the district court of the United States for any judicial district, subpenas issued by such court to compel the attendance of witnesses may be served in any other judicial district, except that in any civil action or proceeding no such subpena shall be issued for service upon any individual who resides in another district at a place more than one hundred miles from the place at which such court is held without approval given by a judge of such court upon a showing of good cause.
(d) All other process in any action or proceeding under this chapter may be served on any person in any judicial district in which such person resides, is found, has an agent, or transacts his affairs.

18 U.S.C. 1966

Expedition of Actions

In any civil action instituted under this chapter by the United States in any district court of the United States, the Attorney General may file with the clerk of such court a certificate stating that in his opinion the case is of general public importance. A copy of that certificate shall be furnished immediately by such clerk to the chief judge or in his absence to the presiding district judge of the district in which such action is pending. Upon receipt of such copy, such judge shall designate immediately a judge of that district to hear and determine action.

18 U.S.C. 1967

Evidence

In any proceeding ancillary to or in any civil action instituted by the United States under this chapter the proceedings may be open or closed to the public at the discretion of the court after consideration of the rights of affected persons.

18 U.S.C. 1968

Civil Investigative Demand

(a) Whenever the Attorney General has reason to believe that any person or enterprise may be in possession, custody, or control of any documentary materials relevant to a racketeering investigation, he may, prior to the institution of a civil or criminal proceeding thereon, issue in writing, and cause to be served upon such person, a civil investigative demand requiring such person to produce such material for examination.

(b) Each such demand shall—
  (1) state the nature of the conduct constituting the alleged racketeering violation which is under investigation and the provision of law applicable thereto;
  (2) describe the class or classes of documentary material produced thereunder with such definiteness and certainty as to permit such material to be fairly identified;
  (3) state that the demand is returnable forthwith or prescribe a return date which will provide a reasonable period of time within which the material so demanded may be assembled and made available for inspection and copying or reproduction; and
  (4) identify the custodian to whom such material shall be made available.

(c) No such demand shall—
  (1) contain any requirement which would be held to be unreasonable if contained in a subpena duces tecum issued by a court of the United States in aid of a grand jury investigation of such alleged racketeering violation; or

(2) require the production of any documentary evidence which would be privileged from disclosure if demanded by a subpena duces tecum issued by a court of the United States in aid of a grand jury investigation of such alleged racketeering violation.

(d) Service of any such demand or any petition filed under this section may be made upon a person by—

(1) delivering a duly executed copy thereof to any partner, executive officer, managing agent, or general agent thereof, or to any agent thereof authorized by appointment or by law to receive service of process on behalf of such person, or upon any individual person;

(2) delivering a duly executed copy thereof to the principal office or place of business of the person to be served; or

(3) depositing such copy in the United States mail, by registered or certified mail duly addressed to such person at its principal office or place of business.

(e) A verified return by the individual serving any such demand or petition setting forth the manner of such service shall be prima facie proof of such service. In the case of service by registered or certified mail, such return shall be accompanied by the return post office receipt of delivery of such demand.

(f)

(1) The Attorney General shall designate a racketeering investigator to serve as racketeer document custodian, and such additional racketeering investigators as he shall determine from time to time to be necessary to serve as deputies to such officer.

(2) Any person upon whom any demand issued under this section has been duly served shall make such material available for inspection and copying or reproduction to the custodian designated therein at the principal place of business of such person, or at such other place as such custodian and such person thereafter may agree and prescribe in writing or as the court may direct, pursuant to this section on the return date specified in such demand, or on such later date as such custodian may prescribe in writing. Such person may upon written agreement between such person and the custodian substitute for copies of all or any part of such material originals thereof.

(3) The custodian to whom any documentary material is so delivered shall take physical possession thereof, and shall be responsible for the use made thereof and for the return thereof pursuant to this

chapter. The custodian may cause the preparation of such copies of such documentary material as may be required for official use under regulations which shall be promulgated by the Attorney General. While in the possession of the custodian, no material so produced shall be available for examination, without the consent of the person who produced such material, by any individual other than the Attorney General. Under such reasonable terms and conditions as the Attorney General shall prescribe, documentary material while in the possession of the custodian shall be available for examination by the person who produced such material or any duly authorized representatives of such person.

(4) Whenever any attorney has been designated to appear on behalf of the United States before any court or grand jury in any case or proceeding involving any alleged violation of this chapter, the custodian may deliver to such attorney such documentary material in the possession of the custodian as such attorney determines to be required for use in the presentation of such case or proceeding on behalf of the United States. Upon the conclusion of any such case or proceeding, such attorney shall return to the custodian any documentary material so withdrawn which has not passed into the control of such court or grand jury through the introduction thereof into the record of such case or proceeding.

(5) Upon the completion of—

(i) the racketeering investigation for which any documentary material was produced under this chapter, and

(ii) any case or proceeding arising from such investigation, the custodian shall return to the person who produced such material all such material other than copies thereof made by the Attorney General pursuant to this subsection which has not passed into the control of any court or grand jury through the introduction thereof into the record of such case or proceeding.

(6) When any documentary material has been produced by any person under this section for use in any racketeering investigation, and no such case or proceeding arising therefrom has been instituted within a reasonable time after completion of the examination and analysis of all evidence assembled in the course of such investigation, such person shall be entitled, upon written demand made upon the Attorney General, to the return of

all documentary material other than copies thereof made pursuant to this subsection so produced by such person.

(7) In the event of the death, disability, or separation from service of the custodian of any documentary material produced under any demand issued under this section or the official relief of such custodian from responsibility for the custody and control of such material, the Attorney General shall promptly—

(i) designate another racketeering investigator to serve as custodian thereof, and

(ii) transmit notice in writing to the person who produced such material as to the identity and address of the successor so designated.

Any successor so designated shall have with regard to such materials all duties and responsibilities imposed by this section upon his predecessor in office with regard thereto, except that he shall not be held responsible for any default or dereliction which occurred before his designation as custodian.

(g) Whenever any person fails to comply with any civil investigative demand duly served upon him under this section or whenever satisfactory copying or reproduction of any such material cannot be done and such person refuses to surrender such material, the Attorney General may file, in the district court of the United States for any judicial district in which such person resides, is found, or transacts business, and serve upon such person a petition for an order of such court for the enforcement of this section, except that if such person transacts business in more than one such district such petition shall be filed in the district in which such person maintains his principal place of business, or in such other district in which such person transacts business as may be agreed upon by the parties to such petition.

(h) Within twenty days after the service of any such demand upon any person, or at any time before the return date specified in the demand, whichever period is shorter, such person may file, in the district court of the United States for the judicial district within which such person resides, is found, or transacts business, and serve upon such custodian a petition for an order of such court modifying or setting aside such demand. The time allowed for compliance with the demand in whole or in part as deemed proper and ordered by the court shall not run during the pendency of such petition in the court. Such petition shall specify each ground upon which the petitioner relies in seeking such relief, and may be based upon any failure of such demand to comply with the provisions of this section or upon any constitutional or other legal right or privilege of such person.

(i) At any time during which any custodian is in custody or control of any documentary material delivered by any person in compliance with any such demand, such person may file, in the district court of the United States for the judicial district within which the office of such custodian is situated, and serve upon such custodian a petition for an order of such court requiring the performance by such custodian of any duty imposed upon him by this section.

(j) Whenever any petition is filed in any district court of the United States under this section, such court shall have jurisdiction to hear and determine the matter so presented, and to enter such order or orders as may be required to carry into effect the provisions of this section.

APPENDIX B. SELECTED BIBLIOGRAPHY

Articles and Books

Abrams, *Crime Legislation and the Public Interest: Lessons From Civil RICO*, 50 SOUTHERN METHODIST UNIVERSITY LAW REVIEW 33 (1996).

Amann, *Spotting Money Launderers: A Better Way to Fight Organized Crime?* 27 SYRACUSE JOURNAL OF INTERNATIONAL LAW & COMMERCE 199 (2000).

American Law Reports, Federal, *Validity, Construction, and Application of Provision of Racketeer Influenced and Corrupt Organizations Act*, 18 *U.S.C.A. §1961 et seq.*, 171 ALR FED. 1 (2011-2012).

Batista, CIVIL RICO PRACTICE MANUAL (2008).

Blakey & Gettings, *Racketeer Influenced and Corrupt Organizations (RICO): Basic Concepts— Criminal and Civil Remedies*, 53 TEMPLE LAW QUARTERLY 1009 (1980).

Blakey & Goldstock, *On the Waterfront: RICO and Labor Racketeering*, 17 AMERICAN CRIMINAL LAW REVIEW 341 (1980).

Blakey & Perry, *An Analysis of the Myths That Bolster Efforts to Rewrite RICO and the Various Proposals for Reform: "Mother of God—Is This the End of RICO?"*, 43 VANDERBILT LAW REVIEW 851 (1990).

Blakey & Roddy, *Reflections on Reves v. Ernst & Young: Its Meaning and Impact on Substantive, Accessory, Aiding Abetting and Conspiracy*

Liability Under RICO, 33 AMERICAN CRIMINAL LAW REVIEW 1345 (1996).

Floyd, RICO STATE BY STATE: A GUIDE TO LITIGATION UNDER THE STATE RACKETEERING STATUTES (1998).

Getzendanner, *Judicial "Pruning" of "Garden Variety Fraud": Civil RICO Cases Does Not Work: it's Time for Congress to Act*, 43 VANDERBILT LAW REVIEW 673 (1990).

Goldberg, *RICO Forfeiture of Sexually Explicit Expressive Materials: Another Weapon in the War on Pornography, or an Impermissible Collateral Attack on Protected Expression? Alexander v. United States, 113 S.Ct. 2766 (1993)*, 21 WILLIAM MITCHELL LAW REVIEW 231 (1995).

Goldsmith, *RICO and Enterprise Criminality: A Response to Gerald E. Lynch*, 88 COLUMBIA LAW REVIEW 774 (1988).

Goldsmith & Keith, *Civil RICO Abuse: The Allegations in Context*, 1986 BRIGHAM YOUNG UNIVERSITY LAW REVIEW 55.

——, *Resurrecting RICO: Removing Immunity for White-Collar Crime*, 41 HARVARD JOURNAL OF LEGISLATION 281 (2004).

Goldsmith & Linderman, *Civil RICO Reform: The Gatekeeper Concept*, 43 VANDERBILT LAW REVIEW 735 (1990).

Jacobs, Cunningham, & Friday, *The RICO Trusteeships After Twenty Years: A Progress Report*, 19 LABOR LAWYER 419 (2004).

Jeffries & Gleeson, *The Federalization of Organized Crime: Advantages of Federal Prosecution*, 46 HASTINGS LAW JOURNAL 1095 (1995).

Lynch, *A Conceptual, Practical and Political Guide to RICO Reform*, 43 VANDERBILT LAW REVIEW 769 (1990).

——, *A Reply to Michael Goldsmith*, 88 COLUMBIA LAW REVIEW 802 (1988).

——, *RICO: The Crime of Being a Criminal, Pts. I & II, III & IV*, 87 COLUMBIA LAW REVIEW 661, 920 (1987).

McClellan, *The Organized Crime Control Act (S.30) or its Critics: Which Threatens Civil Liberties?* 46 NOTRE DAME LAWYER 55 (1970).

Mastin, *RICO Conspiracy: Dismantles the Mexican Mafia & Disables Procedural Due Process*, 27 WILLIAM MITCHELL LAW REVIEW 2295 (2001).

Miller, *RICO and Conspiracy Construction: The Mischief of the Economic Model*, 104 COMMERCIAL LAW JOURNAL 26 (1999).

Nonna & Corrado, *RICO Reform: "Weeding Out" Garden Variety Disputes Under the Racketeer Influenced and Corrupt Organizations Act*, 64 ST. JOHN'S LAW REVIEW 825 (1990).

Northrup & Steen, Union *"Corporate Campaigns" as Blackmail: The RICO Battle at Bayou Steel*, 22 HARVARD JOURNAL OF LAW & PUBLIC POLICY 771 (1999).

Reed, *The Defense Case for RICO Reform*, 43 VANDERBILT LAW REVIEW 691 (1990).

Scallan, *Proximate Cause Under RICO*, 20 SOUTHERN ILLINOIS UNIVERSITY LAW JOURNAL 455 (1996).

Smith & Reed, CIVIL RICO (2012).

Steckman, *RICO Section 1962(c) Enterprises and the Present State of the "Distinctness Requirement" in the Second, Third, and Seventh Circuits*, 21 TOURO LAW REVIEW 1083 (2006).

Stefanou, *Concurrent Jurisdiction Over Federal Civil RICO Claims: Is It Workable? An Analysis of* Taffin v. Levitt, 64 ST. JOHN'S LAW REVIEW 877 (1990).

Tarlow, *RICO: The New Darling of the Prosecutor's Nursery*, 49 FORDHAM LAW REVIEW 165 (1980).

United States Department of Justice, Criminal Division, Organized Crime and Racketeering Section, *Criminal RICO: 18 U.S.C. §§1961-1968 – A Manual for Federal Prosecutors* (5th ed. 2009).

United States House of Representatives, Committee on the Judiciary, Subcommittee on Intellectual Property and Judicial Administration, *RICO Amendments Act of 1991*, 102d Cong., 1st Sess. (1991).

——,Subcommittee on Crime, *RICO Reform Act of 1989*, 101st Cong., 1st Sess. (1989).

——, Subcommittee on Criminal Justice, *RICO Reform*, 100th Cong., 1st & 2d Sess. (1988).

——, *RICO Reform*, Pts. 1 & 2, 99th Cong., 1st & 2d Sess. (1986).

United States Senate, Committee on Governmental Affairs, Permanent Subcommittee on Investigations, *Federal Government's Use of Trusteeships Under the RICO Statute*, 101st Cong., 1st Sess. (1989).

——, Committee on the Judiciary, *Racketeer Influenced and Corrupt Organizations Reform Act*, 101st Cong., 1st Sess. (1989).

——, *Proposed RICO Reform Legislation*, 100th Cong., 1st Sess. (1987).

Vitiello, *More Noise from the Tower of Babel: Making 'Sense' Out of Reves v. Ernst & Young*, 56 OHIO STATE LAW JOURNAL 1363 (1995).

Wallace, *Outgunning the Mob*, 80 AMERICAN BAR ASSOCIATION JOURNAL 60 (1994).

Notes and Comments

Civil Versus Criminal RICO and the "Eradication" of La Cosa Nostra, 28 NEW ENGLAND JOURNAL OF CRIMINAL AND CIVIL CONFINEMENT 279 (2002).

Completing Klehr v. A.O. Smith Corp., and Resolving the Oddity and Lingering Questions of Civil Statute of Limitations Accrual, 1998 BRIGHAM YOUNG UNIVERSITY LAW REVIEW 1273.

Counteracting Theft and Fraud: The Applicability of RICO to Organized Retail Crime, 88 MINNESOTA LAW REVIEW 1391 (2004).

Equity Up in Smoke: Civil RICO, Disgorgement, and United States v. Philip Morris, 74 FORDHAM LAW REVIEW 2461 (2006).

Exercising the Passive Virtues of Interpreting Civil RICO "Business or Property," 75 UNIVERSITY OF CHICAGO LAW REVIEW 1773 (2008).

Forfeiture Law, the Eighth Amendment's Excessive Fines Clause, and United States v. Bajakajian, 74 NOTRE DAME LAW REVIEW 1371 (1999).

From the Mafia to Milking Cows: State RICO Act Expansion, 41 ARIZONA LAW REVIEW 1133 (1999).

Personal Versus Property Harm and Civil RICO Standing, 73 UNIVERSITY OF CHICAGO LAW REVIEW 1513 (2006).

Pimpin' Ain't Easy Under the Eleventh Circuit's Broad RICO Enterprise Standard: United States v. Pipkins, 73 UNIVERSITY OF CINCINNATI LAW REVIEW 1643 (2005).

Preventing Absurd Application of RICO: A Proposed Amendment to Congress's Definition of 'Racketeering Activity' in the Wake of National Organization of Women, Inc. v. Scheidler, 68 TEMPLE LAW QUARTERLY 223 (1995).

Protesters, Extortion, and Coercion: Preventing RICO From Chilling First Amendment Freedoms, 75 NOTRE DAME LAW REVIEW 691 (1999).

RICO and the Legislative Supremacy Approach to Federal Criminal Lawmaking, 31 LOYOLA UNIVERSITY OF CHICAGO LAW JOURNAL 639 (2000).

RICO: Is It a Panacea or a Bitter Pill for Labor Unions, Union Democracy and Collective Bargaining? 11 HOFSTRA LABOR LAW JOURNAL 499 (1994).

Twenty-Seventh Survey of White Collar Crime: Racketeer Influenced and Corrupt Organizations, 49 AMERICAN CRIMINAL LAW REVIEW 1157 (2012).

Appendix C. State RICO Citations[144]

Ariz.Rev.Stat.Ann. §§13-2312 to 13-2315;
Cal.Penal Code §§186 to 186.8;
Colo.Rev.Stat. §§18-17-101 to 18-17-109;
Conn.Gen.Stat.Ann. §§53-393 to 53-403;
Del.Code tit.11 §§1501 to 1511;
Fla.Stat.Ann. §§895.01 to 895.09;
Ga.Code Ann. §§16-14-1 to 16-14-15;
Hawaii Rev.Stat. §§842-1 to 842-12;
Idaho Code §§18-7801 to 18-7805;
Ind.Code Ann. §§35-45-6-1 to 35-45-6-2;
Iowa Code Ann. §§706a.1 to 706a.5;
Ky.Rev.stat. §506.120;
La.Rev.Stat.Ann.§§15:1351 to 15:1356;
Mass.Gen.Laws Ann. Ch. 271a §§1 to 3;
Mich.Comp.Laws Ann. §§750.159f to 750.159x;
Minn.Stat.Ann. §§609.901 to 609.912;
Miss.Code §§97-43-1 to 97-43-11;
Neb.Rev.Stat.Ann. §§28-1352 to 28-1356;
144
Nev.Rev.Stat. §§207.350 to 207.520;
N.J.Stat.Ann. §§2c:41-1 to 2c:41-6.2;
N.M.Stat.Ann. §§30-42-1 to 30-42-6;
N.Y.Penal Law §§460.00 to 460.80;
N.C.Gen. Stat. §§75d-1 to 75d-14;
N.d.Cent.Code §§12.1-06.1-01 to 12.1-06.1-08;
Ohio Rev.Code §§2923.31 to 2923.36;
Okla.Stat.Ann. Tit.22 §§1401 to 1419;
Ore.Rev.Stat. §§166.715 to 166.735;
Pa.Stat. Ann. Tit.18 §911;
R.i.Gen.Laws §§7-15-1 to 7-15-11;
Tenn.Code Ann. §§39-12-201to 39-12-210;
Tex.Penal Code §§71.01 to 71.05;
Utah Code Ann. §§76-10-1601 to 76-10-1610;
Va. Code §§18.2-512 to 18.2-517;
Wash.Rev.Code Ann. §§9a.82.010 to 9a.82.17
W.Va. Code Ann. §§61-13-1 to 61-13-6;
Wis.Stat.Ann. §§946.80 to 946.88.

End Notes

[1] 18 U.S.C. 1961 -1968 (text is appended).

[2] 84 Stat. 941 (1970).

[3] *Boyle v. United States*, 556 U.S. 938, 950-51 (2009); *Sedima, S.P.R.L. v. Imrex Co.*, 473 U.S. 479, 499-500 (1985); *H.J. Inc. v. Northwestern Bell Telephone Co.*, 492 U.S. 229, 236 (1989).

[4] "To avoid classifying defendants according to such ancillary characteristics as group ssociation and national origin, the Act basically says 'racketeer is as racketeer does' and then tries to define what a racketeer does indeed do." Bridges, *Private RICO Litigation Based Upon "Fraud" in the Sale of Securities*, 18 Georgia Law Review 43, 49 (1983); *see also*, Lynch, *RICO: The Crime of Being a Criminal: Parts I & II*, 87 Columbia Law Review 661, 686-88 (1987).

[5] Lynch, *RICO: The Crime of Being a Criminal, Parts III & IV, 87 Columbia Law Review 920, 938-39 (1987); Blakey & Gettings, Racketeer Influenced and Corrupt Organizations(RICO): Basic Concepts—Criminal and Civil Remedies*, 53 Temple Law Quarterly 1009, 1021 n.71 (1980).

[6] The statute describes these underlying offenses as "racketeering activities." They are often referred to as "predicate offenses."

[7] In exact terms, it declares:

"(a) It shall be unlawful for any person who has received any income derived, directly or indirectly, from a pattern of racketeering activity or through collection of an unlawful debt in which such person has participated as a principal within the meaning of section 2, title 18, United States Code, to use or invest, directly or indirectly, any part of such income, or the proceeds of such income, in acquisition of any interest in, or the establishment or operation of, any enterprise which is engaged in, or the activities of which affect, interstate or foreign commerce. A purchase of securities on the open market for purposes of investment, and without the intention of controlling or participating in control of the issuer, or of assisting another to do so, shall not be unlawful under this subsection, if the securities of the issuer held by the purchaser, the members of his immediate family, and his or their accomplices in any pattern of racketeering activity or the collection of an unlawful debt after such purchase do not amount in the aggregate to one percent of the outstanding securities of any one class, and do not confer, either in law or in fact, the power to elect one or more directors of the issuer.

"(b) It shall be unlawful for any person through a pattern of racketeering activity or through collection of an unlawful debt to acquire or maintain, directly or indirectly, any interest in or control of any enterprise which is engaged in, or the activities of which affect, interstate or foreign commerce.

"(c) It shall be unlawful for any person employed by or associated with any enterprise engaged in, or the activities of which affect, interstate or foreign commerce, to conduct, or participate, directly or indirectly, in the conduct of such enterprise's affairs through a pattern of racketeering activity or collection of unlawful debt.

"(d) It shall be unlawful for any person to conspire to violate any of the provisions of subsection (a), (b), or (c) of this section." 18 U.S.C. 1962.

[8] 18 U.S.C. 1963, 3571.

[9] 18 U.S.C. 1963(c).

[10] 18 U.S.C. 1964(a).

[11] 18 U.S.C. 1965.

[12] 18 U.S.C. 1966.

[13] "In any proceeding ancillary to or in any civil action instituted by the United States under this chapter the proceedings may be open or closed to the public at the discretion of the court after consideration of the rights of affected persons." 18 U.S.C. 1967.

[14] 18 U.S.C. 1968. The civil investigative demand process, borrowed from antitrust law like so many of the other features of RICO, permits the Attorney General to demand the production of documentary evidence from anyone prior to the initiation of civil or criminal RICO provisions.

[15] 18 U.S.C. 1962(a), (b), (c), (d).

[16] 18 U.S.C. 1961(3).

[17] *Cedric Kushner Promotions, Ltd. v. King*, 533 U.S. 158, 161 (2001); *Brown v. Cassens Transport Co.*, 675 F.3d 946, 967 (6th Cir. 2012); *Abraham v. Singh*, 480 F.3d 351, 357 (5th Cir. 2007); *Living Designs, Inc. v. E.I. Dupont de Nemours and Co.*, 431 F.3d 353, 361 (9th Cir. 2005); *Branon v. Boatmen's First National Bank*, 153 F.3d 1144, 1146 (10th Cir. 1998); *United States v. London*, 66 F.3d 1227, 1244 (1st Cir. 1995).

[18] *Cedric Kushner Promotions, Ltd. v. King*, 533 U.S. 158, 161 (2001); *Living Designs, Inc. v. E.I. Dupont de Nemours*, 431 F.3d 353, 361 (9th Cir. 2005); *First Capital Asset Management v. Satinwood, Inc.*, 385 F.3d 159, 173 (2d Cir. 2004).

[19] *Gentry v. Resolution Trust Corp.*, 937 F.2d 899, 907 (3d Cir. 1991); *Crowe v. Henry*, 43 F.3d 198, 205 (5th Cir. 1995); *In re Managed Care Litigation*, 150 F.Supp.2d 1330, 1351 (S.D.Fla. 2001); cf., *Churchill Village v. General Electric*, 361 F.3d 566, 574-75 (9th Cir. 2004).

[20] *United States v. Shamah*, 624 F.3d 449, 454 (7th Cir. 2010)(police department); *United States v. Urban*, 404 F.3d 754, 770-71 (3d Cir. 2005)(city department); *United States v. Cianci*, 378 F.3d 71, 83 (1st Cir. 2004)(mayor's office); *Ferluga v. Eickhoff*, 408 F.Supp.2d. 1153, 1162 (D.Kan. 2006)(municipality).

[21] *County of Oakland v. City of Detroit*, 866 F.2d 839, 851 (6th Cir. 1989); *Illinois Department of Revenue v. Phillips*, 771 F.2d 312, 316-17 (7th Cir. 1985).

[22] *Keller v. Central Bank*, 277 F.3d 811, 821 (6th Cir. 2002)(foreign sovereign); Brown v. Nationsbank Corp., 188 F.3d 579, 587 (5th Cir. 1999)(Federal Bureau of Investigation); *Pedrina v. Chun*, 97 F.3d 1296, 1300 (9th Cir. 1996); *McNeily v. United States*, 6 F.3d 343,

350 (5th Cir. 1993)(Federal Deposit Insurance Corp.); *Berger v. Pierce*, 933 F.2d 393, 397 (6th Cir. 1991)(Federal Insurance Administration); *Reyes v. City of Chicago*, 585 F.Supp.2d 1010, 1014 (N.D. Ill. 2008); *Wood v. Incorporated Village of Patchogue*, 311 F.Supp.2d 344, 354 (E.D.N.Y. 2004); *Lathrop v. Juneau & Associates, Inc.*, 220 F.R.D. 330, 334 (S.D.Ill. 2004)(municipality); *Donahue v. Federal Bureau of Investigation*, 204 F.Supp.2d 169, 173-74 (D.Mass. 2002).

[23] *Brittingham v. Mobil Corp.*, 943 F.2d 297, 303 (3d Cir. 1991), citing 116 Cong.Rec. 35199 (1970)(remarks of Rep. St. Germain), 116 Cong.Rec. 607 (1970) (remarks of Sen. Byrd), and 115 Cong.Rec. 6993 (1969)(remarks of Sen. Hruska); ABRAMS, THE LAW OF CIVIL RICO, 206 (1991); *Sadighi v. Daghighfekr*, 36 F.Supp.2d 279, 286 (D.S.C. 1999). RICO predates 18 U.S.C. 1956, 1957, the principal federal money laundering statutes, by close to a decade and a half.

[24] *Gristede's Foods, Inc. v. Unkechauge Nation*, 532 F.Supp.2d 439, 446 (E.D.N.Y. 2007), quoting, Ouaknine v. MacFarlane, 897 F.2d 75, 83 (2d Cir. 1990); *see also, Ideal Steel Supply Corp. v. Anza*, 652 F.3d 310, 321 (2d Cir. 2011)("Subsection (a), in contrast, focuses the inquiry on conduct different from the conduct constituting the pattern of racketeering activity. After there have been sufficient predicate acts to constitute such a pattern, what is forbidden by subsection (a) is the investment or use of the proceeds of that activity to establish or operate a commerce-affecting enterprise").

[25] *BCCI Holdings (Luxembourg) Societe Anonyme v. Khalil*, 56 F.Supp.2d 14, 63 (D.D.C. 1999); Goldstock, *On the Waterfront: RICO and Labor Racketeering*, 17 AMERICAN CRIMINAL LAW REVIEW 341, 356 (1980).

[26] *Rao v. BP Products North American*, Inc., 589 F.3d 389, 398 (7th Cir. 2009); St. Paul Mercury Ins. Co. v. Williamson, 224 F.3d 425, 441 (5th Cir. 2000); *United States v. Vogt*, 910 F.2d 1184, 1194 (4th Cir. 1990); *Republic of Colombia v. Diageo North America*, Inc., 531 F.Supp.2d 365, 427 (E.D.N.Y. 2007); Sadighi v. Daghighfekr, 36 F.Supp.2d 279, 286 (D.S.C. 1999).

More precisely, the subsection declares, "(a) It shall be unlawful for any person who has received any income derived, directly or indirectly, from a pattern of racketeering activity or through collection of an unlawful debt in which such person has participated as a principal within the meaning of section 2, title 18, United States Code, to use or invest, directly or indirectly, any part of such income, or the proceeds of such income, in acquisition of any interest in, or the establishment or operation of, any enterprise which is engaged in, or the activities of which affect, interstate or foreign commerce. A purchase of securities on the open market for purposes of investment, and without the intention of controlling or participating in control of the issuer, or of assisting another to do so, shall not be unlawful under this subsection, if the securities of the issuer held by the purchaser, the members of his immediate family, and his or their accomplices in any pattern of racketeering activity or the collection of an unlawful debt after such purchase do not amount in the aggregate to one percent of the outstanding securities of any one class, and do not confer, either in law or in fact, the power to elect one or more directors of the issuer." 18 U.S.C. 1962(a).

[27] *Churchill Village v. General Electric*, 361 F.3d 566, 574 (9th Cir. 2004)("Where a corporation engages in racketeering activities and is the direct or indirect beneficiary of the pattern of racketeering activity, it can be both the 'person' and the 'enterprise' under section 1962(a)"); *Gentry v. Resolution Trust Corp.*, 937 F.2d 899, 907 (3d Cir. 1991); *Official Publications, Inc. v. Kable News*, 884 F.2d 664, 668 (2d Cir. 1989); *Downing v. Halliburton & Associates*, Inc., 812 F.Supp. 1178 (M.D.Ala. 1995), aff'd without written op., 13 F.3d 410 (11th Cir. 1995).

[28] *Brady v. Dairy Fresh Products* Co., 974 F.2d 1149, 1152 (9th Cir. 1992); *United States v. Wyatt*, 807 F.2d 1480, 1482 (9th Cir. 1987).

[29] *National Organization for Women, Inc. v. Scheidler*, 968 F.2d 612, 625 (7th Cir. 1992), rev'd on other grounds, 510 U.S. 249 (1994); *In re Burzynski*, 989 F.2d 733, 744 (5th Cir. 1993); *Ideal Steel Supply Corp. v. Anza*, 373 F.3d 251, 264 (2d Cir. 2004), rev'd on other grounds,

547 U.S. 451 (2006); *Johnson v. GEICO Casualty Co.*, 516 F.Supp.2d 351, 361 (D.Del. 2007).

[30] "(b) It shall be unlawful for any person through a pattern of racketeering activity or through collection of an unlawful debt to acquire or maintain, directly or indirectly, any interest in or control of any enterprise which is engaged in, or the activities of which affect, interstate or foreign commerce." 18 U.S.C. 1962(b); *Advocacy Organization for Patients and Providers v. Auto Club Insurance Association*, 176 F.3d 315, 322 (6th Cir. 1999); *Tal v. Hogan*, 453 F.3d 1244, 1268 (10th Cir. 2006).

[31] *Churchill Village v. General Electric*, 361 F.3d 566, 574 (9th Cir. 2004); *Landry v. Air Line Pilots Ass'n*, 901 F.2d 404, 425 (5th Cir.1990); *Gentry v. Resolution Trust Corp.*, 937 F.2d 899, 907 (3d Cir. 1991); *Whaley v. Auto Club Insurance Association*, 891 F.Supp. 1237, 1241-242 (E.D.Mich. 1995).

[32] *Wagh v. Metris Direct, Inc.*, 363 F.3d 821, 830 (9th Cir. 2003); *Advocacy Organization for Patients and Providers v. Auto Club Insurance Association*, 176 F.3d at 329; *Banks v. Wolk*, 918 F.2d 418, 421 (3d Cir. 1990); *Andrews Farms v. Calcot*, Ltd., 527 F.Supp.2d 1239, 1256 (E.D.Cal. 2007).

[33] *Tal v. Hogan*, 453 F.3d at 1268-269 ("'Interest in or control of' requires more than a general interest in the results of its actions, or the ability to influence the enterprise through deceit ... Rather, it requires some ownership of the enterprise or an ability to exercise dominion over it"); *Ikuno v. Yip*, 912 F.2d 306, 310 (9th Cir. 1990), *citing Sutliff, Inc. v. Donovan Co.*, 727 F.2d 648, 653 (7th Cir. 1984), and *Cincinnati Gas & Elec.Co. v. General Electric Co.*, 656 F.Supp. 49, 85 (S.D.Ohio 1986); *Nafta v. Fenisk International House of Trade (USA),* Inc., 932 F.Supp. 422, 428 (1996); *Griffin v. NBD Bank*, 43 F.Supp.2d 780, 791-92 (W.D.Mich. 1999)(includes the control evidenced by the ability to select one or more of members of a corporation's board of directors). Control may also be indirect as for example where the defendant exercises a measure of control over a subsidiary by virtue of his control over its parent organization, *BCCI Holding (Luxembourg) Societe Anonyme v. Khalil*, 56 F.Supp.2d 14, 51 (D.D.C. 1999).

[34] "(c) It shall be unlawful for any person employed by or associated with any enterprise engaged in, or the activities of which affect, interstate or foreign commerce, to conduct, or participate, directly or indirectly, in the conduct of such enterprise's affairs through a pattern of racketeering activity or collection of unlawful debt." 18 U.S.C. 1962(c). "A substantive RICO charge requires the Government to prove: (1) the existence of an enterprise which affects interstate or foreign commerce; (2) the defendant's association with the enterprise; (3) the defendant's participation in the conduct of enterprise's affairs; and (4) that the participation was through a pattern of racketeering activity," *United States v. Fowler*, 535 F.3d 408, 418 (6th Cir. 2008); see also, *United States v. Brandao*, 539 F.3d 44, 50-1 (1st Cir. 2008); *Crest Construction II, Inc. v. John Do*e, 660 F.3d 346, 353 (8th Cir. 2011).

[35] Gordon, *Crimes That Count Twice: A Reexamination of RICO's Nexus Requirements Under 18 U.S.C. §§1962(c) and 1964(c),* 32 VERMONT LAW REVIEW 171, 173 (2007).

[36] *Cedric Kushner Promotions, Ltd. v. King*, 533 U.S. 158, 161 (2001); *City of New York v. Smokes-Spirits.Com, Inc.*, 541 F.3d 425, 446-47 (2d Cir. 2008), rev'd on other grounds sub nom., *Hemi Group v. City of New York*, 130 S.Ct. 983, 990 (2010); *Abraham v. Singh*, 480 F.3d 351, 357 (5th Cir. 2007); *Living Designs, Inc. v. E.I. Dupont de Nemours and* Co., 431 F.3d 353, 361 (9th Cir. 2005); *Branon v. Boatmen's First National Bank*, 153 F.3d 1144, 1146 (10th Cir. 1998); *United States v. London*, 66 F.3d 1227, 1244 (1st Cir. 1995).

[37] *Sever v. Alaska Pulp Corp.*, 978 F.2d 1529, 1534 (9th Cir. 1992); *Glessner v. Kenny*, 952 F.2d 702, 711-12 (3d Cir. 1991); but see, *Webster v. Omnitrition International, Inc.*, 79 F.3d 776, 787 (9th Cir. 1996)(holding a corporation could be guilty under subsection 1962(d) of conspiring with its officers and employees to violate RICO in a case in which the corporation appears to have been considered both the enterprise and a person).

[38] *Cedric Kushner Promotions, Ltd. v. King*, 533 U.S. 158, 161 (2001).

[39] *Reves v. Ernst & Young*, 507 U.S. 170, 184-85 (1993); *see also, Ouwinga v. Benistar 419 Plan Services, Inc.*, 694 F.3d 783, 791-92 (6th Cir. 2012); City of New York v. Smokes-Spirits.Com, Inc., 541 F.3d at 449, *rev'd on other grounds sub nom., Hemi Group v. City of New York*, 130 S.Ct. 983, 990 (2010); *United States v. Swan*, 250 F.3d 495, 498 (7th Cir. 2001).

[40] *United States v. Diaz,* 176 F.3d 52, 92 (2d Cir. 1999);*United States v. Owens*, 167 F.3d 739, 753-54 (1st Cir. 1999); *United States v. Urban*, 404 F.3d 754, 769-70 (3d Cir. 2005); *United States v. Fowler*, 535 F.3d at 418; *Walter v. Drayson*, 538 F.3d 1244, 1247-248 (9th Cir. 2008); *Ouwinga v. Benistar 419 Plan Services, Inc.*, 694 F.3d at 792.

[41] *National Organization for Women, Inc. v. Scheidler*, 510 U.S. 249, 256-61 (1994).

[42] 18 U.S.C. 1961(1). Paragraph 1961(1)(G) simply states that the crimes listed in 18 U.S.C. 2332b(g)(5)(B)(i.e., federal crimes of terrorism) are predicate offenses; thus, whenever a crime is added to subparagraph 2332b(g)(5)(B) it becomes a RICO predicate offense, sub silentio.

[43] *Sedima, S.P.L.R. v. Imrex Co.*, 473 U.S. 479, 488 (1985); *American Chiropractic v. Trigon Healthcare,* 367 F.3d 212, 233 (4th Cir 2004). A civil RICO cause of action based on fraud in the purchase or sale of securities requires a prior conviction, 18 U.S.C. 1964(c); *Powers v. Wells Fargo Bank NA*, 439 F.3d 1043, 1046 (9th Cir. 2006); *Vanderbilt Mortgage and Finance, Inc. v. Flores*, 735 F.Supp. 679, 697 (S.D.Tex. 2010).

[44] *McCarthy v. Pacific Loan, Inc*., 629 F.Supp. 1102, 1108 (D.Haw. 1986); cf., *Appley v. West*, 832 F.2d 1021, 1024-25 (7th Cir. 1987); see discussion of double jeopardy constitutional issue infra at 20.

[45] *H.J., Inc. v. Northwestern Bell Telephone Co*., 492 U.S. 229, 239 (1989)(emphasis of the Court), citing S.Rep.No. 617, 91st Cong., 1st Sess. at 158 (1969) and 116 Cong.Rec. 18940 (1970)(remarks of Sen. McClellan).

[46] *H.J., Inc. v. Northwestern Bell Telephone Co.*, 492 U.S. at 240, quoting, 18 U.S.C. 3575(e); see also, *Ouwinga v. Benistar 419 Plan Services, Inc*., 694 F.3d 783, 795 (6th Cir. 2012); *United States v. Eppolito,* 543 F.3d 25, 51 (2d Cir. 2008); *United States v. Brandao,* 539 F.3d 44, 55 (1st Cir. 2008); *United States v. Browne*, 505 F.3d 1229, 1258 (11th Cir. 2007); *Roger Whitmore's Automotive Services, Inc. v. Lake County*, 424 F.3d 659, 672 (7th Cir. 2005); *United States v. Smith*, 413 F.3d 1253, 1269 (10th Cir. 2005). There may be some question whether the predicate offenses must relate to each other as well as to the enterprise. Compare, *United States v. Cain*, 671 F.3d 271, 284 (2d Cir. 2012) ("[A] RICO pattern may not be established without some showing that the racketeering acts are interrelated and that there is continuity or a threat of continuity. Our subsequent decisions have labeled the requirement that the predicate acts be related to one another 'horizontal relatedness' and the requirement they have a nexus to the enterprise 'vertical relatedness'"), with, *United States v. Fowler*, 535 F.3d 408, 420 (6th Cir. 2008)("It may be true that Fowler's predicate acts are not directly interrelated with each other, but that is not required. Instead, the predicate acts must be connected to the affairs and operations of the criminal enterprise").

[47] *H.J., Inc. v. Northwestern Bell Telephone Co.*, 492 U.S. at 242.

[48] *Id.* (emphasis added); *United States v. Richardson*, 167 F.3d 621, 626 (D.C.Cir. 1999) ("fortuitous interruption of racketeering activity such as by arrest does not grant defendants a free pass to evade RICO charges").

[49] *H.J., Inc. v. Northwestern Bell Telephone Co*., 492 U.S. at 242.

[50] *Jackson v. Segwick Claims Management Services, Inc.,* 699 F.3d 466, 483-84 (6th Cir. 2012)(predicate offenses committed over a 19-month period were sufficient to show closed-ended continuity); *Crest Construction II, Inc. v. John Doe*, 660 F.3d 346, 357 (8th Cir. 2011)(predicate offenses committed over a 7-month period were not sufficient to show closed-ended continuity); *United States v. Wilson*, 605 F.3d 985, 1021 (D.C.Cir. 2010)(15 months, sufficient); *Spool v. World Child International Adoption Agency*, 520 F.3d 178, 184 (2d Cir. 2008) (16 months, insufficient); *Jennings v. Auto Meter Products, Inc*., 495 F.3d 466, 474-75 (7th Cir. 2007)(10 months, insufficient); *Roger Whitmore's Automotive*

Services, Inc. v. Lake County, 424 F.3d 659, 672-74 (7th Cir. 2005)(two years with relatively limited activity involving a relatively few individuals, insufficient); *GE Investment Private Placement Partners II v. Parker*, 247 F.3d 543, 550 (4th Cir. 2001)(two years, insufficient; five years, sufficient); *North Bridge Associates, Inc. v. Boldt*, 274 F.3d 38, 43 (1st Cir. 2001)(4 months, insufficient).

"When considering whether a closed period of related conduct is sufficient to establish continuity," the Seventh Circuit considers "the number and variety of predicate acts and the length of time over which they were committed, the number of victims, the presence of separate schemes and the occurrence of distinct injuries," *Corley v. Rosewood Care Center, Inc.*, 142 F.3d 1041, 1049 (7th Cir. 1998).

51 *H.J., Inc. v. Northwestern Bell Telephone Co.*, 492 U.S. at 242; *Heinrich v. Waiting Angels Adoption Services*, Inc., 668 F.3d 393, 411 n.2 (6th Cir. 2012); *Crest Construction II, Inc. v. John Doe*, 660 F.3d 346, 358 (8th Cir. 2011); United States v. Brandao, 539 F.3d 44, 55 (1st Cir. 2008); *United States v. Browne*, 505 F.3d 1229, 1259-260 (11th Cir. 2007); *Abraham v. Singh*, 480 F.3d 351, 355(5th Cir. 2007); DeFalco v. Bernas, 244 F.3d 286, 323 (2*d* Cir. 2001); *GE Investment Private Placement Partners II v. Parker,* 247 F.3d 543, 549 (4th Cir. 2001).

52 *Spool v. World Child International Adoption Agency*, 520 F.3d at 185; cf., *United States v. Burden*, 600 F.3d 204, 219 (2d Cr. 2010).

53 *United States v. Aucoin*, 964 F.2d 1492, 1495-497 (5th Cir. 1992), quoting dicta in H.J., Inc., 492 U.S. at 232 (1989); *United States v. Giovanelli*, 945 F.2d 479, 490 (2d Cir. 1991); *United States v. Eufrasio*, 935 F.2d 553, 563 n.12 (3d Cir. 1991); but see, *Wright v. Shepard*, 919 F.2d 665, 673 (11th Cir. 1990); *United States v. Oreto*, 37 F.3d 739, 751 (1st Cir. 1994).

Oreto also rejected the argument to the effect that the equal protection clause precludes requiring proof of only a single loansharking violation while demanding proof of the patterned commission of at least two violations for every other predicate offense, 37 F.3d at 751-52 ("Congress could rationally have decided that collections of unlawful debt were central to the evils at which RICO was directed. Accordingly, it could rationally have chosen to make guilt more easily provable in unlawful debt cases than in cases involving other forms of racketeering activity").

54 18 U.S.C. 1961(6); *Community State Bank v. Strong*, 651 F.3d 1241, 1259 (11th Cir. 2011)(usurious non-gambling debt); Cannarozzi v. Fiumara, 371 F.3d 1, 3-4 (1st Cir. 2004); *Neild v. Wolpoff & Abramson*, L.L.P., 453 F.Supp.2d 918, 926 (E.D.Va. 2006).

55 18 U.S.C. 1961(4).

56 *United States v. Turkette*, 452 U.S. 575, 580-93 (1981); *United States v. Palacios*, 677 F.3d 234, 248 (4th Cir. 2012); *United States v. Cianci*, 378 F.3d 71, 83 (1st Cir. 2004).

57 *United States v. Warner*, 498 F.3d 666, 694 (7th Cir. 2007)(state); *United States v. Cianci*, 378 F.3d 71, 83 (1st Cir. 2004)(mayor's office); *DeFalco v. Bernas*, 244 F.3d 286, 307-9 (2d Cir. 2001)(town); *United States v. Massey*, 89 F.3d 1433, 1440 (11th Cir. 1995)(state court); *Pelfresne v. Village of Rosemont*, 22 F.Supp.2d 756, 761-62 (N.D.Ill. 1998) (mayor's office); cf., *Salinas v. United States*, 522 U.S. 52 (1997) (sheriff's office).

58 *Cedric Kushner Promotions, Ltd. v. King*, 533 U.S. 158, 161 (2001); *Abraham v. Singh*, 480 F.3d 351, 357 (5th Cir. 2007); *Living Designs, Inc. v. E.I. Dupont de Nemours and Co.*, 431 F.3d 353, 361 (9th Cir. 2005); *Branon v. Boatmen's First National Bank*, 153 F.3d 1144, 1146 (10th Cir. 1998); *United States v. London*, 66 F.3d 1227, 1244 (1st Cir. 1995).

59 *Gentry v. Resolution Trust Corp.*, 937 F.2d 899, 907 (3d Cir. 1991); *Crowe v. Henry*, 43 F.3d 198, 205 (5th Cir. 1995); *In re Managed Care Litigation*, 150 F.Supp.2d 1330, 1351 (S.D.Fla. 2001); cf., *Churchill Village v. General Electric*, 361 F.3d 566, 574-75 (9th Cir. 2004).

60 *Cedric Kushner Promotions, Ltd. v. King*, 533 U.S. 158, 161 (2001); *Living Designs, Inc. v. E.I. Dupont de Nemours*, 431 F.3d 353, 361 (9th Cir. 2005); *First Capital Asset Management v. Satinwood*, Inc., 385 F.3d 159, 173 (2d Cir. 2004).

[61] *Boyle v. United States*, 556 U.S. 938, 948 (2009).

[62] *Id.* at 946; see also, Ouwinga v. Benistar 419 Plan Services, Inc., 694 F.3d 783, 794 (6th Cir. 2012*); United States v. Hosseini*, 679 F.3d 544, 557 (7th Cir. 2012); *Crest Construction II v. John Doe*, 660 F.3d 346, 354 (8th Cir. 2011).

[63] 18 U.S.C. 1962(a), (b), (c).

[64] *United States v. Robertson*, 514 U.S. 669, 671-72 (1995); see also, *United States v. Keltner*, 147 F.3d 662, 669 (8th Cir. 1998)(multistate travel by the participants in furtherance of the enterprise's activities with RICO predicates committed in more than one state); *United States v. Pipkins*, 378 F.3d 1281, 1294-295 (11th Cir. 2004)(same).

[65] *United States v. Flores*, 572 F.3d 1254, 1267 (11th Cir. 2009); *United States v. Gardiner*, 463 F.3d 445, 458 (6th Cir. 2006); *United States v. Johnson*, 440 F.3d 832, 841 (7th Cir. 2006); *United States v. Cianci,* 378 F.3d 71, 98 (1st Cir. 2004); *United States v. Rodriguez*, 360 F.3d 949, 955 (9th Cir. 2004); *Breslin Realty Development Corp. v. Schackner*, 457 F.Supp.2d 132, 136-37 (E.D.N.Y. 2006).

[66] *United States v. White*, 116 F.3d 903, 925-26 (D.C.Cir. 1997); *United States v. Miller*, 116 F.3d 641, 673-74 (2d Cir. 1997).

[67] Waucaush v. United States, 380 F.3d 251, 256 (6th Cir. 2004).

[68] 18 U.S.C. 1962(d)("It shall be unlawful for any person to conspire to violate any of the provisions of subsection (a), (b), or (c) of this section"). *United States v. Harris*, 695 F.3d 1125, 1132 (10th Cir. 2012)("In order to convict a defendant for violating §1962(d), the Government must prove beyond a reasonable doubt that the defendant: (1) by knowing about and agreeing to facilitate the commission of two or more acts (2) constituting a pattern (3) of racketeering activity (4) participates in (5) an enterprise (6) the activities of which affect interstate or foreign commerce").

[69] *Salinas v. United States*, 522 U.S. 52, 63 (1997); *United States v. Tocco*, 200 F.3d 401, 426 (6th Cir. 2003); *United States v. Smith*, 413 F.3d 1253, 1265 (10th Cir. 2005); *United States v. Browne*, 505 F.3d 1229, 1263 (11th Cir. 2007).

[70] *Salinas v. United States*, 522 U.S. at 65-6; *United States v. Harris*, 695 F.3d 1125, 1133 (10th Cir. 2012); *United States v. Tello*, 687 F.3d 785, 793 (7th Cir. 2012); *United States v. Mouzone*, 687 F.3d 207, 218 (4th Cir. 2012); *RSM Production Corp. v. Freshfields Bruckhaus Deringer U.S LLP*, 682 F.3d 1043, 1048 (D.C. Cir. 2012).

[71] *United States v. Cornelius*, 696 F.3d 1307, 1317 (10th Cir. 2012); but see, United States v. Mouzone, 687 F.3d at 218 ("Thus, to satisfy §1962(d), the government must prove that an enterprise affecting interstate commerce existed ... ").

[72] *Salinas v. United States*, 522 U.S. at 65; *United States v. Lawson*, 535 F.3d 434, 445 (6th Cir. 2008); *United States v. Fernandez*, 388 F.3d 1119, 1228 (9th Cir. 2004); *United States v. Warneke,* 310 F.3d 542, 547-48 (7th Cir. 2003); United States v. Posada-Rios, 158 F.3d 832, 857 (5th Cir. 1998).

[73] *Pinkerton v. United States*, 328 U.S. 640, 646-47 (1946); *United States v. Harris*, 695 F.3d 1125, 1136 (10th Cir. 2012); *United States v. Benabe*, 654 F.3d 753, 777 (7th Cir. 2011); cf., *United States v. Moore*, 651 F.3d 30, 91-4 (D.C. Cir. 2011).

[74] *United States v. Harris*, 695 F.3d at 1137; *United States v. Schiro*, 679 F.3d 521, 528-29 (7th Cir. 2012).

[75] 18 U.S.C. 1963(a).

[76] U.S.S.G. §2E1.1. Federal courts were at one time required to sentence an offender within the range provided by the United States Sentencing Guidelines, unless the court found that the case involved factors not sufficiently considered in the Guidelines, 18 U.S.C. 3553(b)(2000 ed.). The once mandatory Guidelines are now advisory, but continue to carry considerable weight, *United States v. Booker*, 543 U.S. 220, 264 (2005)("The district courts, while not bound by the Guidelines, must consult those Guidelines and take them into account when sentencing").

[77] 18 U.S.C. 1963(a), 3571.

[78] 18 U.S.C. 3583(a)("The court, in imposing a sentence to a term of imprisonment for a felony or a misdemeanor may include as part of the sentence a requirement that the defendant be placed on a term of supervised release after imprisonment ... "); 3559(a)(3). Although the language of the statute is discretionary, the Sentencing Guidelines require a term of supervised release in cases in which the term of imprisonment imposed is more than a year, U.S.S.G. §5D1.1(a).

[79] 18 U.S.C. 3663A. Restitution in other cases is discretionary, 18 U.S.C. 3663.

[80] 18 U.S.C. 1963(a) ("Whoever violates any provision of section 1962 ... shall forfeit to the United States, irrespective of any provision of State law – (1) any interest the person has acquired or maintained in violation of section 1962; (2) any – (A) interest in; (B) security of; (C) claim against; or (D) property or contractual right of any kind affording a source of influence over; any enterprise which the person has established, operated, controlled, conducted, or participated in the conduct of, in violation of section 1962; and (3) any property constituting, or derived from, any proceeds which the person obtained, directly or indirectly, from racketeering activity or unlawful debt collection in violation of section 1962 ... ").

[81] 18 U.S.C. 1956("(a)(1) Whoever, knowing that the property involved in a financial transaction represents the proceeds of some form of unlawful activity, conducts or attempts to conduct such a financial transaction which in fact involves the proceeds of specified unlawful activity - (A)(i) with the intent to promote the carrying on of specified unlawful activity; or ... (B) knowing that the transaction is designed in whole or in part - (i) to conceal or disguise the nature, the location, the source, the ownership, or the control of the proceeds of specified unlawful activity ... shall be sentenced to a fine ... or imprisonment for not more than twenty years, or both.... (c) As used in this section ... (7) the term 'specified unlawful activity' means - (A) any act or activity constituting an offense listed in section 1961(1) of this title except an act which is indictable under subchapter II of chapter 53 of title 31 [relating to financial transaction reporting requirements] ... ").

[82] 18 U.S.C. 981("(a)(1) The following property is subject to forfeiture to the United States ... (C) Any property, real or personal, which constitutes or is derived from proceeds traceable to a violation of ... any offense constituting 'specified unlawful activity (as defined in section 1956(c)(7) of this title) ... "). For a general overview of federal forfeiture law, see CRS Report 97-139, *Crime and Forfeiture*.

[83] 18 U.S.C. 1964(c)("Any person injured in his business or property by reason of a violation of section 1962 of this chapter may sue therefor in any appropriate United States district court and shall recover threefold the damages he sustains and the cost of the suit, including a reasonable attorney's fee, except that no person may rely upon any conduct that would have been actionable as fraud in the purchase or sale of securities to establish a violation of section 1962. The exception contained in the preceding sentence does not apply to an action against any person that is criminally convicted in connection with the fraud, in which case the statute of limitations shall start to run on the date on which the conviction becomes final").

[84] *Sedima S.P.R.L. v. Imrex Co, Inc.*, 473 U.S. 479, 493 (1985); *Smith v. Husband*, 376 F.Supp.2d 603, 613 (E.D.Va. 2005).

[85] *Davis-Lynch, Inc. v. Moreno*, 667 F.3d 539, 550 (5th Cir. 2012); *Ideal Steel Supply Corp. v. Anza*, 652 F.3d 310, 321 (2d Cir. 2011); *United States v. BP Products North America*, Inc., 589 F.3d 389, 398 (7th Cir. 2009); but see, *Sadighi v. Daghighfekr*, 36 F.Supp.2d 279, 288 n.9 (D.S.C. 1999)(emphasis added)("[u]nder Fourth Circuit case law, plaintiffs have standing to sue if they allege that their injuries were either (1) proximately caused by the predicate acts underlying the §1962(a) violation, or (2) proximately caused by *the investment and use* of the illegally obtained income").

[86] *Wagh v. Metris Direct, Inc.*, 363 F.3d 821, 830 (9th Cir. 2003); *Vanderbilt Mortgage and Finance, Inc. v. Flores*, 735 F.Supp.2d 679, 701 (S.D.Tex. 2010)(internal quotation marks omitted)("Section 1962(b)'s acquisition requirement necessitates that the plaintiff's alleged

injury be caused by the alleged RICO defendants acquiring or maintaining an interest or control in the alleged enterprise. The injury cause by the acquisition of maintenance must be distinct from the jury caused by the predicate acts").

[87] *Bridge v. Phoenix Bond & Indem. Co.*, 553 U.S. 639, 647 (2008)("RICO provides a private right of action for treble damages to any person injured in his business or property by reason of the conduct of a qualifying enterprise's affairs through a pattern of [predicate] acts ... "); *Brown v. Cassens Transport Co.*, 546 F.3d 347, 353 (6th Cir. 2009).

[88] *Davis-Lynch, Inc. v. Moreno*, 667 F.3d 539, 552 (5th Cir. 2012)("Injury caused by acts that are not racketeering activities or otherwise wrongful under RICO will not establish a viable civil RICO claim"); *Morganroth & Morganroth v. Norris, McLaughlin & Marcus*, 331 F.3d 406, 415 (3d Cir. 2003); *Gagan v. American Cablevision*, Inc., 77 F.3d 951, 958-59 (7th Cir. 1996); *Bowman v. Western Auto Supply Co.*, 985 F.2d 383, 387-88 (8th Cir. 1993); cf., Beck v. Prupis, 529 U.S. 494, 507 (2000).

[89] 18 U.S.C. 1964(c).

[90] *Hemi Group v. City of New York*, 130 S.Ct. 983, 990 (2010)(the City, claiming that Hemi sold untaxed cigarettes to City residents but fraudulently failed to report the sale to state authorities who then would have passed the information on to City tax authorities, did not suffer a direct RICO injury: "the disconnect between the asserted injury and the alleged fraud in this case is even sharper than in *Anza*. There, we viewed the point as important because the same party – National Steel – had both engaged in the harmful conduct and committed the fraudulent act. We nevertheless found the distinction between the relevant acts sufficient to defeat Ideal's RICO claim. Here, the City's theory of liability rests not just on separate actions, but separate actions carried out by separate parties" (emphasis of the Court)); *Anza v. Ideal Steel Supply Corp.*, 547 U.S. 451, 460-61 (2006)(competitors, claiming that Anza could lower prices because he failed to collect sales tax from cash customers and then used mail and wire fraud to cover his tax evasion, did not suffer a direct or proximate RICO injury); *Holmes v. Securities Investor Protection Corp.*, 503 U.S. 258, 265-68 (1992)(the Corporation, that reimbursed the customers of defaulting brokers following the defendant's alleged stock manipulation, did not suffer a direct or proximate RICO injury); *see generally*, CRS Report RS22470, Civil RICO and Standing: *Anza v. Ideal Steel Supply Corporation*.

[91] *Guerrero v. Gates*, 357 F.3d 911, 920 (9th Cir. 2004); *Diaz v. Gates*, 380 F.3d 480, 483-85 (9th Cir. 2004); *Gentry v. Resolution Trust Corp.*, 937 F.2d 899, 918 (3d Cir. 1991).

[92] *Brown v. Cassens Transport Co.*, 675 F.3d 946, 959 (6th Cir. 2012); *Evans v. City of Chicago*, 434 F.3d 916, 924-26 (7th Cir. 2006); *Diaz v. Gates*, 420 F.3d 897, 900-903 (9th Cir. 2005); *Hughes v. Tobacco Inst. Inc.*, 278 F.3d 417, 422 (5th Cir. 2001); *Hamm v. Phone-Poulenc Rorer Pharm., Inc.*, 187 F.3d 941, 954 (8th Cir. 1999); *Bast v. Cohen, Dunn & Sinclair, PC*, 59 F.3d 492, 495 (4th Cir. 1995); *Libertad v. Welch*, 53 F.3d 428, 437 (1st Cir. 1995); *Gentry v. Resolution Trust Corp.*, 937 F.2d 899, 918-19 (3d Cir. 1991); *Grogan v. Platt*, 835 F.2d 844, 847 (11th Cir. 1988); *Bankers Trust Co. v. Rhoades*, 741 F.2d 511, 515 (2d Cir. 1984); *McCormick v. City of Lawrence*, 325 F.Supp.2d 1191, 1209 (D.Kan. 2004); cf., *Serv. Employees Int'l Union Health & Welfare Fund v. Philip Morris Inc.*, 249 F.3d 1068, 1076 (D.C. Cir. 2001); *see generally, Personal Versus Property Harm and Civil RICO Standing*, 73 UNIVERSITY OF CHICAGO LAW REVIEW 1513 (2006).

[93] *Evans v. City of Chicago*, 434 F.3d 916, 924-26 (7th Cir. 2006)(malicious prosecution injuries are personal and cannot provide the basis for a civil RICO suit); *Diaz v. Gates*, 420 F.3d 897, 900-903 (9th Cir. 2005)(false imprisonment injuries may provide the basis for a civil RICO suit); *see generally, Exercising the Passive Virtues in Interpreting Civil RICO "Business or Property,"* 75 UNIVERSITY OF CHICAGO LAW REVIEW 1773, 1774 (2008)("Courts struggling to define 'business or property' as used in §1964(c) have adopted markedly different approaches").

[94] 18 U.S.C. 1961(1)(D).

[95] 18 U.S.C. 1964(c)(emphasis added)("Any person injured in his business or property by reason of a violation of section 1962 of this chapter may sue therefor in any appropriate United States district court and shall recover threefold the damages he sustains and the cost of the suit, including a reasonable attorney's fee, *except that no person may rely upon any conduct that would have been actionable as fraud in the purchase or sale of securities to establish a violation of section 1962. The exception contained in the preceding sentence does not apply to an action against any person that is criminally convicted in connection with the fraud, in which case the statute of limitations shall start to run on the date on which the conviction becomes final*").

[96] *United States v. Bonanno Organized Crime Family*, 879 F.2d 20, 21-7 (2d Cir. 1989); *Peia v. United States*, 152 F.Supp.2d 226, 234 (D.Conn. 2001).

[97] *City of New York v. Smokes-Spirits.Com, Inc.*, 541 F.3d 425, 444-45 (2d Cir. 2008), rev'd on other grounds sub nom., *Hemi Group v. City of New York*, 130 S.Ct. 983 (2010); *County of Oakland v. City of Detroit*, 866 F.2d 839, 851 (6th Cir. 1989); *Illinois Department of Revenue v. Phillips*, 771 F.2d 312, 316-17 (7th Cir. 1985). Some courts, however, believe that a governmental entity may only sue under RICO for injuries related to a commercial transactions, *Canyon County v. Syngenta Seeds*, Inc., 519 F.3d 969, 976 (9th Cir. 2008); *Township of Marlboro v. Scannapuieco*, 545 F.Supp.2d 452, 458 (D.N.J. 2008)(citing dicta subsequently repudiated in *Smokes-Spirits.Com, Inc.*).

[98] *Pedrina v. Chun*, 97 F.3d 1296, 1300 (9th Cir. 1996)(municipality); *McNeily v. United States*, 6 F.3d 343, 350 (5th Cir. 1993)(Federal Deposit Insurance Corp.); *Genty v. Resolution Trust Corp.*, 937 F.2d 899, 908-14 (3d Cir. 1991)(municipality); Berger v. Pierce, 933 F.2d 393, 397 (6th Cir. 1991)(Federal Insurance Administration); *Smith v. Babbitt*, 875 F.Supp. 1353, 1365 (D.Minn. 1995), aff'd, 100 F.3d 556 (8th Cir. 1996)(Indian tribal government); *McMaster v. State of Minnesota*, 819 F.Supp. 1429, 1434 (D.Minn. 1993), aff'd, 30 F.3d 976 (8th Cir. 1994)(state); *Keller v. Central Bank of Nigeria*, 277 F.3d 811, 820 (6th Cir. 2002) (foreign governmental entity); *Donahue v. Federal Bureau of Investigation*, 204 F.Supp.2d 169, 173-74 (D.Mass. 2002); *Banks v. Dept. of Motor Vehicles*, 419 F.Supp.2d 1186, 1192 (C.D.Cal. 2006).

[99] "Many courts have applied the logic of *Central Bank [v. First Interstate Bank*, 511 U.S. 164 (1994)] to RICO and concluded that §1962(c) does not provide for [civil] aiding and abetting liability," *Cobbs v. Sheahan*, 385 F.Supp.2d 731, 738 (N.D.Ill. 2005); accord, *DeFalco v. Bernas*, 244 F.3d 286, 330 (2d Cir. 2001);*Pennsylvania Association of Edwards Heirs v. Rightenour*, 235 F.3d 839, 840 (3d Cir. 2000); *In re Countrywide Financial Corp.* Mortgage Marketing and Sales Practice, 601 F.Supp.2d 1201, 1219 (S.D.Cal. 2009); *Rolo v. City Investing Co. Liquidating Trust*, 155 F.3d 644, 656-68 (3d Cir. 1998); *In re MasterCard International Inc., Internet Gambling Litigation*, 132 F.Supp.2d 468, 493-95 (E.D.La. 2001), aff'd, 313 F.3d 257 (5th Cir. 2002); contra, *In re Managed Care Litigation*, 298 F.Supp.2d at 1272; see also, *First American Corp. v. Al-Nah*yan, 17 F.Supp.2d 10, 23-4 (D.D.C. 1998)(preliminarily finding Central Bank distinguishable, but finding it unnecessary to resolve the issue in light of the prospect of the defendants' possible direct RICO liability); *American Automotive Accessories, Inc. v. Fishman*, 991 F.Supp. 987, 993 (N.D.Ill. 1998)("to be held liable as an aider and abettor, a person must in some sort associate himself with the venture, participate in it as something he wishes to bring about, and seek by his action to make it succeed")(noting that the Seventh Circuit has yet to "comment on the possibility of aiding and abetting liability in civil RICO actions").

[100] 18 U.S.C. 1964("(a) The district courts of the United States shall have jurisdiction to prevent and restrain violations of section 1962 of this chapter by issuing appropriate orders, including, but not limited to: ordering any person to divest himself of any interest, direct or indirect, in any enterprise; imposing reasonable restrictions on the future activities or investments of any person, including, but not limited to, prohibiting any person from engaging in the same type of endeavor as the enterprise engaged in, the activities of which affect interstate or foreign commerce; or ordering dissolution or reorganization of any

enterprise, making due provision for the rights of innocent persons. (b) The Attorney General may institute proceedings under this section. Pending final determination thereof, the court may at any time enter such restraining orders or prohibitions, or take such other actions, including the acceptance of satisfactory performance bonds, as it shall deem proper"); e.g., *United States v. Local 560*, 780 F.2d 267, 295-96 (3d Cir. 1985)(equitable remedies available under RICO include court authority to remove union officials and place the union in trusteeship); *United States v. Sasso*, 215 F.3d 283, 292 (2d Cir. 2000)(RICO grants the court authority to order a defendant to contribute to cost of monitoring a previously corrupted union).

The courts, however, have treated RICO requests to order disgorgement cautiously. "Ordinarily, the disgorgement of gains ill-gotten long in the past will not serve the goal of 'preventing and restraining future violations' unless there is a finding that the gains are being used to fund or promote the illegal conduct, or constitute capital available for that purpose," *United States v. Carson*, 52 F.3d 1173, 1182 (2d Cir. 1995). *Richard v. Hoechsty Celanese Chemical Group*, Inc., 355 F.3d 345, 354-55(5th Cir. 2003); in fact one circuit has concluded that disgorgement is not a remedy available under RICO under any circumstances, *United States v. Philip Morris USA, Inc.*, 396 F.3d 1190, 1197-1202 (D.C.Cir. 2005); see, *Equity Up in Smoke: Civil RICO, Disgorgement, and United States v. Philip Morris*, 74 FORDHAM LAW REVIEW 2461 (2006).

[101] E.g., *United States v. Private Sanitation Industry Association*, 995 F.2d 375 (2d Cir. 1993); *United States v. Local* 560, 974 F.2d 315 (3d Cir. 1992); *United States v. Local* 30, 871 F.2d 401 (3d Cir. 1989); *United States v. International Brotherhood of Teamsters, Chauffeurs*, Warehousemen and Helpers (IBT), 931 F.2d 177 (2d Cir. 1991).

The *Teamsters* case, perhaps the best known and most heavily litigated of these instances, has involved issues arising under the consent decree negotiated to settle the government's RICO suit rather than issues as to the government's prerogatives under civil RICO, *United States v. IBT*, 172 F.3d 217 (2d Cir. 1999); *United States v. IBT*, 170 F.3d 136 (2d Cir. 1999); *United States v. IBT*, 168 F.3d 645 (2d Cir. 1999); *United States v. Boggia*, 167 F.3d 113 (2d Cir. 1999); *United States v. IBT*, 156 F.3d 354 (2d Cir. 1998); *United States v. IBT*, 141 F.3d 405 (2d Cir. 1998); *United States v. IBT*, 120 F.3d 341 (2d Cir. 1997); *United States v. IBT*, 86 F.3d 271 (2d Cir. 1996); *United States v. IBT*, 19 F.3d 816 (2d Cir. 1994); *United States v. IBT*, 12 F.3d 360 (2d Cir. 1993); *United States v. IBT*, 3 F.3d 634 (2d Cir. 1993); *United States v. IBT*, 998 F.2d 1101 (2d Cir. 1993); *United States v. IBT*, 998 F.2d 120 (2d Cir. 1993); *United States v. IBT*, 986 F.2d 15 (2d Cir. 1993); *United States v. IBT*, 981 F.2d 1362 (2d Cir. 1992); *United States v. IBT*, 970 F.2d 1132 (2d Cir. 1996); *United States v. IBT*, 968 F.2d 1506 (2d Cir. 1992); *United States v. IBT*, 968 F.2d 1472 (2d Cir. 1992); *United States v. IBT*, 965 F.2d 15 (2d Cir. 1993); *United States v. IBT*, 964 F.2d 1224 (2d Cir. 1992); *United States v. IBT*, 964 F.2d 180 (2d Cir. 1992); *United States v. IBT*, 955 F.2d 171 (2d Cir. 1992); *United States v.IBT*, 950 F.2d 94 (2d Cir. 1991); *United States v. IBT*, 948 F.2d 98 (2d Cir. 1992); 931 F.2d 177 (2d Cir. 1991).

The United States has also sought to invoke it in its RICO litigation against various tobacco companies, *United States v. Philip Morris Inc.*, 396 F.3d 1190, 1191 (D.C.Cir. 2005).

[102] *National Organization for Women, Inc. v. Scheidler*, 267 F.3d 687, 695-700 (7th Cir. 2001)(concluding that private RICO plaintiffs are entitle to equitable relief), *rev'd on other grounds*, 537 U.S. 393 (2003); *In re Managed Care Litigation*, 298 F.Supp.2d 1259, 1282-283 (S.D.Fla. 2003); *contra*, *Religious Technology Center v. Wollersheim*, 796 F.2d 1076, 1080-89(9th Cir. 1986); *In re Fredeman Litigation*, 843 F.2d 821, 828-30 (5th Cir. 1988); *Sedima, S.P.R.L. v.Imrex*, 741 F.2d 482, 489 n.20 (2d Cir. 1984), *rev'd on other grounds*, 473 U.S. 479 (1985); *Wheeling-Pittsburgh Steel Corp. v. Mitsui & Co., Inc.*, 221 F.3d 924, 927 n.2 (6th Cir. 2000); *Dan River v. Icahn*, 701 F.2d 278, 290 (4th Cir. 1983); *Minter v. Wells Fargo Bank*, 593 F.Supp.2d 788, 795-96 (D.Md. 2009); *American Medical Association v.United Healthcare Corp.*, 588 F.Supp.2d 432, 444-46 (S.D.N.Y. 2008).

[103] 18 U.S.C. 1965. The circuits are divided, however, over the question of whether the section permits the exercise of jurisdiction over other defendants outside the district only when the court has personal jurisdiction over at least one of the defendants, *FC Investment Group v. IFX Martkets, Ltd.*, 529 F.3d 1087, 1099 (D.C. Cir. 2008)(citing cases on either side of the divide); *see also*, *Cory v. Aztec Steel Building, Inc.*, 468 F.3d 1226, 1231-233 (10th Cir. 2006); *Koch v. Royal Wine Merchants, Ltd.*, 847 F.Supp. 1370, 1374-375 & n.3 (S.D.Fla. 2012).

[104] *Tafflin v. Lavitt*, 493 U.S. 455, 458 (1990).
An injured party may also have a cause of action under an applicable state RICO statute, citations for which are appended.

[105] *Shearson/American Express Inc. v. McMahon*, 482 U.S. 220, 242 (1987); cf., *Pacificare Health Systems, Inc. v. Book*, 538 U.S. 401, 406-407 (2003).

[106] *Agency Holding Corp. v. Malley-Duff & Associates*, 483 U.S. 143, 156 (1987); *Klehr v. A.O.Smith Corp.*, 521 U.S. 179, 183 (1997). The Court also held that a plaintiff must have exercised due diligence to discover the violation before statute of limitations will be tolled because of the defendant's fraudulent concealment, *id.* at 194, and that unlike the statute of limitations in criminal cases, a civil cause of action does not date from the "last predicate act" of the RICO violation, *id.* at 186-87. The statute of limitations for a RICO criminal prosecution is five years, 18 U.S.C. 3282; *United States v. Schiro*, 679 F.3d 521, 528 (7th Cir. 2012).

[107] *Rotella v. Wood*, 528 U.S. 549, 551 (2000); *Potomac Electric Power Co. v. Electric Motor and Supply, Inc.*, 262 F.3d 260, 266 (4th Cir. 2001); *Mathews v. Kidder, Peabody & Co., Inc.*, 260 F.3d 239, 244-50 (3d Cir. 2001); *Indiana ex rel. Carter v. Pastrick*, 384 F.Supp.2d 1261, 1269-270 (N.D.Ind. 2005).

[108] *Humana, Inc. v. Forsyth*, 525 U.S. 299, 303 (1999); *American Chiropractic Ass'n, Inc. v. Trigon Healthcare, Inc.*, 367 F.3d 212, 230-32 (4th Cir. 2004); *Bankoklahoma Mortgage Corp. v. Capital Title Co., Inc.*, 194 F.3d 1089, 1198-1100 (10th Cir. 1999); *LeBarre v. Credit Acceptance Corp.*, 175 F.3d 640, 642-43 (8th Cir. 1999).

[109] *RICO Overreach: How the Federal Government's Escalating Offensive Against Gangs Has Run Afoul of the Constitution, 62 VANDERBILT LAW REVIEW 211 (2009); Federalizing Street Crime: The Improper Broadening of RICO's "Affecting Commerce" Requirement*, 46 HOUSTON LAW REVIEW 139 (2009).

[110] *United States v. Nascimento*, 491 F.3d 25, 40-3(1st Cir. 2007); *United States v. Palfrey*, 515 F.Supp.2d 120, 124-25 (D.D.C. 2007).

[111] U.S. Const. Amend.V.

[112] *Blockburger v. United States*, 284 U.S. 299, 304 (1932).

[113] *United States v. Marino*, 277 F.3d 11, 39 (1st Cir. 2002); *United States v. Coonan*, 938 F.2d 1553, 1566 (2d Cir. 1991); *United States v. Beale*, 921 F.2d 1412, 1437 (11th Cir. 1991); *United States v. Massino*, 311 F.Supp.2d 316, 318 (E.D.N.Y. 2004); see also, *United States v. Ayala*, 601 F.3d 256, 265 (4th Cir. 2010)(conspiracy to murder in aid of a RICO enterprise and RICO conspiracy each have at least one disparate element and thus both may be prosecuted without a breach of the Double Jeopardy Clause).

[114] *United States v. Kehoe*, 310 F.3d 579, 587-88 (8th Cir. 2002); *United States v. Marino*, 277 F.3d 11, 39 (1st Cir. 2002); *United States v. Diaz*, 176 F.3d 52, 115-16 (2d Cir. 1999); *United States v. Rone*, 598 F.2d 564, 569-71 (9th Cir. 1979); *United States v. Dionisio*, 415 F.Supp.2d 191, 195-200 (E.D.N.Y. 2006).

[115] *United States v. Schiro*, 679 F.3d 521, 526 (7th Cir. 2012); *United States v. DeCologero*, 530 F.3d 36, 71 (1st Cir. 2008); *United States v. Jones*, 482 F.3d 60, 71-2 (2d Cir. 2006).

[116] *United States v. Wheeler*, 535 F.3d 446, 449-50 (6th Cir. 2008), quoting, *United States v. Russotti*, 717 F.2d 27, 33 (2d Cir. 1983); and *United States v. Dean*, 647 F.2d 779, 788 (8th Cir. 1981).

[117] U.S. Const. Art. I, §9, cl.3; Art .I, §10, cl.1; *Collins v. Youngblood*, 497 U.S. 37, 52 (1990).

[118] *United States v. Flemmi*, 245 F.3d 24, 27 n.3 (1st Cir. 2001)("The government did not seek to indict Flemmi for the crime of murder because there is no federal statute that can be applied to the 1967 slayings without violating the Ex Post Facto Clause. This fact, however, does not prohibit reference to the slayings as predicate acts in connection with the RICO counts. See also, *United States v. Brown*, 555 F.2d 407, 416-17 (5th Cir. 1977)(upholding, against constitutional challenge, government's use of predicate acts occurring prior to RICO's effective date in conjunction with predicate acts occurring after that date)"); *United States v. Caporale*, 806 F.2d 1487, 1516 (11th Cir. 1986).

The fact that the defendant may be adversely affected by a procedural change likewise does not trigger ex post facto concerns. Thus, when Congress amended RICO to permit the confiscation of substitute assets should the forfeitable property become unavailable, the ex post facto clause did not preclude application of the change to cases arising before the amendment, *United States v. Reed*, 924 F.2d 1014, 1016-17 (11th Cir. 1991); *United States v. Martenson*, 780 F.Supp. 492, 495 (N.D.Ill. 1991).

[119] *Posters 'N' Things, Ltd. v. United States*, 511 U.S. 513, 525 (1994), quoting, *Kolender v. Lawson*, 461 U.S. 352, 357 (1983).

[120] *H.J., Inc. v. Northwestern Bell Telephone Co.*, 492 U.S. 251, 254-55 (1989)(Scalia, J., concurring in the judgment)("Four terms ago ... we gave lower courts ... four clues concerning the meaning of the enigmatic term 'pattern of racketeering activity'.... Today, four years and countless millions in damages and attorney's fees later (not to mention prison sentences under the criminal provisions of RICO), the Court does little more than repromulgate those hints as to what RICO means.... It is, however, unfair to be so critical of the Court's effort, because I would be unable to provide an interpretation of RICO that gives significantly more guidance concerning its application.... Today's opinion has added nothing to improve our prior guidance, which has created a kaleidoscope of Circuit positions, except to clarify that RICO may additionally be violated when there is a 'threat of continuity.' It seems to me this increases rather than removes the vagueness").

[121] *United States v. Burden*, 600 F.3d 204, 228 (2d Cir. 2010); *United States v. Keltner*, 147 F.3d 662, 667 (8th Cir. 1998); *United States v. Krout*, 66 F.3d 1420, 1432 (5th Cir. 1995); *Columbia Natural Resources, Inc. v. Tatum*, 58 F.3d 1101, 1106-109 (6th Cir. 1995); *United States v. Oreto*, 37 F.3d 739, 752 (1st Cir. 1994); *United States v. Korando*, 29 F.3d 1114, 1119 (7th Cir. 1994); *Cox v. Administrator*, U.S. Steel & Carnegie, 17 F.3d 1386, 1398 (11th Cir. 1994); *United States v. Bennett*, 984 F.2d 597, 606 (4th Cir. 1993); *United States v. Dischner*, 974 F.2d 1502, 1509-510 (9th Cir. 1992); *United States v. Woods*, 915 F.2d 854, 862-64 (3d Cir. 1990); *Buchanan County v. Blankenship*, 545 F.Supp.2d 553, 555 (W.D. Va. 2008); *United States v. Stevens*, 778 F.Supp.2d 683, 694-95 (W.D.La. 2011).

[122] "Excessive bail shall not be required, nor excessive fines imposed, nor cruel and unusual punishments inflicted." U.S. Const. Amend. VIII.

[123] *Harmelin v. Michigan*, 501 U.S. 957 (1991), upheld the imposition of a state mandatory term of life in prison without the possibility of parole upon conviction for possession of more than 650 grams of cocaine. Of the nine Justices, two (Justice Scalia and Chief Justice Rehnquist) voted to affirm and would limit proportionality analysis to capital punishment cases; three others (Justices O'Connor, Kennedy and Souter) voted to affirm but pursuant to a proportionality analysis where the seriousness of the offense carried the day, 501 U.S. at 996; and the remaining four (Justices White, Marshall, Blackmun and Stevens) dissented in favor of a proportionality test placing greater emphasis on the comparative harshness of the penalty and a comparison with the penalties imposed for other crimes, 501 U.S. at 1009, 1027, 1028.

[124] *United States v. Busher*, 817 F.2d 1409, 1413-414 (7th Cir. 1987); *United States v. Feldman*, 853 F.2d 648, 663 (9th Cir. 1988); cf., *United States v. Vriner*, 921 F.2d 710, 712-13 (7th Cir. 1991) (criminal forfeiture under 21 U.S.C. 853).

[125] Palm, *RICO Forfeiture and the Eighth Amendment: When Is Everything Too Much?* 53 UNIVERSITY OF PITTSBURGH LAW REVIEW 1 (1991).

[126] *Alexander v. United States*, 509 U.S. 544 (1993).

[127] *United States v. Bajakajian*, 522 U.S. 321, 334-37 (1998). Whether a forfeiture should be considered grossly disproportionate turns upon "(1) whether the defendant falls into the class of persons at whom the criminal statute was principally directed; (2) other penalties authorized by the legislature (or the Sentencing Commission); and (3) the harm caused by the defendant," *United States v. Browne*, 505 F.3d 1229, 1281 (11th Cir; 2007); *United States v. Heldeman*, 402 F.3d 220, 223 (1st Cir. 2005).

[128] See e.g., *United States v. Najjar*, 300 F.3d 466, 485-86 (4th Cir. 2002)(confiscation of $2.76 million was not excessive in light of the seriousness of the offense and the extent of the wrong doing); *United States v. Segal*, 495 F.3d 826, 840 (7th Cir. 2007)(confiscation of $30 million in proceeds and the defendant's 60% interest in a business enterprise was similarly not excessive); *United States v. Browne*, 505 F.3d at 1281-282 (confiscation of $592,271.32 was not excessive).

[129] *United States v. Levesque*, 546 F.3d 78, 83-5 (1st Cir. 2008); contra, *United States v. Dicter*, 198 F.3d 1284, 1292 n.11 (11th Cir. 1999); *United States v. 817 N.E.* 29th Drive, 175 F.3d 1304, 1311 (11th Cir. 1999).

[130] "Congress shall make no law ... abridging the freedom of speech, or of the press.... " U.S.Const. Amend.I.

[131] *Near v. Minnesota ex rel. Olson*, 283 U.S. 697 (1931); *Alexander v. United States*, 509 U.S. 544, 550 (1993).

[132] *Ginzburg v. United States*, 383 U.S. 463, 464-65 (1966); *Smith v. United States*, 431 U.S. 291, 296 (1977).

[133] *Alexander v. United States*, 509 U.S. 544, 550-58 (1993).

[134] *United States v. Monsanto*, 491 U.S. 600, 614-16 (1989); *Caplin & Drysdale v. United States*, 491 U.S. 617, 624-32 (1989).

[135] *United States v. Borromeo*, 954 F.2d 245, 249 (4th Cir. 1992); *In re Assets of Tom Billman*, 915 F.2d 916, 922 (4th Cir. 1990); *United States v. Wingerter*, 369 F.Supp.2d 799, 810-12 (E.D.Va. 2005).

[136] *United States v. Saccoccia*, 564 F.3d 502, 504-507 (1st Cir. 2009).

[137] *Libretti v. United States*, 516 U.S. 29, 48-9 (1995)(parallel citations omitted)("Libretti would have us equate [his] statutory right to a jury determination of forfeitability with the familiar Sixth Amendment right to a jury determination of guilt or innocence. See, e.g., *United States v. Gaudin*, 515 U.S. 506, 511 (1995) ('The Constitution gives a criminal defendant the right to demand that a jury find him guilty of all the elements of the crime with which he is charged'). Without disparaging the importance of the right provided by Rule 31(e), our analysis of the nature of criminal forfeiture as an aspect of sentencing compels the conclusion that the right to a jury verdict on forfeitability does not fall within the Sixth Amendment's constitutional protection. Our cases have made abundantly clear that a defendant does not enjoy a constitutional right to a jury determination as to the appropriate sentence to be imposed. See e.g., McMillan v. *Pennsylvania*, 477 U.S. 789, 93 (1986) ('[T]here is no Sixth Amendment right to jury sentencing, even where the sentence turns on specific findings of fact'); Cabana v. Bullock, 474 U.S. 376, 385 (1986) ('The decision whether a particular punishment ... is appropriate in any given case is not one that we have ever required to be made by a jury')").

[138] *Apprendi v. New Jersey*, 530 U.S. 466 (2000); *Blakely v. Washington*, 542 U.S. 296 (2004); *United States v. Booker*, 543 U.S. 220 (2005).

[139] *Id.*, 543 U.S. at 244.

[140] "Most of the statute [(the Sentencing Reform Act)]is perfectly valid. See, e.g., 18 U.S.C.... 3554 (forfeiture).... " Id. at 258. Section 3554 declares that "The court, in imposing a sentence on a defendant who has been found guilty of an offense described in section 1962 [RICO] of this title ... shall order ... that the defendant forfeit property to the United States in accordance with the provisions of section 1963 of this title.... " 18 U.S.C. 3554 (emphasis added).

[141] *United States v. Saccoccia*, 564 F.3d 502, 505-507 (1st Cir. 2009); *United States v. Huber*, 462 F.3d 945, 948-49 (8th Cir. 2006); *United States v. Leahy*, 438 F.3d 328, 331-39 (3d Cir. 2006); *United States v. Fruchter*, 411 F.3d 377, 382-83 (2d Cir. 2005).

[142] U.S. Const. Art. III, §3, cl.2.

[143] *United States v. Thevis*, 474 F.Supp. 134, 140-41 (N.D.Ga. 1979); *United States v. Grande*, 620 F.2d 1026, 1037-39 (4th Cir. 1980).

[144] For an early comparative analysis of the content of many of the state RICO provisions, *see*, Blakey & Perry, *An Analysis of the Myths that Bolster Efforts to Rewrite RICO and the Various Proposals for Reform: "Mother of God—Is This the End of RICO?*, 43 VANDERBILT LAW REVIEW 851, 988-1011 (1990); *see also*, Floyd, RICO STATE BY STATE: A GUIDE TO LITIGATION UNDER THE STATE RACKETEERING STATUTES (1998).
Several of the states do not have RICO statutes as such, but have enacted provisions which enhance the penalties for, and provide procedural tools against, various forms of commercialized criminal activity, frequently modeled after the federal drug kingpin statute, 21 U.S.C. 848, see e.g., ARK.CODE ANN. §§5-74-101 to 5-74-109 (criminal gangs, organizations or enterprises); ILL.COMP. LAWS ANN. ch.725 §§175/1 to 175/9 (narcotics racketeering); LA.REV.STAT. ANN. §§15:1351 to 15:1356 (narcotics racketeering); MD.CODE ANN. art.27 §286(g)(drug kingpin); VA.CODE §18.2-248 (drug kingpin).

In: Conspiratorial Crimes ...
Editors: L. C. Wright and J. C. Miller
ISBN: 978-1-62618-426-8

Chapter 3

MONEY LAUNDERING: AN ABRIDGED OVERVIEW OF 18 U.S.C. 1956 AND RELATED FEDERAL CRIMINAL LAW*

Charles Doyle

SUMMARY

This is an overview of the elements of federal criminal money laundering statutes and the sanctions imposed for their violation. The most prominent is 18 U.S.C. 1956. Section 1956 outlaws four kinds of money laundering—promotional, concealment, structuring, and tax evasion laundering of the proceeds generated by designated federal, state, and foreign underlying crimes (predicate offenses)—committed or attempted under one or more of three jurisdictional conditions (i.e., laundering involving certain financial transactions, laundering involving international transfers, and stings). Its companion, 18 U.S.C. 1957, prohibits depositing or spending more than $10,000 of the proceeds from a Section 1956 predicate offense. Violations of Section 1956 are punishable by imprisonment for not more than 20 years; Section 1957 carries a maximum penalty of imprisonment for 10 years. Property involved in either case is subject to confiscation. Misconduct which implicates Sections 1956 and 1957 may implicate other federal criminal

---

* This is an edited, reformatted and augmented version of a Congressional Research Service publication, CRS Report for Congress RS22401, prepared for Members and Committees of Congress, from www.crs.gov, dated February 8, 2012.

statutes as well. Federal racketeer influenced and corrupt organization (RICO) provisions outlaw acquiring or conducting the affairs of an enterprise (whose activities affect interstate or foreign commerce) through the patterned commission of a series of underlying federal or state crimes. RICO violations are also 20-year felonies. Every RICO predicate offense, including each "federal crime of terrorism," is automatically a Section 1956 money laundering predicate offense. A second related statute, the Travel Act (18 U.S.C. 1952), punishes interstate or foreign travel, or the use of interstate or foreign facilities, conducted with the intent to distribute the proceeds of a more modest list of predicate offenses or to promote or carry on such offenses when an overt act is committed in furtherance of that intent. Such misconduct is punishable by imprisonment for not more than five years. Other federal statutes proscribe, with varying sanctions, bulk cash smuggling, layering bank deposits to avoid reporting requirements, failure to comply with federal anti-money laundering provisions, or conducting an unlawful money transmission business.

The Supreme Court has held that the Section 1956 ban on attempted international transportation of tainted proceeds for the purpose of concealing their ownership, source, nature, or ultimate location is limited to instances where concealment is a purpose rather than an attribute of the transportation (simple smuggling is not proscribed as such), United States v. Cuellar, 553 U.S. 550 (2008). In a second case, the Court indicated that for purposes of Section 1956 the "proceeds" of a predicate offense often referred to the profits rather than the gross receipts realized from the offense, United States v. Santos, 553 U.S. 507 (2008). Congress responded by defining "proceeds" for purposes of Sections 1956 and 1957 as the property obtained or retained as a consequence of a predicate offense, including gross receipts, P.L. 111-21, 123 Stat. 1618 (2009)(S. 386)(111th Cong.).

INTRODUCTION

Money laundering is commonly understood as the process of cleansing the taint from the proceeds of crime.

In federal criminal law, however, it is more. In the principal federal criminal money laundering statutes, 18 U.S.C. 1956 and 1957, and to varying degrees in several other federal criminal statutes, money laundering involves the flow of resources to and from several hundred other federal, state, and foreign crimes.

18 U.S.C. 1956

Section 1956 outlaws four kinds of money laundering—promotional, concealment, smurfing, and tax evasion committed or attempted under one or more of three jurisdictional conditions— laundering involving certain financial transactions, laundering involving international transfers, and stings. More precisely, Section 1956(a)(1) outlaws financial transactions involving the proceeds of other certain crimes—predicate offenses referred to as "specified unlawful activities"—committed or attempted (1) with the intent to promote further predicate offenses; (2) with the intent to evade taxation; (3) knowing the transaction is designed to launder the proceeds; or (4) knowing the transaction is designed to avoid anti-laundering reporting requirements.

Section 1956(a)(2) outlaws the interstate or international transportation or transmission (or attempted transportation or transmission) of funds (1) with the intent to promote a predicate offense; (2) knowing that the purpose is to conceal laundering of the funds and knowing that the funds are the proceeds of a predicate offense; or (3) knowing that the purpose is to avoid reporting requirements and knowing that the funds are the proceeds of a predicate offense.

Section 1956(a)(3) is a sting section. It outlaws financial transactions (or attempted transactions) that the defendant believes involve the proceeds of a predicate offense and that are intended to (1) promote a predicate offense, (2) launder the proceeds, or (3) avoid reporting requirements.

All but 2 of the 10 Section 1956 crimes are related in one way or another to the commission or purported commission of at least one of a list of predicate offenses, "specified unlawful activities." The predicate offenses come in three varieties: state crimes, foreign crimes, and federal crimes. The list of state crimes is relatively short and consists of any state crime that is a RICO predicate offense, that is, any act or threat involving murder, kidnapping, gambling, arson, robbery, bribery, extortion, dealing in obscene matter, or dealing in a controlled substance or listed chemical (as defined in Section 102 of the Controlled Substances Act), which is chargeable under state law and punishable by imprisonment for more than one year. The list of foreign crimes recognized as Section 1956 predicate offenses is very much the same—violations of the laws of another country involving murder, kidnapping, bribery, drug trafficking and the like—but it only applies in cases involving a financial transaction occurring in whole or in part in this country. The list of federal predicate offenses is considerably longer if for no other reason than it is specific rather than generic.

Each of the 10 criminal proscriptions found in Section 1956 outlaws both the completed offense and the attempt to commit it. Section 1956(h) outlaws conspiracy to violate any of these proscriptions.

Consequences: Prison terms, fines, civil penalties, and confiscation may follow as a consequence of conviction of a money laundering offense. Any violation of Section 1956 is punishable by imprisonment for not more than 20 years. Violations of Section 1956(a)(1) and (a)(2), the financial institution and interstate or foreign transmission offenses, are punishable by a fine of no more than the greater of $500,000 or twice the value of the property involved in the offense. Sting violations are punishable by a fine of not more than the greater of $250,000 ($500,000 for an organization) or twice the amount involved in the offense. Violators of any provisions of Section 1956 are subject to a civil penalty of no more than the greater of $10,000 or the value of the property involved in the offense. Forfeiture is the confiscation of property to the government as a consequence of the property's proximity to some form of criminal activity. The proceeds of a confiscation are generally shared among the law enforcement agencies that participate in the investigation and prosecution of the forfeiture. Section 1956 provides a vehicle for confiscation in two very distinct ways. First, the "proceeds" of any Section 1956 predicate offense (and any property traceable to such proceeds) are subject to confiscation without the necessity of any actual violation of Section 1956. Second, property "involved" in a Section 1956 money laundering offense (or property traceable to such involved property) may be confiscated. The Eighth Amendment prohibits excessive fines. Fines are excessive if they are grossly disproportionate to the gravity of the offender's misconduct. While the excessive fines clause may impose limits upon the permissible extent of the confiscation for failure to comply with anti-money laundering reporting statutes, forfeitures under Section 1956 are not ordinarily considered excessive because of the gravity of the offense and its predicate offenses.

The Supreme Court recently held that the proscription in Section 1956 against attempted international transportation of tainted proceeds for the purpose of concealing their ownership, source, nature, or ultimate location is limited to instances where concealment is a purpose rather than an attribute of the transportation (simple smuggling is not proscribed as such), *United States v. Cuellar*, 553 U.S. 550 (2008). In a second case, the Court indicated that for purposes of Section 1956, in many instances the "proceeds" of a predicate offense referred to net receipts or profits realized from the offense, *United States v. Santos*, 553 U.S. 507 (2008). Congress preferred a different reading of "proceeds," which in an amendment to Section 1956, it defined to mean any property obtained or retained through the commission of a predicate offense, including gross receipts, 18 U.S.C. 1956(c)(9)(P.L. 111-21, 123 Stat. 1618 (2009)(S. 386)).

18 U.S.C. 1957

Unless there is some element of promotion, concealment, or evasion, Section 1956 does not make simply spending or depositing tainted money a crime. Section 1957 does. It outlaws otherwise innocent transactions contaminated by the origin of the property involved in the transaction. Using most of the same definitions as Section 1956, the elements of 1957 cover anyone who:

1. A. in the United States,
   B. in the special maritime or territorial jurisdiction of the United States, or
   C. outside the United States if the defendant is an American,
2. knowingly
3. A. engages or
   B. attempts to engage in
4. a monetary transaction
5. in or affecting U.S. interstate or foreign commerce
6. in criminally derived property that
   A. is of a greater value than $10,000 and
   B. is derived from specified unlawful activity.

Section 1957 also proscribes attempts to violate its provisions. Section 1956(h) outlaws conspiracy to violate Section 1957. Violations of Section 1957 and conspiracy to violate Section 1957 are each punishable by imprisonment for not more than 10 years and/or by a fine of not more than the greater of $250,000 ($500,000 for an organization) or twice the amount involved in the transaction. Violators of Section 1957 are subject to a civil penalty of no more than the greater of $10,000 or the value of the property involved in the offense. Any property involved in a violation of Section 1957 or traceable to property involved in a violation of Section 1957 is subject to confiscation under either civil or criminal procedures, and the applicable law is essentially the same as in the case of Section 1956.

TRAVEL ACT

The money laundering provisions of Sections 1956, 1957 punish transactions involving promotion, concealment, evasion, spending, and depositing. The Travel Act, 18 U.S.C. 1952, punishes interstate or foreign travel (or use of the facilities of interstate or foreign commerce) conducted with the intent to distribute the proceeds of a more modest list of predicate offenses or to promote or carry on such offenses when there is an overt act in furtherance of that intent. The Travel Act is a Section 1956 and 1957 predicate offense (specified unlawful activity); Section 1956 and 1957 are Travel Act predicate offenses (unlawful activity); and although the money laundering predicate offense list is more extensive, several of the Travel Act predicate offenses are also money laundering predicates. The Travel Act essentially condemns three crimes each with an interstate element: the distribution of the proceeds of a predicate offense, the promotion of a predicate offense, or the commission of a violent crime in aid of a predicate offense. The first two variants bear some resemblance to the concealment and promotion offenses of Section 1956 and somewhat more remotely to the deposit/spending proscriptions of Section 1957. The violent crime component of the Travel Act is only coincidentally related to money laundering and consequently will be mentioned only in passing.

The courts often abbreviate their statement of the elements to encompass only whichever of the three versions is at issue:

> Distribution – The essential elements of a violation under section 1952(a) are: "(1) travel in interstate or foreign commerce; (2) with the specific intent to distribute the proceeds of an unlawful activity; and (3) knowing and willful commission of an act in furtherance of that intent," United States v. Hinojosa, 958 F.2d 624, 629 (5th Cir. 1992).
>
> Facilitation – The government must prove that the defendant "(1) travels in interstate or foreign commerce [or uses an interstate facility] (2) with intent to ... promote ... any unlawful activity and (3) that the defendant thereafter performs or attempts to perform an act of promotion ... of any unlawful activity," United States v. Driver, 535 F.3d 424, 430 (6th Cir. 2008).
>
> Violence – "To prove a violation of the Travel Act, the government was required to establish that [the defendant]: (1) used a facility of interstate or foreign commerce; (2) with intent to commit any unlawful activity (including arson ...); and (3) thereafter performed an additional act to further the unlawful activity," United States v. Salameh, 152 F.3d 88, 152 (2d Cir. 1998).

The distribution and facilitation offenses of the Travel Act, 18 U.S.C. 1952(a)(1) and 18 U.S.C. 1952(a)(3), are punishable by imprisonment for not more than five years; the crime-of-violencein-furtherance offense is punishable by imprisonment for not more than 20 years. Offenders of any of the three offenses are subject to a fine of the greater of not more than $250,000 ($500,000 for organizations) or twice the gain or loss associated with the offense. Property associated with a violation of Section 1952 is not subject to confiscation solely by virtue of that fact, although the property may be confiscated by operation of the laws governing 1952 predicate offenses.

31 U.S.C. 5322—Reporting Requirements

Section 5322 penalizes willful violation of several monetary transaction reporting requirements found in Subtitle 53-II of title 31 of the United States Code and elsewhere. The section's coverage extends to violations of:

-31 U.S.C. 5313 - financial institution reports of cash transactions involving $10,000 or more (31 C.F.R. §103.22);

-31 U.S.C. 5314 - reports by persons in the U.S. of foreign financial agency transactions (31 C.F.R. §103.24);

-31 U.S.C. 5316 - reports by any person taking $10,000 in cash out of the U.S. or bringing it in;

-31 U.S.C. 5318 - suspicious transaction reports by financial institutions;

-31 U.S.C. 5325 - reports by financial institutions issuing cashier's checks in amounts of $3000 or more (31 C.F.R. §103.29);

-31 U.S.C. 5326 - cash transaction reports by financial institutions and/or various trades or businesses pursuant to Treasury Department geographical orders (31 C.F.R. §103.26);

-31 U.S.C. 5331 - reports of trades and businesses other than financial institutions of cash transactions involving $10,000 or more (31 C.F.R. §103.30);

-12 U.S.C. 1829b - record keeping requirements of federally insured depository institutions; -12 U.S.C. 1953 - record keeping by uninsured banks or similar institutions.

Simple violations of Section 5322 are punishable by imprisonment for not more than five years, a fine of not more than $250,000, or both. Violations committed during the commission of another federal crime or as part of a pattern of illegal activity involving more than $100,000 over the course of a year are punishable by imprisonment for not more than 10 years; a fine of not more than $500,000 (not more than $1 million for a special measures violation (31 U.S.C. 5318A) or a violation involving a breach of due diligence with respect to private banking for foreign customers or foreign shell banks (31 U.S.C. 5318(i), (j)); or both. Section 5322 is a Travel Act predicate offense and RICO predicate offense, but not a Section 1956 or 1957 money laundering predicate offense. Property associated with violations of two of the sections within its coverage is subject to confiscation. Under Section 5317(c), property becomes forfeitable when it is involved in, or traceable to, a violation of 31 U.S.C. 5313 (reports relating to cash transactions involving $10,000 or more) or of 31 U.S.C. 5316 (reports relating to taking $10,000 or more out of the United States or to bring it into the United States).

31 U.S.C. 5324—Anti-Structuring

Section 5324 condemns causing a financial institution to fail to file a required report, causing the submission of a false report, structuring transactions to evade a reporting requirement, or attempting to do so. Violations are punishable by imprisonment for not more than 5 years (not more than 10 years if committed in conjunction with another federal offense or if committed as part of a pattern of activity involving $100,000 or more) and a fine of not more than $250,000 (not more than $500,000 for organizations), with the maximum fine doubled if the offense is committed in conjunction with another federal crime or as part of a pattern of activity involving $100,000.

31 U.S.C. 5332—Bulk Cash Smuggling

Section 5332 outlaws carrying or attempting to transport more than $10,000 in unreported, "concealed" cash across a U.S. border with the intent to evade 31 U.S.C. 5316 reporting requirements. The proscribed methods of concealment seem to envelope any method short of public display. The offense carries a prison term of not more than five years, but also calls for confiscation of the cash and related property.

18 U.S.C. 1960—Money Transmitters

Section 1960 prohibits unlicensed money transmitting businesses and defines such businesses as (A) those that are required by state law to be licensed and are not; (B) those that fail to comply with federal regulatory provisions; or (C) those that transmit money they know is derived from, and intended to finance, criminal activity. Offenders face imprisonment for not more than five years and/or a fine of not more than $250,000 (not more than $500,000 for organizations).

18 U.S.C. 1961-1964—Racketeer Influenced and Corrupt Organizations (RICO)

All the racketeering predicate offenses listed in 18 U.S.C. 1961(1) are by definition money laundering predicate offenses under Sections 1956 and 1957. RICO makes it a federal crime for any person to:

1. conduct or participate, directly or indirectly, in the conduct of
2. the affairs of an enterprise
3. engaged in or the activities of which affect, interstate or foreign commerce
4. through the collection of an unlawful debt, or
5. through a pattern of racketeering activity (predicate offenses).

RICO violations are punishable by imprisonment for not more than 20 years (not more than life imprisonment if any of the applicable predicate offenses carries a life sentence). Offenders also face fines of up to $250,000 (up to $500,000 for organizations) as well as the confiscation of any property associated with the offense. They may also be liable to their victims for triple damages and attorneys fees, and at least when sued by the government, subject to the equitable remedies.

In: Conspiratorial Crimes ... ISBN: 978-1-62618-426-8
Editors: L. C. Wright and J. C. Miller

Chapter 4

MAIL AND WIRE FRAUD: A BRIEF OVERVIEW OF FEDERAL CRIMINAL LAW*

Charles Doyle

SUMMARY

It is a federal crime to devise a scheme to defraud another of property, when either mail or wire communications are used in furtherance of the scheme, 18 U.S.C. 1341, 1343. Mail or wire fraud includes schemes to defraud another of honest services, when the scheme involves bribery or a kick back, 18 U.S.C. 1346; *Skilling v. United States*, 130 S.Ct. 2896 (2010). In order to convict, the government must prove beyond a reasonable doubt that the defendant (1) used either mail or wire communications in the foreseeable furtherance, (2) of a scheme to defraud, (3) involving a material deception, (4) with the intent to deprive another of, (5) either property or honest services.

Offenders face the prospect of imprisonment for not more than 20 years, a fine of not more than $250,000 (not more than $500,000 for organizations), an order to pay victim restitution, and the confiscation of any property realized from the offense.

Misconduct that constitutes mail or wire fraud may also constitute a violation of one or more other federal crimes. Principal among these are

* This is an edited, reformatted and augmented version of a Congressional Research Service publication, CRS Report for Congress R41930, from www.crs.gov, dated July 21, 2011.

predicate offense crimes, frauds based on jurisdictional factors other than use of mail or wire communications, and other honest services frauds in the form of bribery or kickbacks. The other federal bribery and kickback offenses include bribery of public officials, federal program bribery, extortion under color of official right, and Medicare/Medicaid kickbacks. Mail and wire fraud are money laundering and racketeering predicate offenses. Numbered among the fraud offenses based on other jurisdiction grounds are the false claims and false statement offenses, bank fraud, health care fraud, securities fraud, and foreign labor contracting fraud.

INTRODUCTION

The federal mail and wire fraud statutes outlaw schemes to defraud that involve the use of mail or wire communications.[1] Both condemn fraudulent conduct that may also come within the reach of other federal criminal statutes. Both may serve as racketeering and money laundering predicate offenses. Both are punishable by imprisonment for not more than 20 years; for not more than 30 years, if the victim is a financial institution or the offense is committed in the context of major disaster or emergency. Both entitle their victims to restitution. Both may result in the forfeiture of property.

BACKGROUND

The mail fraud statute was first enacted in the late nineteenth century in order to prevent city slickers from using the mail to cheat guileless country folks.[2] But for penalty increases and amendments calculated to confirm its breath, the prohibition has come down to us essentially unchanged.[3] Speaking in 1987, the Supreme Court noted that "the last substantive amendment to the statute . . . was the codification of the holding of *Durland* . . . in 1909 [that is, (*Durland v. United States*, 161 U.S. 306 (1896)(rejecting the argument that the statute was limited to the common law crime of false pretenses)].[4] Congress did amend it thereafter to confirm that the statute and the wire fraud statute reached schemes to defraud another of the right to honest services [5] and to encompass the use of commercial postal carriers.[6]

The wire fraud statute is of more recent vintage. Enacted as part of the Communications Act Amendments of 1952,[7] it was always intended to mirror the provisions of the mail fraud statute.[8]

Since its inception, changes in the mail fraud statute have come with corresponding changes in the wire fraud statute in most instances.[9]

ELEMENTS

The mail and wire fraud statutes are essentially the same, except for the medium associated with the offense – the mail in the case of mail fraud and wire communication in the case of wire fraud. As a consequence, the interpretation of one is ordinarily considered to apply to the other.[10] In construction of the terms within the two, the courts will frequently abbreviate or adjust their statement of the elements of a violation to focus on the questions at issue before them.[11] As treatment of the individual elements makes clear, however, there seems little dispute that conviction requires the government to prove:

1) the use of either mail or wire communications in the foreseeable furtherance
2) of a scheme to defraud
3) involving a material deception
4) with the intent to deprive another of
5) either property or honest services.

Use of Mail or Wire Communications

The wire fraud statute applies to anyone who "transmits or causes to be transmitted by wire, radio, or television communication in interstate or foreign commerce any writings . . . for the purpose executing [a]. . . scheme or artifice."[12] The mail fraud statute is similarly worded and applies to anyone who ". . . for the purpose of executing [a] . . . scheme or artifice . . . places in any post office . . . or causes to be delivered by mail. . . any . . . matter."[13]

The statutes require that a mailing or wire communication be in furtherance of a scheme to defraud. It need not be an essential element of the scheme, as long as it "is incident to an essential element of the scheme."[14] A qualifying mailing or communication, standing alone, may be routine, innocent or even self-defeating, because "[t]he relevant question at all times is whether the mailing is part of the execution of the scheme as conceived by the perpetrator at the time, regardless of whether the mailing later, through hindsight, may prove to have been counterproductive."[15] The element may also be satisfied by mailings or communications "designed to lull the victim into a false sense of security, postpone inquiries or complaints, or make the transaction less suspect."[16]

A defendant need not personally have mailed or wired a communication; it is enough that he "caused" a mailing or transmission of a wire communication in the sense that the mailing or transmission was the reasonable foreseeable consequence of his intended scheme.[17]

Scheme to Defraud

The mail and wire fraud statutes "both prohibit, in pertinent part, 'any scheme or artifice to defraud[,]' or to obtain money or property 'by means of false or fraudulent pretenses, representations, or promises,"[18] or deprive another of the right to honest services by such means.[19] From the beginning, Congress intended to reach a wide range of schemes to defraud, and has expanded the concept whenever doubts arose. It added the second prong – obtaining money or property by false pretenses, representations, or promises – after defendants had suggested that the term "scheme to defraud" covered false pretenses concerning present conditions but not representations or promises of future conditions.[20] More recently, it added Section 1346 to make it clear the term "scheme to defraud" encompassed schemes to defraud another of the right to honest services.[21] Even before that adornment, the words were understood to "refer 'to wronging one in his property rights by dishonest methods or schemes,' and 'usually signify the deprivation of something of value by trick, deceit, chicane or overreaching.'"[22]

The statutes condemn schemes to defraud – both the successful and the unsuccessful.[23] Nevertheless, there may be some question whether the statutes reach those schemes designed to deceive the gullible though they could not ensnare the reasonably prudent. It is not uncommon for the courts to declare that to demonstrate a scheme to defraud the government needs to show that the defendant's "communications were reasonably calculated to deceive persons of ordinary prudence and comprehension."[24] One court considered these statements no more than an identification of a point at which the government has satisfied its burden in a particular case, without addressing whether a lesser quantum of evidence might suffice in other cases.[25] In any event, the question may be more clearly present in the context of the defendant's intent and the materiality of deception, matters discussed below.

Materiality

Neither the mail nor the wire fraud statute include a reference to materiality. Yet materiality is an element of each offense, because at the time of the statutes' enactment, the word "defraud" was understood to "require[] a misrepresentation or concealment of [a] material fact."[26] "[A] statement is material for [mail or] wire fraud purposes only if it has the natural tendency to influence or be capable of influencing the person to whom it was addressed."[27]

Intent

"Under both statutes, intent to defraud requires a willful act by the defendant with the intent to deceive or cheat, usually [, but not necessarily,] for the purpose of getting financial gain for one's self or causing financial loss to another."[28] A defendant has a complete defense if he believes the deceptive statements or promises to be true or otherwise acts in good faith.[29] A defendant has no such defense, however, if he blinds himself to the truth.[30] Nor is it a defense if he intends to deceive but feels his victim will ultimately profit or be unharmed.[31]

Money, Property, or Honest Services

The mail and wire fraud statutes speak of schemes to defraud or to obtain money or property.[32] They clearly protect against deprivations of tangible property. Their protection of intangibles has not always been as clear. They do protect intangible *property* rights,[33] although they do not apply to certain intangible rights in property that have no value in the hands of the victim of a scheme.[34]

Some time ago, the Supreme Court held in *McNally v. United States* that the protection does not extend to "the intangible right of the citizenry to good government."[35] Soon after *McNally*, Congress enlarged the mail and wire fraud statute coverage to include the intangible right to honest services, by defining the "term 'scheme or artifice to defraud' [to] include[s] a scheme or artifice to deprive another of the intangible right to honest services."[36] Lest the expanded definition be found unconstitutionally vague, the Court in *Skilling v. United States* limited its application to cases of bribery or kickbacks.[37]

Aiding and Abetting, Attempt, and Conspiracy

Attempting or conspiring to commit mail or wire fraud or aiding and abetting the commission of those offenses carries the same penalties as the underlying offense.[38] "In order to aid and abet another to commit a crime it is necessary that a defendant in some sort associate himself with the venture, that he participate in it as in something that he wishes to bring about, that he seek by his action to make it succeed."[39]

To prove conspiracy to commit either wire or mail fraud, the government must establish that: "(1) two or more persons, directly or indirectly, reached an agreement to devise and execute a scheme to defraud; (2) the defendant knew the unlawful purpose of the agreement; and (3) the defendant joined in the agreement willfully, that is, with the intent to further the unlawful purpose."[40] The offense is complete upon agreement without the necessity of an overt act committed in its furtherance.[41] As a general rule, a conspirator is liable for any other offenses that a co-conspirator commits in the foreseeable furtherance of the conspiracy.[42] Such liability, however, extends only until the objectives of the conspiracy have been accomplished or the defendant has withdrawn from the conspiracy.[43]

Where attempt has been made a separate offense, conviction ordinarily requires that the defendant commit a substantial step towards the completion of the underlying offense with the intent to commit it.[44] It does not, however, require the attempt to have been successful.[45] Unlike conspiracy, a defendant may not be convicted of both the substantive offense and the lesser included crime of attempt to commit it.[46]

Sentencing

A mail and wire fraud are punishable by imprisonment for not more than 20 years and a fine of not more than $250,000 (not more than $500,000 for organizations), or fine of not more than $1 million and imprisonment for not more than 30 years if the victim is a financial institution or the offense was committed in relation to a natural disaster.[47] Conviction may also result in probation, a term of supervised release, a special assessment, a restitution order, and/or a forfeiture order.

Sentencing Guidelines

Sentencing in federal court begins with the federal Sentencing Guidelines.[48] The Guidelines are essentially a score keeping system. A defendant's ultimate sentence under the Guidelines is determined by reference first to a basic guideline, which sets a base "offense level." Offense levels are then added or subtracted to reflect his prior criminal record as well as the aggravating and mitigating circumstances attending his offense.[49] One of two basic guidelines applies to mail and wire fraud. Section 2C1.1 applies to mail and wire fraud convictions involving corruption of public officials.[50] Otherwise, Section 2B1.1 applies. Both sections include enhancements based on the amount of loss associated with the fraud.[51]

After all the calculations, the final offense level determines the Guidelines' recommendation concerning probation, imprisonment, and fines. The Guidelines convert final offense levels into 43 sentencing groups, which are in turn each divided into 6 sentences ranges based on the defendant's criminal history.[52] Thus, for instance, the recommended sentencing range for a first time offender (i.e., one with a category I criminal history) with a final offense level of 15 is imprisonment for between 18 and 24 months.[53] A defendant with the same offense level 15 but with a criminal record placing him in criminal history category VI, would face imprisonment from between 41 and 51 months.[54] The Guidelines also provide offense level determined fine ranges for individuals and organizations.[55]

As a general rule, sentencing courts may place a defendant on probation for a term of from 1 to 5 years for any crime punishable by a maximum of term of imprisonment of less than 25 years.[56] The Guidelines, however, recommend "pure" probation, that is probation without any term of incarceration, only with respect to defendants with an offense level of 8 or below, i.e., levels where the sentencing range is between 0 and 6 months.[57]

Once a court has calculated the Guideline recommendations, it must weigh the other statutory factors found in 18 U.S.C. 3553(a) before imposing sentence.[58] Sentences will be upheld on appeal if they are procedural and substantively reasonable. A sentence is reasonable procedurally if it is free of procedural defects, such as a failure to accurately calculate the Guidelines recommendations and to fully explain the reasons for the sentence selected.[59] A sentence is reasonable substantively if it is reasonable in light of circumstances which a case presents.[60]

Supervised Release and Special Assessments

Supervised release is form of parole-like supervision imposed after a term of imprisonment has been served.[61] Although imposition of a term of supervised release is discretionary in mail and wire fraud cases,[62] the Sentencing Guidelines recommend its imposition in all felony cases.[63] The maximum supervised release term for wire and mail fraud generally is 3 years – 5 years when the defendant is convicted of the mail or wire fraud against a financial institution that carries a 30- years maximum term of imprisonment.[64] Release will be subject to a number of conditions, violation of which may result in a return to prison for not more than 2 years (not more than 3 years if the original crime of conviction carried a 30-year maximum).[65] There are three mandatory conditions: (1) commit no new crimes; (2) allow a DNA sample to be taken; and (3) submit to periodic drug testing.[66] The court may suspend the drug testing condition,[67] although it is under no obligation to do so even though the defendant has no history of drug abuse and drug abuse played no role in the offense.[68]

Most courts will impose a standard series of conditions in addition to the mandatory condition of supervised release.[69] The Sentencing Guidelines recommend that these include the payment of any fines, restitution, and special assessments that remain unsatisfied.[70] Defendants convicted of mail or wire fraud must pay a special assessment of $100.[71]

Restitution

Restitution is ordinarily required of those convicted of mail or wire fraud.[72] The victims entitled to restitution include those directly and proximately harmed by the defendant's crime of conviction, and "in the case of an offense that involves as an element a scheme, conspiracy, or patterns of criminal activity" – like mail and wire fraud – "any person directly harmed by the defendant's conduct in the course of the scheme, conspiracy, or pattern."[73]

Forfeiture

Property that constitutes the proceeds of mail or wire fraud is subject to confiscation by the United States.[74] It may be confiscated pursuant to either civil forfeiture or criminal forfeiture procedures. Civil forfeiture proceedings are conducted treating the property itself as the defendant.[75] Criminal forfeiture proceedings are conducted as part of the criminal prosecution of the property owner.[76] The provision authorizing the civil confiscation of property associated with mail or wire fraud is somewhat convoluted:

The following property is subject to forfeiture to the United States . . . (C) Any property, real or personal, which constitutes or is derived from proceeds traceable to . . . any offense constituting 'specified unlawful activity' (as defined in Section 1956(c)(7) of this title). . . ." 18 U.S.C. 981(a)(1)(C). "The term 'specified unlawful activity' means – any act or activity constituting an offense listed in Section 1961(1). . . ." 18 U.S.C. 1956(c)(7)(A). "(1) As used in this chapter – (1) 'racketeering activity' means . . . (B) any which is indictable under any of the following provisions of Title 18, United States Code . . . Section 1341 (relating to mail fraud), Section 1343 (relating to wire fraud). . . . 18 U.S.C. 1961(1)(B).[77]

Any property subject to civil forfeiture may be confiscated instead using criminal forfeiture procedures, unless Congress has specifically provided otherwise.[78]

A number of defendants, convicted of either mail or wire fraud, have argued to no avail that they should not be held liable for restitution and forfeiture.[79]

Related Criminal Provisions

The mail and wire fraud statutes essentially outlaw dishonesty. Due to their breadth, misconduct that constitutes mail or wire fraud may constitute a violation of one or more other federal criminal statutes as well. This overlap occurs perhaps most often with respect to (1) crimes for which mail or wire fraud are predicate offenses;[80] (2) fraud proscribed under jurisdictional circumstances other than mail or wire use;[81] and (3) honest services fraud in the form of bribery or kick backs.[82]

Predicate Offense Crimes

Some federal crimes have as an element the commission of some other federal offense. The money laundering statute, for example, outlaws laundering the proceeds of various predicate offenses. The racketeering statute outlaws committing predicate offense to operate a racketeering enterprise. Mail and wire fraud are predicate racketeering and money laundering predicate offenses.

RICO

The Racketeering Influenced and Corrupt Organization (RICO) provisions outlaw acquiring or conducting the affairs of an enterprise, engaged in or whose activities affect interstate commerce, through loan sharking or the patterned commission of various other predicate offenses.[83] The elements under the more commonly prosecuted conduct prong are: (1) conducting the affairs; (2) of an enterprise; (3) through a pattern; (4) of racketeering activity.[84] "Racketeering activity" means, among other things, any act which is indictable under either the mail or wire fraud statutes.[85] As for pattern, "a person cannot be subjected to the sanctions [of RICO] simply for committing two widely separate and isolated criminal offenses. Instead, the term 'pattern' itself requires the showing of a relationship between the predicates and of the threat of continuing activity. It is this factor of *continuity plus relationship* which combines to produce a pattern."[86]

The pattern of predicate offenses must be used by someone employed by or associated with a qualified enterprise to conduct or participate in its activities. "The 'conduct or participate' element requires a defendant to have some part in directing those" activities.[87] The element is not satisfied unless "one has participated in the operation or management of the enterprise itself."[88] Nevertheless, an "enterprise is operated not just by upper management but also by lower rung participants in the enterprise who are under the direction of upper management."[89]

The enterprise may be either any group of individuals, any legal entity, or any group "associated in fact."[90] An enterprise "associated in fact" "must have at least three structural elements: a purpose, relationships among those associated with the enterprise, and longevity sufficient to permit these associates to pursue the enterprise's purpose."[91] Qualified enterprises are only those that "engaged in, or the activities of which affect, interstate or foreign commerce."[92]

RICO violations are punishable by imprisonment for not more than 20 years and a fine of not more than $250,000 (not more than $500,000 for organizations).[93] The crime is one for which restitution must be ordered when one of the predicate offenses is mail or wire fraud.[94] RICO has one of the first contemporary forfeiture provisions covering property and interests acquired through RICO violations.[95] As noted earlier, any RICO predicate offense is by virtue of that fact a money laundering predicate.[96] Victims enjoy a cause of action for treble damages when injured in their business or property by reason of a RICO violation.[97]

Money Laundering

Mail and wire fraud are both money laundering predicate offenses.[98] Among other things, the most commonly prosecuted federal money laundering statute, 18 U.S.C. 1956, outlaws knowingly engaging in a financial transaction involving the proceedings of a "specified unlawful activity"(a predicate offense) for the purpose (1) of laundering the such proceeds or (2) of promoting further predicating offenses.[99]

To establish the laundering or concealment offense, the government must establish that: "(1) [the] defendant conducted, or attempted to conduct a financial transaction which in any way or degree affected interstate commerce or foreign commerce; (2) the financial transaction involved proceeds of illegal activity; (3) [the] defendant knew the property represented proceeds of some form of unlawful activity; and (4) [the] defendant conducted or attempted to conduct the financial transaction knowing the transaction was designed in whole or in part to conceal or disguise the nature, the location, the source, the ownership or the control of the proceeds of specified unlawful activity."[100]

To prove the promotional offense, "the government must demonstrate that [the defendant]: (1) conducted a financial transaction that involved the proceeds of unlawful activity; (2) knew the property involved was proceeds of unlawful activity; and (3) intended to promote that unlawful activity."[101]

Nothing in the either provision suggests that the defendant must be shown to have committed the predicate offense. Yet, simply establishing that the defendant spent or deposited the proceeds of the predicate offense is not enough without proof of an intent to promote or conceal.[102]

Either offense is punishable by imprisonment for not more than 20 years and a fine of not more than $500,000.[103] Property involved in a transaction in violation of Section 1956 is subject to civil and criminal forfeiture.[104]

Merely depositing the proceeds of a predicate offense does not alone constitute a violation of Section 1956. It is enough for a violation of Section 1957, if more than $10,000 is involved.[105] Section 1957 uses Section 1956's definition of specified unlawful activities.[106] Thus, mail and wire fraud are predicate offenses for purposes of Section 1957.[107] "Section 1957 differs from Section 1956 in two critical respects: It requires that the property have a value greater than $10,000, but it does not require that the defendant know of [the] design to conceal [or promote] aspects of the transaction or that anyone have such a design."[108]

Violations are punishable by imprisonment for not more than 10 years and a fine of not more than $250,000 (not more than $500,000) for organizations.[109] The property involved in a violation is subject to forfeiture under either civil or criminal procedures.[110]

Fraud under Other Jurisdictional Circumstances

This category includes the offenses that were made federal crimes because they involve fraud against the United States, as well as, the other frauds that share chapter 63 with the mail and wire fraud sections. The most prominent are the proscriptions against defrauding the United States by the submission of false claims, conspiracy to defraud the United States, and material false statements in matters within the jurisdiction of the United States.[111] Bank fraud, health care fraud, securities and commodities fraud, and fraud in foreign labor contracting are all chapter 63 companions of mail and wire fraud.[112]

Defrauding the United States

False Claims

Section 287 outlaws the knowing submission of a false claim against the United States.[113] "[T]o sustain a conviction under §287, the government must prove: (1) that the defendant presented a false or fraudulent claim against the United States; (2) that the claim was presented to an agency of the United States; and (3) that the defendant knew that the claim was false or fraudulent."[114] The offense carries a sentence of imprisonment for not more than 5 years and a fine of not more than $250,000 (not more than $500,000 for organizations).[115] The crime is one for which restitution must be ordered.[116] There is no explicit authority for confiscation of property tainted by the offense,[117] but either a private individual or the government may bring a civil action for treble damages.[118] It is neither a RICO nor a money laundering predicate offense.[119]

Conspiracy to Defraud the U.S.

The general conspiracy statute has two parts.[120] It outlaws conspiracies to violate the laws of the United States.[121] More relevant here, it also outlaws conspiracies to defraud the United States.[122] To prove conspiracy to defraud the United States, the government must show (1) an agreement between two or more persons, (2) to defraud the United States, and (3) an overt act on the part of one of them in furtherance of the conspiracy.[123] The "fraud covered by the statute reaches any conspiracy for the purpose of impairing, obstructing or defeating the lawful functions of any department of the Government" by "deceit, craft or trickery, or at least by means that are dishonest."[124] Unlike mail and wire fraud, the government need not show that the scheme was designed to deprive another of money, property, or honest services; it is enough that to show that the scheme is designed to obstruct governmental functions.[125]

Conspiracy to defraud the United States is punishable by imprisonment for not more than 5 years and a fine of not more than $250,000 (not more than $500,000 for organizations).[126] It is neither a RICO nor a money laundering predicate offense.[127] It is an offense for which restitution must be ordered.[128] There is no explicit authority for confiscation of property tainted by the offense.[129]

False Statements

Section 1001 outlaws knowingly and willfully making a material false statement on a matter within the jurisdiction of the executive, legislative, or judicial branch of the federal government.[130] A matter is material for purposes of Section 1001 when "it has a natural tendency to influence, or is capable of influencing, the decision of" the individual or entity to whom it is addressed.[131] A matter is within the jurisdiction of a federal entity "when it has the power to exercise authority in a particular matter" and "may exist when false statements [are] made to state or local government agencies receiving federal support or subject to federal regulation."[132]

A violation of Section 1001 is punishable by imprisonment for not more than 5 years and a fine of not more than $250,000 (not more than $500,000 for organizations).[133] It is neither a RICO nor a money laundering predicate offense.[134] It is an offense for which restitution must be ordered.[135] There is no explicit authority for confiscation of property tainted by the offense, unless the offense relates to the activities of various federal financial entities.[136] However, in a situation where the offense involves the submission of a false claim either a private individual or the government may bring a civil action for treble damages.[137]

Fraud Elsewhere in Chapter 63

Chapter 63 contains four other fraud proscriptions in addition to mail and wire fraud: bank fraud, health care fraud, securities and commodities fraud, and fraud in foreign labor contracting.[138] Each relies on a jurisdictional base other than use of the mail or wire communications.

Bank Fraud

The bank fraud statute outlaws schemes to (1) defraud a federally insured financial institution, or (2) to falsely obtain property from such an institution.[139] To establish the scheme to defraud offense, "the government must prove . . . (1) the defendant knowingly executed or attempted to execute a scheme or artifice to defraud a financial institution; (2) the defendant had the intent to defraud a financial institution; and (3) the bank involved was federally insured."[140]

To establish the "falsely obtain" violation, "the government must show that: (1) a scheme existed to obtain money, funds, or credit in the custody or control of a federally insured financial institution; (2) the defendant participated in the scheme by means of a material false pretenses, representations, or promises; and (3) the defendant acted knowingly."[141]

Violation of either offense is punishable by imprisonment for not more than 30 years and a fine of not more than $1 million.[142] Bank fraud is both a RICO and a money laundering predicate offense.[143] Conviction also requires an order for victim restitution.[144] Property constituting the proceeds of a violation are subject to forfeiture under either civil or criminal procedure.[145]

Health Care Fraud

The health care fraud proscription in Section 1347 has two prongs as well. It outlaws knowingly and willfully executing a scheme either (1) to defraud a health care benefit program, or (2) to falsely obtain property from a health care benefit program – in connection with the delivery of, or payment for, health care products or services.[146] Construction of the two prongs mirrors the effort elsewhere, e.g., "To obtain a conviction for health care fraud under 18 U.S.C. §1347, the Government is required to prove beyond a reasonable doubt that [the defendant]: (1) knowingly devised a scheme or artifice to defraud a health care benefit program in connection with the delivery of or payment for health care benefits, items, or services; (2) executed or attempted to execute this scheme or artifice to defraud; and (3) acted with intent to defraud.[147] The intent element, however, is a little different. Conviction requires a knowing and willful intent. "To establish knowledge and willfulness, the Government must prove that the defendant acted with knowledge that his conduct was unlawful,"[148] but it need show that the defendant knew of or intended to violation Section 1347 specifically.[149]

Section 1347's penalty structure is also somewhat distinctive. General violations are punishable by imprisonment for not more than 10 years and fines of not more than $250,000.[150] If serious bodily injury results, however, the maximum penalty is increased to imprisonment for not more than 20 years, and to imprisonment for life or any term of years should death result.[151] Section 1347 offenses are neither money laundering nor RICO predicate offenses.[152] They do entitle the government to restitution,[153] but not to forfeiture of any tainted property.[154]

Securities and Commodities Fraud

The securities and commodities fraud prohibition in Section 1348 features the same two pronged approach.[155] It outlaws knowingly executing or attempt to execute a scheme (1) to defraud or (2) to falsely obtain money or property – with respect to commodities or securities.[156] "Under § 1348(1), the Government must provide sufficient evidence to establish that [the defendant] had (1) 'fraudulent intent'; (2) 'a scheme or artifice to defraud'; and (3) 'a nexus with a security.' Alternatively, pursuant to § 1348(2), the Government can show that [the defendant] executed: (1) a scheme or artifice; (2) 'to obtain, by means of false or fraudulent pretenses, representations, or promises, any money or property;' while possessing (3) fraudulent intent. . . ." Moreover, "the Government must also show that the false and misleading statements . . . were material."[157]

Offenders face imprisonment for not more than 25 years and fines of not more than $250,000 (not more than $500,000 for organizations).[158] The offense is neither a money laundering nor a RICO predicate offense.[159] Victim restitution must be ordered upon conviction,[160] but forfeiture is not authorized.[161]

Fraud in Foreign Labor Contracting

The recently enacted fraud in foreign labor contracting, 18 U.S.C. 1351, provides that:

> Whoever knowingly and with intent to defraud recruits, solicits or hires a person outside the United States for purposes of employment in the United States by means of materially false or fraudulent pretenses, representations or promises regarding that employment shall be fined under this title or imprisoned for not more than 5 years, or both.

The offense is neither a money laundering nor a RICO predicate offense.[162] A restitution order is required at sentencing,[163] but forfeiture is not authorized.[164]

Honest Services Fraud Elsewhere

After *Skilling*, honest services mail and wire fraud consists of bribery and kickback schemes furthered by use of the mail or wire communications. Mail and wire fraud aside, the principal bribery and kickback statutes include 18 U.S.C. 201 (bribery of public officials), 666 (bribery relating to federal programs), 1951 (extortion under color of official right); 15 U.S.C 78dd-1 to 78dd-3 (foreign corrupt practices); and 42 U.S.C. 1320a-7b (Medicare/Medicaid anti-kickback).

Bribery of Public Officials

Conviction for violation of Section 201 "requires a showing that something of value was corruptly . . . offered or promised to a public official . . . or corruptly . . . sought . . . or agreed to be received by a public official with intent . . . to influence any official act . . . or in return for 'being influenced in the performance of any official act."[165]

The hallmark of the offense is a corrupt quid pro quo, "a specific intent to give or receive something of value in exchange for an official act."[166] The public officials covered include federal officers and employees, those of the District of Columbia, and those who perform tasks for or on behalf the United States or any its departments or agencies.[167] The official acts that constitute the objective of the corrupt bargain include any decision or action relating to any matter coming before an individual in his official capacity.[168]

Section 201 punishes bribery with imprisonment for up to 15 years, a fine of up to $250,000 (up to $500,000 for an organization), and disqualification from future federal office or employment.[169] Section 201 is a RICO predicate offense and consequently also a money laundering predicate offense.[170] The proceeds of a bribe in violation of Section 201 are subject to forfeiture under either civil or criminal procedure.[171]

Bribery Related to Federal Programs

Section 666 outlaws bribes offered to, or solicited by, agents of any state, local, tribal, or private entity – that receives more than $10,000 in federal benefits – in relation to a transaction of $5,000 or more.[172] Agents are statutorily defined as "person[s] authorized to act on behalf of another person or a government and, in the case of an organization or government, includes a servant or employee, and a partner, director, officer, manager, and representative."[173] "Where the bribe-giver receives an intangible benefit, the bribe amount may be used as a proxy to stand for the value of the business or transaction."[174] The circuits appear divided over whether the government must establish a quid pro quo as in a Section 201 bribery case.[175] The government, however, need not establish that the tainted transaction involves federal funds.[176]

Violations of Section 666 are punishable by imprisonment for not more than 10 years and a fine of not more than $250,000 (not more than $500,000 for organizations).[177] Section 666 offenses are money laundering predicate offenses.[178] Section 666 offenses are not among the RICO federal predicate offenses, although bribery in violation of state felony laws is a RICO predicate offense.[179] The proceeds of a bribe in violation of Section 666 are subject to forfeiture under either civil or criminal procedure.[180]

Hobbs Act

The Hobbs Act, 18 U.S.C. 1951, outlaws obtaining the property of another under "color of official right," in a manner that has an effect on interstate commerce.[181] Conviction requires the government to prove that the defendant: "(1) was a government official; (2) who accepted property to which she was not entitled; (3) knowing that she was not entitled to the property; and (4) knowing that the payment was given in return for officials acts: (5) which had at least a de minimis effect on commerce."[182] Conviction does not require that the public official sought or induced payment, "the government need only show that a public official has obtained a payment to which he was not entitled, knowing that the payment was made in return for official acts."[183]

Hobbs Act violations are punishable by imprisonment for not more than 20 years and a fine of not more than $250,000 (not more than $500,000 for an organization).[184] Hobbs Act violations are RICO predicate offenses and thus money laundering predicates as well.[185] The proceeds of a Hobbs Act violation are subject to forfeiture under either civil or criminal procedure.[186]

Foreign Corrupt Practices

The bribery provisions of the Foreign Corrupt Practices Act are three: 15 U.S.C. 78dd-1(trade practices by issuers), 78dd-2 (trade practices by domestic concerns), 78dd-3 (trade practices by others within the United States).[187] Other than class of potential defendants, the elements of the three are comparable. They "make[] it a crime to: (1) willfully; (2) make use of the mail or any means or instrumentality of interstate commerce; (3) corruptly; (4) in furtherance of an offer, payment, promise to pay, or authorization of the payment of any money, or offer, gift, promise to give, or authorization of the giving of anything of value to; (5) any foreign official; (6) for purposes of [either] influencing any act or decision of such foreign official in his official capacity [or] inducing such foreign official to do or omit to do any act in violation of the lawful duty of such official [or] securing any improper advantage; (7) in order to assist such [corporation] in obtaining or retaining business for or with, or directing business to, any person."[188]

None of the three proscriptions apply to payments "to expedite or to secure the performance of a routine governmental action,"[189] and each affords defendants an affirmative defense for payments that are lawful under the applicable foreign law or regulation.[190]

Violations are punishable by imprisonment for not more than 5 years and by a fine of not more than $100,000 (not more than $2 million for organizations).[191] Foreign Corrupt Practices Act violations are not RICO predicate offenses,[192] but they are money laundering predicates.[193] The proceeds of a violation are subject to forfeiture under either civil or criminal procedure.[194]

Medicare Kickbacks

The Medicare/Medicaid kickback prohibition in 42 U.S.C. 1320a-7b(b)[195] outlaws "knowingly and willfully [offering or paying], soliciting [or] receiving, any remuneration (including any kickback) . . . to induce the referral of[, or the purchase with respect to] Medicare [or] Medicaid beneficiaries . . . any item or service for which payment may be made in whole or in part under the Medicare [or] Medicaid programs. . . 42 U.S.C §1320a-7b(b)[(1),](2)."[196]

Violations are punishable by imprisonment for not more than 5 years and by a fine of not more than $25,000. Section 1320a-7b kickback violations are money laundering, but not RICO, predicate offenses.[197] The proceeds of a violation are subject to forfeiture under either civil or criminal procedure.[198]

APPENDIX. MAIL AND WIRE FRAUD STATUTES

18 U.S.C. 1341. Frauds and Swindles (Text)

Whoever, having devised or intending to devise any scheme or artifice to defraud, or for obtaining money or property by means of false or fraudulent pretenses, representations, or promises, or to sell, dispose of, loan, exchange, alter, give away, distribute, supply, or furnish or procure for unlawful use any counterfeit or spurious coin, obligation, security, or other article, or anything represented to be or intimated or held out to be such counterfeit or spurious article, for the purpose of executing such scheme or artifice or attempting so to do, places in any post office or authorized depository for mail matter, any matter or thing whatever to be sent or delivered by the Postal Service, or deposits or causes to be deposited any matter or thing whatever to be sent or delivered by any private or commercial interstate carrier, or takes or receives therefrom, any such matter or thing, or knowingly causes to be delivered by mail or such carrier according to the direction thereon, or at the place at which it is directed to be delivered by the person to whom it is addressed, any such matter or thing, shall be fined under this title or imprisoned not more than 20 years, or both. If the violation occurs in relation to, or involving any benefit authorized, transported, transmitted, transferred, disbursed, or paid in connection with, a presidentially declared major disaster or emergency (as those terms are defined in Section 102 of the Robert T. Stafford Disaster Relief and Emergency Assistance Act (42 U.S.C. 5122)), or affects a financial institution, such person shall be fined not more than $1,000,000 or imprisoned not more than 30 years, or both.

18 U.S.C. 1343. Fraud by Wire, Radio, or Television (Text)

Whoever, having devised or intending to devise any scheme or artifice to defraud, or for obtaining money or property by means of false or fraudulent pretenses, representations, or promises, transmits or causes to be transmitted by means of wire, radio, or television communication in interstate or foreign commerce, any writings, signs, signals, pictures, or sounds for the purpose of executing such scheme or artifice, shall be fined under this title or imprisoned not more than 20 years, or both. If the violation occurs in relation to, or involving any benefit authorized, transported, transmitted, transferred, disbursed, or paid in connection with, a presidentially declared major disaster or emergency (as those terms are defined in Section 102 of the Robert T. Stafford Disaster Relief and Emergency Assistance Act (42 U.S.C. 5122)), or affects a financial institution, such person shall be fined not more than $1,000,000 or imprisoned not more than 30 years, or both.

End Notes

[1] 18 U.S.C. 1341(mail fraud), 1343(wire fraud).

[2] The prohibition was thought necessary "to prevent the frauds which are mostly gotten up in the large cities . . . by thieves, forgers, and rapscallions generally, for the purpose of deceiving

and fleecing the innocent people in the country," *McNally v. United States*, 483 U.S. 350, 356 (1987), quoting, 43 *Cong. Globe* 35 (1870)(remarks of Representative Farnsworth).

[3] Act of June 8, 1872, ch. 335, §302, 17 Stat. 323 (1872): "That if any person having devised or intending to devise any scheme or artifice to defraud, or be effected by either opening or intending to open correspondence or communication with any other person (whether resident within or outside of the United States), by means of the post-office establishment of the United States, or by inciting such other person to open communication with the person so devising or intending, shall, in and for executing such scheme or artifice (or attempting so to do), place any letter or packet in any post-office of the United States, or take or receive any therefrom, such person, so misusing the post-office establishment, shall be guilty of a misdemeanor, and shall be punished with a fine of not more than five hundred dollars, with or without such imprisonment, as the court shall direct, not exceeding eighteen calendar months. . . ."

[4] *McNally v. United States*, 483 U.S. at 357 n.6. The penalty for general violations remained at imprisonment not more than 18 months until the 1909 criminal code revision when it was increased to imprisonment for not more than 5 years, Act of March 4, 1909, ch. 321, §217, 35 Stat. 1130 (1909). So it stayed until 2002, when it was increased to imprisonment for not more than 20 years, P.L. 107-204, §903(a), 116 Stat. 805 (2002). The penalty enhancement for defrauding a financial institution was added in 1989, P.L. 101-73, §961(i), 103 Stat. 500 (1989), and increased from a maximum of imprisonment for not more than 20 years to its present maximum of imprisonment for not more than 30 years in 1990, P.L. 101-647, §2504(h), 104 Stat. 4861 (1990). The application of the 30-year maximum to disaster related frauds appeared in 2008, P.L. 110-179, §4, 121 Stat. 2257 (2008).

[5] 18 U.S.C. 1346.

[6] P.L. 103-322, §250006, 108 Stat. 2087 (1994).

[7] Act of July 16, 1952, ch. 879, §18(a), 66 Stat. 722 (1952).

[8] H. Rept. 82-388, at 1 (1951)("The general object of the bill is to amend the Criminal Code . . . making it a Federal criminal offense to use wire or radio communications as instrumentalities for perpetrating frauds upon the public. In principal it is not dissimilar to the post fraud statute (18 U.S.C. 1341)"); S. Rept. 82-44, at 14 (1951)("This section . . . is intended merely to establish for radio a parallel provision now in the law for fraud by mail, so that fraud conducted or intended to be conducted by radio shall be amenable to the same penalties now provided for fraud by means of the mails"); H. Rept. 82-1750, at 22 (1952).

[9] There was no need to amend the wire fraud statute, when commercial carriers were included in the mail fraud statute or when references to the Postal Service were substituted to references to the Post Office, P.L. 103-322, §250006(1), 108 Stat. 2087 (1994); P.L. 91-375, §6(j)(11), 84 Stat. 778 (1970).

[10] *Pasquantino v. United States*, 544 U.S. 349, 355 n.2 (2005)("we have construed identical language in the wire and mail fraud statutes *in pari materia*"), citing, *Neder v. United States*, 527 U.S. 1, 20 (1999) and *Carpenter v. United States*, 484 U.S. 19, 25 and n.6 (1987); see also, *United States v. Mullins*, 613 F.3d 1273, 1281 n.2 (10th Cir. 2010) ("[I]nterpretations of the mail fraud statute are, of course, authoritative on questions of wire fraud"); *United States v. McKanry*, 628 F.3d 1010, 1017 (8th Cir. 2011)("The elements of wire fraud are nearly identical except they involve the use of interstate wiring instead of mail").

[11] E.g., *United States v. Washington*, 634 F.3d 1180, 1183 (10th Cir. 2011)(here and elsewhere internal quotation marks and citations have usually been omitted)("To establish guilt under the mail-fraud statute, the government had to prove that (1) Mr. Washington engaged in a

scheme or artifice to defraud or to obtain money by means of false and fraudulent pretences; (2) he did so with the intent to defraud; and (3) he used a private or commercial interstate carrier to facilitate that scheme"); *United States v. Schmitz*, 634 F.3d 1247, 1260 (11th Cir. 2011)("Mail fraud consists of the following elements: (1) an intentional participation in a scheme to defraud a person of money or property, and (2) the use of the mails in furtherance of the scheme"); *United States v. Jenkins*, 633 F.3d 788, 804 (9th Cir. 2011)("Wire fraud has three elements: (1) a scheme to defraud; (2) use of wires in furtherance of the scheme; and (3) a specific intent to deceive or defraud"); *United States v. Radley*, 632 F.3d 177, 184 (5th Cir. 2011)("To prove wire fraud, the government must prove: (1) a scheme to defraud and (2) the use of, or causing the use of, wire communications in furtherance of the scheme"); *United States v. McKanry*, 628 F.3d 1010, 1017 (8th Cir. 2011)("To establish mail fraud, the government must prove: (1) a scheme to defraud by means of material false representations or promises, (2) intent to defraud, (3) reasonable foreseeability that the mail would be used, and (4) that the mail was used in furtherance of some essential step in the scheme"); *United States v. Riley*, 621 F.3d 312, 325 (3d Cir. 2010)("In order to find a defendant guilty of mail fraud under §1341, the prosecution must prove that (1) there was a scheme to defraud; (2) the defendant acted with the intent to defraud; and (3) the defendant used the mails to further or carry out the scheme").

[12] 18 U.S.C. 1343.

[13] 18 U.S.C. 1341.

[14] *Schmuck v. United States*, 489 U.S. 705, 712 (1989), quoting, *Pereira v. United States*, 347 U.S. 1, 8 (1954); *United States v. Washington*, 634 F.3d 1183-184 (10th Cir. 2011); *United States v. Dowl*, 619 F.3d 494, 499 (5th Cir. 2010).

[15] *Schmuck v. United States*, 489 U.S. at 715, citing by way of example, *Carpenter v. United States*, 484 U.S. 19, 28 (1987); *United States v. Coughlin*, 610 F.3d 89, 98 (D.C.Cir. 2010).

[16] *United States v. Lane*, 474 U.S. 438, 451-52 (1986), quoting, *United States v. Maze*, 414 U.S. 395; 403 (1974); *United States v. Faulkenberry*, 614 F.3d 573, 582 (6th Cir. 2010); *United States v. Phipps*, 595 F.3d 243, 246-47 (5th Cir. 2010).

[17] *Pereira v. United States*, 347 U.S. at 8-9 ("Where one does an act with knowledge that the use of the mails will follow in the ordinary course of business, or where such use can reasonably be foreseen, even though not actually intended, then he 'causes' the mails to be used"); *United States v. Dooley*, 578 F.2d 582, 588 (7th Cir. 2009); *United States v. Weiss*, 630 F.3d 1263, 1269-270 (10th Cir. 2010); *United States v. Green*, 592 F.3d 1057, 1069-70 (9th Cir. 2010).

[18] *Neder v. United States*, 527 U.S. 1, 20 (1999).

[19] 18 U.S.C. 1346.

[20] *McNally v. United States*, 483 U.S. 350, 356-57 & n.6 (footnote 6 in brackets)("*Durland v. United States*, 161 U.S. 306 (1986), the first case in which this Court construed the meaning of the phrase 'any scheme or artifice to defraud,' held that the phrase is to be interpreted broadly insofar as property rights are concerned. . . . the Court rejected the argument that 'the statute reaches only such as cases as, at common law, would come within the definition of false pretences, in order to make out which there must be a misrepresentation as to some existing fact and not a mere promise as to the future. Instead, it construed the statute to 'include everything designed to defraud by representations as to the past or present, or suggestions and promises as to the future.' . . .Congress codified the holding of *Durland* in 1909. . . . [Prior to *Durland* Congress amended the statute to add language expressly reaching schemes of the period . . . . The addition of this language appears to have been noting more than a reconfirmation of the statute's original purpose in the face of some

disagreement among the lower federal courts as to whether the statute should be broadly or narrowly read"].

[21] 18 U.S.C. 1346. The phrase "deprivation of the right to honest services" extends only to bribery and kick-back schemes, *Skilling v. United States*, 130 S.Ct. 2896, 2931 (2010).

[22] *McNally v. United States*, 483 U.S. at 358, quoting, *Hammerschmidt v. United States*, 265 U.S. 182, 188 (1924).

[23] *Pasquantino v. United States*, 544 U.S. 349, 371 (2005)("[T]he wire fraud statute punishes the scheme, not its success"); *United States v. Warshak*, 631 F.3d 266, 310 (6th Cir. 2010); *United States v. Lupton*, 620 F.3d 790, 805 (7th Cir. 2010); *United States v. Valencia*, 600 F.3d 389, 429 (5th Cir. 2010).

[24] *United States v. Williams*, 527 F.3d 1235, 1245 (11th Cir. 2008).

[25] *United States v. Svete*, 556 F.3d 1157, 1168-169 (11th Cir. 2009)("Svete and Girardot cite decisions that use the 'ordinary prudence' language as evidence that fraud requires a scheme capable of defrauding the reasonably prudent, but none of the decisions cited by Svete and Girardot overturned a conviction on the ground that the scheme was incapable of deceiving persons of ordinary prudence. The 'ordinary prudence' language was invoked instead to affirm convictions. Two sister circuits have stated that 'ordinary prudence' has a place in the proof of mail fraud, but both held that the jury instructions about materiality were sufficient to establish that the jury had found the fraudulent schemes reliable. . . None of these decisions reversed a conviction of mail fraud for failure to instruct the jury that the alleged scheme had to be capable of deceiving people of ordinary prudence, and none reached the perverse result of insulating criminals who target those least likely to protect themselves").

[26] *Neder v. United States*, 527 U.S. 1, 22-3, 25 (1999).

[27] *United States v. Jenkins*, 633 F.3d 788, 802 n.3 (9th Cir. 2011)(parenthetical indications omitted); *United States v. Wetherald*, 636 F.3d 1315, 1324 (11th Cir. 2011); *United States v. Radley*, 632 F.3d 177, 185 (5th Cir. 2011); *United States v. Weldon*, 606 F.3d 912, 918 (6th Cir. 2010).

[28] *United States v. Howard*, 619 F.3d 723, 727 (7th Cir. 2010); *United States v. Phipps*, 595 F.3d 243, (2010)("Mail and wire fraud are both specific intent crimes that require the Government to prove that a defendant knew the scheme involved false representations"); *United States v. Stalnaker*, 571 F.3d 428, 436 (5th Cir. 2009).

[29] *United States v. Coughlin*, 610 F.3d 89, 98 (D.C.Cir. 2010); cf., *United States v. Maxwell*, 579 F.3d 1282, 1301 (11th Cir. 2009)("[A]n intent to defraud is not present if the defendant knew that he could not deceive the recipient of his statements").

[30] *United States v. Alston-Graves*, 435 F.3d 331, 336-38 (D.C.Cir. 2006*); United States v. Ramirez*, 574 F.3d 869, 876-77 (7th Cir. 2009); *United States v. Clay*, 618 F.3d 946, 953 (8th Cir. 2010).

[31] *United States v. Hamilton*, 499 F.3d 734, 736-37 (7th Cir. 2007); *United States v. Chavis*, 461 F.3d 1201, 1209 (10th Cir. 2006)("A defendant's honest belief that a venture will ultimately succeed does not constitute good faith if, in carrying out the plan, he knowingly uses false representations or pretenses with intent to deceive").

[32] 18 U.S.C. 1341, 1343.

[33] *Carpenter v. United States*, 484 U.S. 19, (1987)("*McNally* did not limit the scope of §1341 to tangible as distinguished from intangible property rights"); see also, *Pasquantino v. United States*, 544 U.S. 349, 356 (2005) ("Canada's right to uncollected excise taxes . . . is 'property' in its hands. This right is an entitlement to collect money. . . Valuable entitlements like these are 'property' as that term ordinarily is employed").

[34] *Cleveland v. United States*, 531 U.S. 12, 20 (2000)(Section "1341 does not reach fraud in obtaining a state or municipal license of the kind here involved, for such a license is not 'property' in the government regulator's hands")

[35] *McNally v. United States*, 483 U.S. 350, 356 (1987).

[36] 18 U.S.C. 1346.

[37] *Skilling v. United States*, 130 S.Ct. 2896, 2907 (2010).

[38] 18 U.S.C. 2(a)("Whoever commits an offense against the United States or aids, abets, counsels, commands, induces or procures its commission, is punishable as a principal"); 1349("Any person who attempts or conspires to commit any offense under this chapter shall be subject to the same penalties as those prescribed rot he offense, the commission of which was the object of the attempt or conspiracy").

[39] *Nye & Nissen v. United States*, 336 U.S. 613, 619 (1949); *United States v. Devries*, 630 F.3d 1130, 1133 (8th Cir. 23011); *United States v. Mullins*, 613 F.3d 1273, 1290 (10th Cir. 2010)(emphasis of the court)("It's enough that *someone* [else] committed wire fraud, and that Ms. Edwards sought to make it succeed"); *United States v. Reifler*, 446 F.3d 65, 96-7 (2d Cir. 2006)("[A] defendant may be convicted of aiding and abetting a given crime where the government proves that the underlying crime was committed by a person other than the defendant, that the defendant knew of the crime, and that the defendant acted with the intent to contribute to the success of the underlying crime. To prove that the defendant acted with that specific intent, the government must show that he knew of the crime, but it need not show that he knew all of the details of the crime, so long as the evidence shows that he joined the venture, that he shared in it, and that his efforts contributed towards its success. A defendant may not properly be convicted of aiding and abetting a crime that was completed before his accessorial acts were performed. However, where the crime has more than one stage, the defendant may be convicted of aiding and abetting even if he did not learn of the crime at its inception but knowingly assisted at a later stage. The latter principle has been applied to charges of wire fraud, allowing a defendant to be convicted of that offense on an aiding-and-abetting theory even if the wire transmission preceded his conduct, so long as the fraudulent scheme was ongoing at the time of his conduct. In *United States v. Phillips*, for example, the court ruled that the defendant's act of cashing a money order that had been fraudulently wired aided and abetted the wire fraud").

[40] *United States v. Ford*, 558 F.3d 371, 375 (5th Cir. 2009); see also, *United States v. Brockenborrugh*, 575 F.3d 726, 733-34 (D.C.Cir. 2009); *United States v. Warshak*, 631 F.3d 266, 308 (6th Cir. 2010); see generally, CRS Report R41223, *Federal Conspiracy Law: A Brief Overview*, by Charles Doyle.

[41] *United States v. Fishman*, ___ F.3d ___, ___ (10th Cir. May 27, 2011), citing, *Whitfield v. United States*, 543 U.S. 209 (2005), but see, *United States v. Warshak*, 631 F.3d 266, 308 (6th Cir. 2010).

[42] *Pinkerton v. United States*, 328 U.S. 640, 647 (1946); *United States v. Vazquez-Castro*, 640 F.3d 19, 24 (1st Cir. 2011); *United States v. Luong*, 627 F.3d 1306, 1308 (9th Cir. 2010).

[43] *United States v. Thornburgh*, ___ F.3d ___, ___ (10th Cir. May 27, 2011).

[44] *United States v. Manzo*, 636 F.3d 56, 66 (3d Cir. 2011); *United States v. Farhane*, 634 F.3d 127, 146-47 (2d Cir. 2011).

[45] *Pasquantino v. United States*, 544 U.S. 349, 371 (2005); *United States v. Warshak*, 631 F.3d 266, 310 (6th Cir. 2010); *United States v. Lupton*, 620 F.3d 790, 805 (7th Cir. 2010); *United States v. Valencia*, 600 F.3d 389, 429 (5th Cir. 2010).

[46] *United States v. Brooks*, 438 F.3d 1231, 1242 (10th Cir. 2006).

[47] 18 U.S.C. 1341, 1343, 3751. The maximum for both individuals and organizations may be increased to twice the amount of gain or loss associated with the offense, 18 U.S.C. 3571(d). Both mail and wire fraud statutes contain the financial institution and disaster enhancement (". . . If the violation occurs in relation to, or involving any benefit authorized, transported, transmitted, transferred, disbursed, or paid in connection with, a presidentially declared major disaster or emergency (as those terms are defined in Section 102 of the Robert T. Stafford Disaster Relief and Emergency Assistance Act (42 U.S.C. 5122)), or affects a financial institution, such person shall be fined not more than $1,000,000 or imprisoned not more than 30 years, or both").

[48] *Gall v. United States*, 552 U.S. 38, 49 (2007)("[A] district should begin all sentencing proceedings by correctly calculating the applicable Guidelines range").

[49] See generally, CRS Report R41696, *How the Federal Sentencing Guidelines Work: An Overview*, by Charles Doyle.

[50] U.S.S.G. §2C1.1 cmt. ("Statutory Provisions: . . . 18 U.S.C. . . . 1341 (if the scheme or artifice to defraud was to deprive another of the intangible right of honest services of a public official) . . . 1343 (if the scheme or artifice to defraud was to deprive another of the intangible right of honest services of a public official) . . .").

[51] U.S.S.G. §§2B1.1(b)(1); 2C1.1(b)(2). E.g., *United States v. Martinez*, 610 F.3d 1216, 1222 (10th Cir. 2010)("[T]he PSR [(presentence report)]determined Martinez's base offense level was 14 under U.S.S.G. §2C1.1(a)(1), applied a 16- level enhancement under §2B1.1(b)(1) because Martinez was responsible for a loss between $ 1.5 and $ 2.5 million, and applied a 4-level enhancement under §2C1.1(b)(3). When Martinez's base offense level was adjusted three levels for acceptance of responsibility, his total offense level was 31, which when combined with Martinez's criminal history category I, produced a guideline range of 108-135 months"); *United States v. Skys*, 637 F.3d 146, 150 (2d Cir. 2011) ("The PSR's calculation of Sky's advisory-Guidelines offense level began with a base offense level of 7 pursuant to §2B1.1(a)(1); it recommended increases for the following specific offense characteristics: 24 steps pursuant to §2B1.1(b)(1)(M) for an intended loss amount of more than $50 million but not more than $100 million; two steps pursuant to §2B1.1(b)(2)(A) for an offense involving 10 or more, but fewer than 50, victims; and two steps pursuant to §2B1.1(b)(9)(C) for an offense that involved sophisticated means. The PSR also recommended a four-step upward adjustment pursuant to §3B1.1(a) on the ground that Skys was an organizer or leader of criminal activity that involved five or more participants or was otherwise extensive, and a two-step downward adjustment pursuant to §3E1.1(a) for Skys's acceptance of responsibility prior to the imposition of sentence. The total offense level was 37. Given Sky's criminal history category of II, the Guidelines-recommended range of imprisonment was 235 to 293 months").

[52] U.S.S.G. ch.5A, Sentencing Table.

[53] *Id.*

[54] *Id.*

[55] U.S.S.G. §§5E1.2, 8C12.4.

[56] 18 U.S.C. 3561, 3581(b).

[57] U.S.S.G. §5B1.1. Probation in conjunction with some combination of incarceration is possible up to offense level 11, U.S.S.G. §5B1.2.

[58] 18 U.S.C. §3553(a) ("The court shall impose a sentence sufficient, but not greater than necessary, to comply with the purposes set forth in paragraph (2) of this subsection. The court, in determining the particular sentence to be imposed, shall consider – (1) the nature and circumstances of the offense and the history and characteristics of the defendant; (2) the

need for the sentence imposed – (A) to reflect the seriousness of the offense, to promote respect for the law, and to provide just punishment for the offense; (B) to afford adequate deterrence to criminal conduct; (C) to protect the public from further crimes of the defendant; and (D) to provide the defendant with needed educational or vocational training, medical care, or other correctional treatment in the most effective manner; (3) the kinds of sentences available; (4) the kinds of sentence and the sentencing range established for – (A) the applicable category of offense committed by the applicable category of defendant as set forth in the guidelines – (i) issued by the Sentencing Commission pursuant to Section 994(a)(1) of Title 28, United States Code, subject to any amendments made to such guidelines by act of Congress (regardless of whether such amendments have yet to be incorporated by the Sentencing Commission into amendments issued under Section 994(p) of Title 28); and (ii) that, except as provided in Section 3742(g), are in effect on the date the defendant is sentenced; or (B) in the case of a violation of probation or supervised release, the applicable guidelines or policy statements issued by the Sentencing Commission pursuant to Section 994(a)(3) of Title 28, United States Code, taking into account any amendments made to such guidelines or policy statements by act of Congress (regardless of whether such amendments have yet to be incorporated by the Sentencing Commission into amendments issued under Section 994(p) of Title 28); (5) any pertinent policy statement – (A) issued by the Sentencing Commission pursuant to Section 994(a)(2) of Title 28, United States Code, subject to any amendments made to such policy statement by act of Congress (regardless of whether such amendments have yet to be incorporated by the Sentencing Commission into amendments issued under Section 994(p) of Title 28); and (B) that, except as provided in Section 3742(g), is in effect on the date the defendant is sentenced. (6) the need to avoid unwarranted sentence disparities among defendants with similar records who have been found guilty of similar conduct; and (7) the need to provide restitution to any victims of the offense").

[59] *Gall v. United States*, 552 U.S. 38, 51 (2007); *United States v. Schlueter*, 634 F.3d 965, 967 (7th Cir. 2011).

[60] *Id.*

[61] *United States v. Martin*, 363 F.3d 25, 35 n.17 (1st Cir. 2004)("'Supervised release' is a punishment in addition to incarceration, served after completion of a prison term"). See generally, CRS Report RL31653, *Supervised Release: A Brief Sketch of Federal Law*, by Charles Doyle and United States Sentencing Commission, *Federal Offenders Sentenced to Supervised Release* (July 2010), available at http://www.ussc.gov/Research/Research_Publications/Supervised_Release/20100722_Supervised_Release.pdf.

[62] 18 U.S.C. 3583(a)(emphasis added)("The court, in imposing a sentence to a term of imprisonment for a felony . . . *may* include as a part of the sentence as requirement that the defendant be placed on a term of supervised release after imprisonment, except that the court shall include as a part of the sentence a requirement that the defendant be placed on a term of supervised release if such a term is required by statute. . ."). There are no statutory provisions requiring a term of supervised release upon conviction for either mail or wire fraud, cf., 18 U.S.C. 1341, 1343.

[63] U.S.S.G. §5D1.1(a)(emphasis added)("The court *shall* order a term of supervised release to follow imprisonment when a sentence of imprisonment of more than one year is imposed, or when required by statute").

[64] 18 U.S.C. 3583(b), 3559(a), 1341, 1343.

[65] 18 U.S.C. 3583(e), 3559(a), 1341, 1343.

[66] 18 U.S.C. 3583(d).

[67] 18 U.S.C. 3583(d), 3563(a)(5).

[68] *United States v. Paul*, 542 F.3d 596, 600-601(7th Cir. 2008)(the sentencing court did not abuse its discretion in imposing the condition upon a defendant convicted of wire fraud who had not history of drug abuse but who did have a history of alcohol abuse and "gambling problems").

[69] U.S.S.G. §5D1.3(a), (c).

[70] U.S.S.G. §5D1.3(a)(5), (6).

[71] 18 U.S.C. 3013(a)(2), 3559, 1341, 1343.

[72] 18 U.S.C. 3663A("(a)(1) Notwithstanding any other provision of law, when sentencing a defendant convicted of an offense described in subsection (c), the court shall order . . . that the defendant make restitution to the victim of the offense or, if the victim is deceased, to the victim's estate. . . . (c)(1) This section shall apply in all sentencing proceedings for convictions of, or plea agreements relating to charges for, any offense . . . (A) that is . . . (ii) an offense against property under this title, . . . including any offense committed by fraud or deceit"); *United States v. Dokich*, 614 F.3d 314, 318 (7th Cir. 2010); see generally, CRS Report RL34138, *Restitution in Federal Criminal Cases*, by Charles Doyle.

[73] 18 U.S.C. 3663A(a)(2); *United States v. Gregoire*, 638 F.3d 962, 972-73 (8th Cir. 2011); *United States v. Matos*, 611 F.3d 31, 44 (1st Cir. 2010).

[74] See generally, CRS Report 97-139, *Crime and Forfeiture*, by Charles Doyle

[75] E.g., 18 U.S.C. 983.

[76] E.g., 18 U.S.C. 982.

[77] *United States v. Taylor*, 582 F.3d 558, 565 (5th Cir. 2009)(rejecting the contention that civil forfeiture under 981(a)(1)(C), 1956(c)(7)(A), and 1961(1) is limited to cases in which a RICO (18 U.S.C. 1962) violation is shown).

[78] 28 U.S.C. 2461(c).

[79] *United States v. Venturella*, 585 F.3d 1013, 1019, 1020 (7th Cir. 2009)("We have rejected the theory that forfeiture and restitution cannot be imposed for the same offense. . . . Furthermore, outside the rare occasion where the same party stands to benefit from both payments, Biks does not cite to any authority which holds that restitution must be offset by the forfeiture amount; *United States v. Hoffman-Vaile*, 568 F.3d 1335, 1344 (11th Cir. 2009)(rejecting defendant's argument that forfeiture should be reduced because she paid restitution); *United States v. Bright*, 353 F.3d 1114, 1123 (9th Cir. 2004)(rejecting argument that the district court should have 'offset his forfeited funds against his restitution obligation.')"); *United States v. Taylor*, 582 F.3d 558, 565-66 (5th Cir. 2009)(rejecting challenge of a restitution order for the benefit of the Department of Homeland Security and a forfeiture order for the benefit of the Department of Justice); but see, *United States v. Martinez*, 610 F.3d 1216, 1232 (10th Cir. 2010)("Convinced by the reasoning of our sister circuits, we conclude that the plain language of the [restitution statute] prohibits a district court form considering the value of defendant's forfeited property in initially determining the full amount of restitution. Whether a defendant's restitution obligation may be offset by the value of forfeited property a victim has received is an issue we need not decide").

[80] E.g. *United States v. Wetherald*, 636 F.3d 1315, 1318 (11th Cir. 2011)(conviction for money laundering, mail and wire fraud, and securities fraud); *United States v. Whitfield*, 590 F.3d 325, 335-36 (5th Cir. 2009)(convicted for racketeering, mail and wire fraud, and federal program bribery).

[81] E.g., *United States v. Jones*, 641 F.3d 706, 709 (6th Cir. 2011)(conviction for mail fraud and health care fraud); *United States v. Ford*, 639 F.3d 718, 719 (6th Cir. 2011)(conviction for

wire fraud and false statements in matter within the jurisdiction of a United States agency or department); *United States v. Skys*, 637 F.3d 146, 148 (2d Cir. 2011)(conviction for securities fraud, wire fraud and bank fraud).

[82] E.g., *United States v. Siegelman*, 640 F.3d 1159, 1164 (11th Cir. 2011)(conviction for mail fraud (honest services) and federal program bribery); *United States v. Inzunza*, 638 F.3d 1006, 1012 (9th Cir. 2011)(convicted for wire fraud and extortion under color of official right); *Sotirion v. United States*, 617 F.3d 27, 30 (1st Cir. 2010)(convicted for mail and wire fraud (honest services), racketeering, bribery of public officials, and conspiracy).

[83] 18 U.S.C. 1962. See generally, CRS Report 96-950, *RICO: A Brief Sketch*, by Charles Doyle.

[84] *Rezner v. Bayerische Hypo-Und Vereinsbank AG,* 630 F.3d 866, 873 (9th Cir. 2010), citing, *Sedima, S.P.R.L. v. Imrex Co., Inc.*, 473 U.S. 479, 496 (1985); *United States v. Shamah*, 624 F.3d 449, 454 (7th Cir. 2010); *United States v. Burden*, 600 F.3d 204, 216 (2d Cir. 2010).

[85] 18 U.S.C. 1961(1)(B).

[86] *H.J., Inc. v. Northwestern Bell Telephone Co.*, 492 U.S. 229, 239 (1989)(emphasis of the Court); *US Airlines Pilots Ass'n v. AWAPP,LLC*, 615 F.3d 312, 318-20 (4th Cir. 2010); *United States v. Bruden*, 600 F.3d 204, 216-17 (2d Cir. 2010).

[87] *In re Insurance Brokerage Antitrust Litigation*, 618 F.3d 300, 371 (3d Cir. 2010), quoting, *Reves v. Ernst & Young*, 507 U.S. 170, 183-85 (1993).

[88] *Id.*

[89] *Id.; United States v. Burden*, 600 F.3d 204, 219 (2d Cir. 2010).

[90] 18 U.S.C. 1961(4).

[91] *United States v. Applins*, 637 F.3d 59, (2d Cir. 2011), quoting, *Boyle v. United States*, 129 S.Ct. 2237, 2244 (2009); *United States v. Burden*, 600 F.3d 204, 214-15 (2d Cir. 2010).

[92] 18 U.S.C. 1962(c).

[93] 18 U.S.C. 1963(a), 3571.

[94] 18 U.S.C. 3663A(c)(1)(A)(ii); *United States v. Browne*, 505 F.3d 1229, 1281 (11th Cir. 2007); *United States v. Reifler*, 446 F.3d 65, 121 (2d Cir. 2006).

[95] 18 U.S.C. 1963(a), (b).

[96] 18 U.S.C. 1956(c)(7)(A).

[97] 18 U.S.C. 1964(c).

[98] 18 U.S.C. 1956(c)(7)(A), 1961(1)(B).

[99] 18 U.S.C.1956(a)(1). See generally, CRS Report RL33315, *Money Laundering: An Overview of 18 U.S.C. 1956 and Related Federal Criminal Law,* by Charles Doyle.

[100] *United States v. Dvorak*, 617F.3d 1017, 1021-22 (8th Cir. 2010); see also, *United States v. Baldridge*, 559 F.3d 1126, 1141 (10th Cir. 2009); *United States v. Quinones*, 635 F.3d 590, 597 (2d Cir. 2011).

[101] *United States v. Warshak*, 631 F.3d 266, 317 (6th Cir. 2010); see also, *United States v. Lee*, 558 F.3d 638, 641 (7th Cir. 2009); *United States v. Quinones*, 635 F.3d 590, 597 (2d Cir. 2011).

[102] *United States v. Naranjo*, 634 F.3d 1198, 1208 (11th Cir. 2011)("The spending of illegal proceeds alone is insufficient to prove concealment money laundering"); *United States v. Faulkenberry*, 614 F.3d 573, 586 (6th Cir. 2010)("What is required, rather, is that concealment be an animating purpose of the transaction"); *United States v. Trejo*, 610 F.3d 308, 314 (5th Cir. 2010)(emphasis of the court)("Instead, there must be evidence of *intentional* promotion").

[103] 18 U.S.C. 1956(a)(1).

[104] 18 U.S.C. 981(a)(1)(A); 982(a)(1).

[105] 18 U.S.C. 1957(a)("Whoever, in any of the circumstances set forth in subsection (d)[(including that the offense takes place in the United States)], knowingly engages or attempts to engage in a monetary transaction in criminally derived property of a value greater than $10,000 and is derived from specified unlawful activity, shall be punished as provided in subsection (b)").

[106] 18 U.S.C. 1957(f)(3).

[107] 18 U.S.C. 1957(f)(3), 1956(c)(7)(A), 1961(1)(B).

[108] *United States v. Wetherald*, 636 F.3d 1315, 1325 n.2 (11th Cir. 2011)

[109] 18 U.S.C. 1957(b), 3571.

[110] 18 U.S.C. 981(a)(1)(A), 982(a)(1).

[111] 18 U.S.C. 287, 351, and 1001, respectively.

[112] 18 U.S.C. 1344, 1347, 1348, and 1351, respectively.

[113] 18 U.S.C. 287.

[114] *United States v. Clark*, 577 F.3d 273, 285 (5th Cir. 2009); *United States v. Refert*, 519 F.3d 752, 757 (8th Cir. 2008).

[115] 18 U.S.C. 287, 3571.

[116] 18 U.S.C. 3663A(c)(1)(A)(ii).

[117] Cf., 18 U.S.C. 981, 982.

[118] 31 U.S.C. 3729-3733; see generally, CRS Report R40785, *Qui Tam: The False Claims Act and Related Federal Statutes*, by Charles Doyle.

[119] Cf., 18 U.S.C. 1956(c)(7), 1961(1).

[120] 18 U.S.C. 371; see generally, CRS Report R41223, *Federal Conspiracy Law: A Brief Overview*, by Charles Doyle.

[121] "If two or more persons conspire either *to commit an offense against the United States* or to defraud the United States, or any agency thereof in any manner or for any purpose. . . ." 18 U.S.C. 371(emphasis added).

[122] "If two or more persons conspire either to commit an offense against the United States or *to defraud the United States, or any agency thereof in any manner or for any purpose*. . . ." 18 U.S.C. 371(emphasis added).

[123] *United States v. Stewart*, 590 F.3d 93, 109 (2d Cir. 2009); *United States v. Root*, 585 F.3d 145, 157 (3d Cir. 2009); *United States v. World Wide Moving, N.V.*, 411 F.3d 502, 516 (4th Cir. 2005).

[124] *Hammerschmidt v. United States*, 265 U.S. 182, 188 (1924); *Glasser v. United States*, 315 U.S. 60, 66 (1942); *Tanner v. United States*, 483 U.S. 107, 128 (1987).

[125] *United States v. McKee*, 506 F.3d 225, 238 (3d Cir. 2007); *Hammerschmidt v. United States*, 265 U.S. at 188; *Tanner v. United States*, 483 U.S. at 128.

[126] 18 U.S.C. 371.

[127] Cf., 18 U.S.C. 1961(1), 1956(c)(7).

[128] 18 U.S.C. 3663A(c)(1)(A)(ii).

[129] Cf., 18 U.S.C. 981, 982.

[130] 18 U.S.C. 1001; *United States v. Kieffer*, 621 F.3d 825, 833 (8th Cir. 2010); *United States v. Geisen*, 612 F.3d 471, 489 (6th Cir. 2010); *United States v. Moore*, 612 F.3d 698, 700 (D.C.Cir. 2010).

[131] *United States v. Staad*, 636 F.3d 630, 638 (D.C.Cir. 2011), quoting, *Neder v. United States*, 527 U.S. 1, 6 (1999); *United States v. Garcia-Ochoa*, 607 F.3d 371, 375 (4th Cir. 2010); *United States v. Boffil-Rivera*, 607 F.3d 736, 741-42 (11th Cir. 2010)("The government is not required to prove that the statute had actual influence. The false statement must simply have the capacity to impair or pervert the functioning of a government agency. The

statement does not have to be relied upon and can be material even if it is ignored and never read").

132 *United States v. Ford,* 639 F.3d 718, 720 (6th Cir. 2011), quoting, *United States v. Rodgers*, 466 U.S. 475, 479 (1984); see also, *United States v. Jackson*, 608 F.3d 193, (4th Cir. 2010), also quoting, *Rodgers*, 466 U.S. at 479 ("[T]he 'within the jurisdiction' language of the statute merely differentiates the official, or authorized functions of an agency or department from matters that are peripheral to the business of that body").

133 18 U.S.C. 1001. It is punishable by imprisonment for not more than 8 years if the offense involves international or domestic terrorism as defined in 18 U.S.C. 2331 or if the matter relates to an offense under 18 U.S.C. 1591 (relating to commercial sexual trafficking), ch. 109A (relating to sexual abuse), ch. 109B (relating to sex offender registration), ch. 110 (relating to sexual exploitation of children), or ch. 117 (relating to transportation for illicit sexual purposes).

134 Cf., 18 U.S.C. 1961(1), 1956(c)(7).

135 18 U.S.C. 3663A(c)(1)(A)(ii).

136 Cf., 18 U.S.C. 981, 982; but see, 18 U.S.C. 981(a)(1)(D)(civil forfeiture)("(a)(1) The following property is subject to forfeiture to the United States . . . (D) Any property, real or personal, which represents or is traceable to the gross receipts obtained, directly or indirectly, from a violation of . . . (ii) Section 1001 (relating to fraud and false statements) . . . if such violation relates to the sale of assets acquired or held by the Resolution Trust Corporation, the Federal Deposit Insurance Corporation, as conservator or receiver for a financial institution, or any other conservator for a financial institution appointed by the Office of the Comptroller of the Currency or the Office of Thrift Supervision or the National Credit Union Administration, as conservator or liquidating agent for a financial institution"); 982(a)(3)(criminal forfeiture)(same).

137 31 U.S.C. 3729-3733.

138 18 U.S.C. 1344, 1347, 1348, and 1351, respectively.

139 18 U.S.C. 1344 ("Whoever knowingly executes, or attempts to execute, a scheme or artifice – (1) to defraud a financial institution; or (2) to obtain any of the moneys, funds, credits, assets, securities, or other property owned by, or under the custody or control of, a financial institution, by means of false or fraudulent pretenses, representations, or promises; shall be fined not more than $1,000,000 or imprisoned not more than 30 years, or both"). 18 U.S.C. 20 ("As used in this title, the term 'financial institution' means – (1) an insured depository institution (as defined in Section 3(c)(2) of the Federal Deposit Insurance Act); (2) a credit union with accounts insured by the National Credit Union Share Insurance Fund; (3) a Federal home loan bank or a member, as defined in Section 2 of the Federal Home Loan Bank Act (12 U.S.C. 1422), of the Federal home loan bank system; (4) a System institution of the Farm Credit System, as defined in Section 5.35(3) of the Farm Credit Act of 1971; (5) a small business investment company, as defined in Section 103 of the Small Business Investment Act of 1958 (15 U.S.C. 662); (6) a depository institution holding company (as defined in Section 3(w)(1) of the Federal Deposit Insurance Act; (7) a Federal Reserve bank or a member bank of the Federal Reserve System; (8) an organization operating under Section 25 or Section 25(a) of the Federal Reserve Act; (9) a branch or agency of a foreign bank (as such terms are defined in paragraphs (1) and (3) of Section 1(b) of the International Banking Act of 1978); or (10) a mortgage lending business (as defined in Section 27 of this title) or any person or entity that makes in whole or in part a federally related mortgage loan as defined in Section 3 of the Real Estate Settlement Procedures Act of 1974"). See

generally, CRS Report R40549, *Mortgage Fraud: Federal Criminal Provisions*, by Anna C. Henning.

[140] *United States v. Bowling*, 619 F.3d 1175, 1181 (10th Cir. 2010); *United States v. Hall*, 613 F.3d 249, 252 (D.C.Cir. 2010); *United States v. Jackson*, 540 F.3d 578, 594 (7th Cir. 2008).

[141] *United States v. Hill*, ___ F.3d ___, ___ (11th Cir. June 14, 2011); *United States v. Williams*, 390 F.3d 1319, 1324 (11th Cir. 2004); *United States v. Crisci*, 273 F.3d 235, 239-40 (2d Cir. 2001).

[142] 18 U.S.C. 1344.

[143] 18 U.S.C. 1961(1), 1956(c)(7)(A).

[144] 18 U.S.C. 3663A(c)(1)(A)(ii).

[145] 18 U.S.C. 981(a)(1)(C), 982(a)(2)(A).

[146] 18 U.S.C. 1347(a).

[147] *United States v. Martinez*, 588 F.3d 301, 314 (6th Cir. 2009).

[148] *United States v. Franklin-el*, 555 F.3d 1115, 1122 (10th Cir. 2009).

[149] 18 U.S.C. 1347(b).

[150] 18 U.S.C. 1347(a).

[151] *Id.* In such cases, the government must show that the offense was the proximate cause of the injury or death, that is, that the injury or death followed as the foreseeable and nature consequence of the offense, *United States v. Martinez*, 588 F.3d at 317-19.

[152] Cf., 18 U.S.C. 1956(c)(7), 1961(1).

[153] 18 U.S.C. 3663A(c)(1); *United States v. Mateos*, 623 F.3d 1350, 1369-370 (11th Cir. 2010).

[154] Cf., 18 U.S.C. 981, 982, 1347. Nevertheless, the same facts may constitute a violation either the mail or wire fraud statute which would permit forfeiture under either civil or criminal forfeiture procedures, 18 U.S.C. 981(a)(1)(C), 1956(c)(7), 1961(1); 28 U.S.C. 2461(c).

[155] 18 U.S.C. 1348.

[156] 18 U.S.C. 1348 ("Whoever knowingly executes, or attempts to execute, a scheme or artifice – to defraud any person in connection with any commodity for future delivery, or any option on a commodity for future delivery, or any security of an issuer with a class of securities registered under Section 12 of the Securities Exchange Act of 1934 or that is required to file reports under Section 15(d) of the Securities Exchange Act of 1934; or to obtain, by means of false or fraudulent pretenses, representations, or promises, any money or property in connection with the purchase or sale of any commodity for future delivery, or any option on a commodity for future delivery, or any security of an issuer with a class of securities registered under Section 12 of the Securities Exchange Act of 1934 or that is required to file reports under Section 15(d) of the Securities Exchange Act of 1934; shall be fined under this title, or imprisoned not more than 25 years, or both").

[157] *United States v. Hatfield*, 724 F.Supp.2d 321, 324 (E.D.N.Y. 2010); see also, *United States v. Motz*, 652 F.Supp.2d 284, 296 (E.D.N.Y. 2009)("The parties agree that because the text and legislative history of 18 U.S.C. §1348 clearly establish that it was modeled on the mail and wire fraud statutes, the Court's analysis should be guided by the caselaw construing those statutes").

[158] 18 U.S.C. 1348.

[159] Cf., 18 U.S.C. 1961(1), 1956(c)(7).

[160] 18 U.S.C. 3663A(c)(1)(A)(ii).

[161] Cf., 18 U.S.C. 1348, 981, 982.

[162] Cf., 18 U.S.C. 1956(c)(7), 1961(1).

[163] 18 U.S.C. 3663A(c)(1)(A)(ii).

[164] Cf., 18 U.S.C. 1351, 981, 982.

[165] *United States v. Sun Diamond Growers*, 526 U.S. 398, 404 (1999); *United States v. Whitfield*, 590 F.3d 325, 348 (9th Cir. 2009); *United States v. Harvey*, 532 F.3d 326, 334-35 (4th Cir. 2008).

[166] *United States v. Sun Diamond Growers*, 526 U.S. at 404; *United States v. Peleti*, 576 F.3d 377, 382 (7th Cir. 2009); *United States v. Valle*, 538 F.3d 341, 346-47 (5th Cir. 2008).

[167] 18 U.S.C. 201(a)(1); *Dixon v. United States*, 465 U.S. 482, 496 (1984); *United States v. Franco*, 632 F.3d 880, 884 (5th Cir. 2011).

[168] 18 U.S.C. 201(a)(3); *United States v. Sun Diamond Growers*, 526 U.S. at 404; *United States v. Ozcelik*, 527 F.3d 88, 96-7 (3d Cir. 2008).

[169] 18 U.S.C. 201(b), 3571.

[170] 18 U.S.C. 1961(1)(B), 1956(c)(7)(A).

[171] 18 U.S.C. 981(a)(1)(C), 1956(c)(7)(A); 28 U.S.C. 2461(c).

[172] 18 U.S.C. 666 ("(a) Whoever, if the circumstance described in subsection (b) of this section exists - (1) being an agent of an organization, or of a State, local, or Indian tribal government, or any agency thereof . . . (B) corruptly solicits . . . or accepts . . . anything of value from any person, intending to be influenced or rewarded in connection with any business, transaction, or series of transactions of such organization, government, or agency involving any thing of value of $5,000 or more . . . [or corruptly offers a thing of value to any such agent for any such purposes and in relation to such matters] shall be fined under this title, imprisoned not more than 10 years, or both. "(b) The circumstance referred to in subsection (a) of this section is that the organization, government, or agency receives, in any one year period, benefits in excess of $10,000 under a Federal program involving a grant, contract, subsidy, loan, guarantee, insurance, or other form of Federal assistance . . .").

[173] 18 U.S.C. 666(d)(1).

[174] *United States v. Townsend*, 630 F.3d 1003, 1011 (11th Cir. 2011).

[175] *United States v. McNair*, 605 F.3d 1152, (11th Cir. 2010)("In concluding §666 does not require a specific *quid pro quo*, we align ourselves with the Sixth and Seventh Circuits. See, *United States v. Abbey*, 560 F.3d 513, 520 (6th Cir. . . . 2009) . . . *United States v. Gee*, 432 F.3d 713, 714-15 (7th Cir. 2005)"); but see, *United States v. Redzic*, 627 F.3d 683, 692 (8th Cir. 2010)("To prove the payment of an illegal bribe, the government must present evidence of a quid pro quo, but an illegal bribe may be paid with the intent to influence a general course of conduct. It was not necessary for the government to link any particular payment to any particular action. . ."); *United States v. Jennings*, 160 F.3d 1006, 1014 (4th Cir. 1998); cf., *United States v. Ganim*, 510 F.3d 134, 141-42 (2d Cir. 2007).

[176] *Sabri v. United States*, 541 U.S. 600, 605(2004).

[177] 18 U.S.C. 666(a), 3571.

[178] 18 U.S.C. 1956(c)(7)(D).

[179] 18 U.S.C. 1961(1).

[180] 18 U.S.C. 981(a)(1)(C), 1956(c)(7)(A); 28 U.S.C. 2461(c).

[181] 18 U.S.C. 1951("(a) Whoever in any way or degree obstructs, delays, or affects commerce or the movement of any article or commodity in commerce, by . . . extortion or attempts or conspires so to do . . . shall be fined under this title or imprisoned not more than twenty years, or both. (b) As used in this section . . . (2) The term 'extortion' means the obtaining of property from another, with his consent, induced by wrongful use of actual or threatened force, violence, or fear, or under color of official right . . .").

[182] *United States v. Kincaid-Chauncey*, 556 F.3d 923, 936 (9th Cir. 2009), citing, *Evans v. United States*, 504 U.S. 255, 268 (1992).

[183] *Evans v. United States*, 504 U.S. at 268; *United States v. Siegelman*, 640 F.3d 1159, 1171 (11th Cir. 2010); *United States v. Manzo*, 636 F.3d 56, 60 (3d Cir. 2011).

[184] 18 U.S.C. 1951, 3571.

[185] 18 U.S.C. 1961(1)(B), 1956(c)(7)(A).

[186] 18 U.S.C. 981(a)(1)(C), 1956(c)(7)(A); 28 U.S.C. 2461(c).

[187] See generally, CRS Report R41466, *Foreign Corrupt Practices Act (FCPA): Congressional Interest and Executive Enforcement*, by Michael V. Seitzinger.

[188] *United States v. Kay*, 513 F.3d 432, 439-40 (5th Cir. 2007).

[189] 15 U.S.C. 78dd-1(b), 78dd-2(b), 78dd-3(b).

[190] 15 U.S.C. 78dd-1(c), 78dd-2(c), 78dd-3(c).

[191] 15 U.S.C. 78dd-2(g), 78dd-3(e), 78ff(c).

[192] Cf., 18 U.S.C. 1961(1).

[193] 18 U.S.C. 1956(c)(7)(D).

[194] 18 U.S.C. 981(a)(1)(C), 1956(c)(7)(D); 28 U.S.C. 2461(c).

[195] See generally, CRS Report RS22743, *Health Care Fraud and Abuse Laws Affecting Medicare and Medicaid: An Overview,* by Jennifer Staman.

[196] *United States v. Mauska*, 557 F.3d 219, 226 (5th Cir. 2009); 42 U.S.C. 1320a-7b("(1) Whoever knowingly and willfully solicits or receives any remuneration (including any kickback, bribe, or rebate) directly or indirectly, overtly or covertly, in cash or in kind – (A) in return for referring an individual to a person for the furnishing or arranging for the furnishing of any item or service for which payment may be made in whole or in part under a Federal health care program, or (B) in return for purchasing, leasing, ordering, or arranging for or recommending purchasing, leasing, or ordering any good, facility, service, or item for which payment may be made in whole or in part under a Federal health care program . . . . (2) Whoever knowingly and willfully offers or pays any remuneration (including any kickback, bribe, or rebate) directly or indirectly, overtly or covertly, in cash or in kind to any person to induce such person – (A) to refer an individual to a person for the furnishing or arranging for the furnishing of any item or service for which payment may be made in whole or in part under a Federal health care program, or (B) to purchase, lease, order, or arrange for or recommend purchasing, leasing, or ordering any good, facility, service, or item for which payment may be made in whole or in part under a Federal health care program, shall be guilty of a felony and upon conviction thereof, shall be fined not more than $25,000 or imprisoned for not more than five years, or both").

[197] 18 U.S.C. 1956(c)(7)(E), 24(a)(1), 1961(1).

[198] 18 U.S.C. 981(a)(1)(C), 1956(c)(7)(E); 28 U.S.C. 2461(c).

In: Conspiratorial Crimes …
Editors: L. C. Wright and J. C. Miller
ISBN: 978-1-62618-426-8

Chapter 5

ATTEMPT: AN OVERVIEW OF FEDERAL CRIMINAL LAW*

Charles Doyle

SUMMARY

It is not a crime to attempt to commit most federal offenses. Unlike state law, federal law has no generally applicable crime of contempt. Congress, however, has outlawed the attempt to commit a substantial number of federal crimes on an individual basis. In doing so, it has proscribed the attempt, set its punishment, and left to the federal courts the task of further developing the law in the area.

The courts have identified two elements in the crime of attempt: an intent to commit the underlying substantive offense and some substantial step towards that end.

The point at which a step may be substantial is not easily discerned; but it seems that the more serious and reprehensible the substantive offense, the less substantial the step need be. Ordinarily, the federal courts accept neither impossibility nor abandonment as an effective defense to a charge of attempt. Attempt and the substantive offense carry the same penalties in most instances.

A defendant may not be convicted of both the substantive offense and the attempt to commit it. Commission of the substantive offense,

* This is an edited, reformatted and augmented version of a Congressional Research Service publication, CRS Report for Congress R42001, from www.crs.gov, prepared for Members and Committees of Congress, dated September 13, 2011.

however, is neither a prerequisite for, nor a defense against, an attempt conviction.

Whether a defendant may be guilty of an attempt to attempt to commit a federal offense is often a matter of statutory construction. Attempts to conspire and attempts to aid and abet generally present less perplexing questions.

INTRODUCTION

Attempt is a crime of general application in every state in the Union, and is largely defined by statute in most.[1] The same cannot be said of federal law. There is no generally applicable federal attempt statute. In fact, it is not a federal crime to attempt to commit most federal offenses. Here and there, Congress has made a separate crime of conduct that might otherwise have been considered attempt. Possession of counterfeiting equipment and solicitation of a bribe are two examples that come to mind.[2] More often, Congress has outlawed the attempt to commit a particular crime, such as attempted murder, or the attempt to commit one of a particular block of crimes, such as the attempt to violate the controlled substance laws.[3] In those instances, the statute simply outlaws attempt, sets the penalties, and implicitly delegates to the courts the task of developing the federal law of attempt on a case by case basis. Over the years, proposals have surfaced that would establish attempt as a federal crime of general application and in some instances would codify federal common law of attempt.[4] Thus far, however, Congress has preferred to expand the number of federal attempt offenses on a much more selective basis.[5]

BACKGROUND

Attempt was not recognized as a crime of general application until the 19th century.[6] Before then, attempt had evolved as part of the common law development of a few other specific offenses. The vagaries of these individual threads frustrated early efforts to weave them into a cohesive body of law.[7] At mid-20th century, the Model Penal Code suggested a basic framework that has greatly influenced the development of both state and federal law.[8] The Model Penal Code grouped attempt with conspiracy and solicitation as "inchoate" crimes of general application.[9] It addressed a number of questions that had until then divided commentators, courts, and legislators.

A majority of the states use the Model Penal Code approach as a guide, but deviate with some regularity.[10] The same might be said of the approach of the National Commission established to recommend revision of federal criminal law shortly after the Model Penal Code was approved.[11] The National Commission recommended a revision of title 18 of the United States Code that included a series of "offenses of general applicability"—attempt, facilitation, solicitation, conspiracy, and regulatory offenses.[12]

In spite of efforts that persisted for more than a decade, Congress never enacted the National Commission's recommended revision of title 18.[13] It did, however, continue to outlaw a growing number of attempts to commit specific federal offenses. In doing so, it rarely did more than outlaw an attempt to commit a particular substantive crime and set its punishment. Beyond that, development of the federal law of attempt has been the work of the federal courts.

Definition

Attempt may once have required little more than an evil heart.[14] That time is long gone. The Model Penal Code defined attempt as the intent required of the predicate offense coupled with a substantial step: "A person is guilty of an attempt to commit a crime, if acting with the kind of culpability otherwise required for commission of the crime, he ... purposely does or omits to do anything that, under the circumstances as he believes them to be, is an act or omission constituting a substantial step in a course of conduct planned to culminate in his commission of the crime."[15] The Model Penal Code then provided several examples of what might constitute a "substantial step"—lying in wait, luring the victim, gathering the necessary implements to commit the offense, and the like.[16]

The National Commission recommended a similar definition: "A person is guilty of criminal attempt if, acting with the kind of culpability otherwise required for commission of a crime, he intentionally engages in conduct which, in fact, constitutes a substantial step toward commission of the crime."[17]Rather than mention the type of conduct that might constitute a substantial step, the Commission defined it: "A substantial step is any conduct which is strongly corroborative of the firmness of the actor's intent to complete the commission of the crime."[18]

Most of the states follow the same path and define attempt as intent coupled to an overt act or some substantial step towards the completion of the substantive offense.[19] Only rarely does a state include examples of substantial step conduct.[20]

Intent and a Substantial Step

The federal courts are in accord and have said, "As was true at common law, the mere intent to violate a federal criminal statute is not punishable as an attempt unless it is also accompanied by significant conduct," that is, unless accompanied by "an overt act qualifying as a substantial step toward completion" of the underlying offense.[21]

The courts seem to have encountered little difficulty in identifying the requisite intent standard. In fact, they rarely do more than note that the defendant must be shown to have intended to commit the underlying offenses.[22] What constitutes a substantial step is a little more difficult to discern.[23] It is said that a substantial step is more than mere preparation.[24] A substantial step is action strongly or unequivocally corroborative of the individual's intent to commit the underlying offense.[25] It is action which if uninterrupted will result in the commission of that offense,[26] although it need not be the penultimate act necessary for completion of the underlying offense.[27] Furthermore, the point at which preliminary action becomes a substantial step is fact specific; action that constitutes a substantial step under some circumstances and with respect to some underlying offenses may not qualify under other circumstances and with respect to other offenses.[28]

It is difficult to read the cases and not find that the views of Oliver Wendell Holmes continue to hold sway: the line between mere preparation and attempt is drawn where the shadow of the substantive offense begins.[29] The line between preparation and attempt is farthest from the predicate offense where the harm and the opprobrium associated with that offense are greatest.

Since conviction for attempt does not require commission of the predicate offense, conviction for attempt does not necessitate proof of every element of the predicate offense,[30] or any element of the predicate offense for that matter. Recall that the only elements of the crime of attempt are intent to commit the predicate offense and a substantial step in that direction. Nevertheless, a court will sometimes demand proof of one or more of the elements of a predicate offense in order to avoid sweeping application of an attempt provision. For instance, the Third Circuit recently held that "acting 'under color of official right' is a required element of an extortion Hobbs Act offense, inchoate or substantive," apparently for that very reason.[31]

Defenses

Impossibility

Defendants charged with attempt have often offered one of two defenses—impossibility and abandonment. Rarely have they prevailed. The defense of impossibility is a defense of mistake, either a mistake of law or a mistake of fact. Legal impossibility exists when "the actions which the defendant performs or sets in motion, even if fully carried out as he desires, would not constitute a crime. The traditional view is that legal impossibility is a defense to the charge of attempt – that is, if the competed offense would not be a crime, neither is a prosecution for attempt permitted."[32]

Factual impossibility exists when "the objective of the defendant is proscribed by criminal law but a circumstance unknown to the actor prevents him from bringing about that objective."[33] Since the completed offense would be a crime if circumstances were as the defendant believed them to be, prosecution for attempt is traditionally permitted.[34]

Unfortunately, as the courts have observed, "the distinction between legal impossibility and factual impossibility [is] elusive."[35] Moreover, "the distinction ... is largely a matter of semantics, for every case of legal impossibility can reasonably be characterized as a factual impossibility."[36] Thus, shooting a stuffed deer when intending to shoot a deer out of season is offered as an example of legal impossibility. Yet, shooting into the pillows of an empty bed when intending to kill its presumed occupant is considered an example of factual impossibility.[37]

The Model Penal Code avoided the problem by defining attempt to include instances when the defendant acted with the intent to commit the predicate offense and "engage[d] in conduct that would constitute the crime if the attendant circumstances were as he believe[d] them to be."[38]

Under the National Commission's Final Report, "[f]actual or legal impossibility of committing the crime is not a defense if the crime could have been committed had the attendant circumstances been as the actor believed them to be."[39] Several states have also specifically refused to recognize an impossibility defense of any kind.[40]

The federal courts have been a bit more cautious. They have sometimes conceded the possible vitality of legal impossibility as a defense,[41] but generally have judged the cases before them to involve no more than unavailing factual impossibility.[42] In a few instances, they have found it unnecessary to enter the quagmire, and concluded instead that Congress intended to eliminate legal impossibility with respect to attempts to commit a particular crime.[43]

Abandonment

The Model Penal Code recognized an abandonment or renunciation defense.[44] A defendant, however, could not claim the defense if his withdrawal was merely a postponement or was occasioned by the appearance of circumstances that made success less likely.[45] The revised federal criminal code recommended by the National Commission contained similar provisions.[46] Some states recognize an abandonment or renunciation defense;[47] the federal courts do not.

Admittedly, a defendant cannot be charged with attempt if he has abandoned his pursuit of the substantive offense at the mere preparation stage. Yet, this is for want of an element of the offense of attempt—a substantial step—rather than because of the availability of an affirmative abandonment defense. Although the federal courts have recognized an affirmative voluntary abandonment defense in the case of conspiracy, the other principal inchoate offense,[48] they have declined to recognize a comparable defense to a charge of attempt.[49]

Sentencing

The Model Penal Code and the National Commission's Final Report both imposed the same sanctions for attempt as for the predicate offense as a general rule. However, both set the penalties for the most serious offenses at a class below that of the predicate offense, and both permitted the sentencing court to impose a reduced sentence in cases when the attempt failed to come dangerously close to the attempted predicate offense.[50] The states set the penalties for attempt in one of two ways. Some set sanctions at a fraction of, or a class below, that of the substantive offense, with exceptions for specific offenses in some instances;[51] others set the penalty at the same level as the crime attempted, again with exceptions for particular offenses in some states.[52]

Most federal attempt crimes carry the same penalties as the substantive offense.[53] The Sentencing Guidelines, which greatly influence federal sentencing beneath the maximum penalties set by statute, reflect the equivalent sentencing prospective.[54] Except for certain terrorism, drug trafficking, assault, and tampering offenses, however, the Guidelines recommend slightly lower sentences for defendants who have yet to take all the steps required of them for commission of the predicate offense.[55]

Relation to Other Offenses

The relation of attempt to the predicate offense is another of the interesting features of the law of attempt. It raises those questions which the Model Penal Code and the National Commission sought to address. May a defendant be charged with attempt even if he has not completed the underlying offense? May a defendant be charged with attempt even if he has also committed the underlying offense? May a defendant be convicted for both attempt and commission of the underlying offense? May a defendant be charged with attempting to attempt an offense? May a defendant be charged with conspiracy to attempt or attempt to conspire? May a defendant be charged with aiding and abetting an attempt or with attempting to aid and abet?

Relation to the Predicate Offense

A defendant need not commit the predicate offense to be guilty of attempt.[56] On the other hand, some 19th century courts held that a defendant could not be convicted of attempt if the evidence indicated that he had in fact committed the predicate offense.[57] This is no longer the case in federal court—if it ever was. In federal law, "[n]either common sense nor precedent supports success as a defense to a charge of attempt."[58]

The Double Jeopardy Clause ordinarily precludes conviction for both the substantive offense and the attempt to commit it. The clause prohibits both dual prosecutions and dual punishment for the same offense.[59] Punishment for both a principal and a lesser included offense constitutes such dual punishment,[60] and attempt ordinarily constitutes a lesser included offense of the substantive crime.[61]

Instances where the federal law literally appears to create an attempt to attempt offense present an intriguing question of interpretation. Occasionally, a federal statute will call for equivalent punishment for attempt to commit any of a series of offenses proscribed in other statutes, even though the other statutes already proscribe attempt. For example, 18 U.S.C. 1349 declares that any attempt to violate any of the provisions of chapter 63 of title 18 of the United States Code "shall be subject to the same penalties as those prescribed for the offense, the commission of which was the object of the attempt."[62] Within chapter 63 are sections that make it a crime to attempt to commit bank fraud, health care fraud, and securities fraud.[63] There may be some dispute over whether provisions like those of Section 1349 are intended to outlaw attempts to commit an attempt or simply to reiterate a determination to punish equally the substantive offenses and attempts to commit them.[64]

Relation to Other General Provisions

Conspiracy

The Model Penal Code and National Commission resolved attempt to attempt and conspiracy to attempt questions by banning dual application. Crimes of general application would not have applied to other crimes of general application.[65] A few states have comparable provisions.[66] The federal code does not. The attempting to conspire or conspiring to attempt questions do not offer as many issues of unsettled interpretation as the attempt to attempt questions, for several reasons. First, the courts have had more occasion to address them. For instance, it is already clearly established that a defendant may be simultaneously prosecuted for conspiracy to commit and for attempt to commit the same substantive offense.[67] Second, as a particular matter, conspiracies to attempt a particular crime are relatively uncommon; most individuals conspire to accomplish, not to attempt.

Third, in a sense, attempting to conspire is already a separate crime, or alternatively, is a separate basis for criminal liability. Solicitation is essentially an invitation to conspire, and solicitation to commit a crime of violence is a separate federal offense.[68] Moreover, an attempt that takes the form of counseling, commanding, inducing, or procuring another to commit a federal crime is already a separate basis for criminal liability.[69]

Fourth, a component of the general conspiracy statute allows simultaneous prosecution of conspiracy and a substantive offense without having to addressing the conspire to attempt quandary. The conspiracy statute outlaws two kinds conspiracies: conspiracy to violate a federal criminal statute and conspiracy to defraud the United States.[70] Conspiracy to defraud the United States is a separate crime, one that need not otherwise involve the violation of a federal criminal statute.[71] Consequently, when attempt or words of attempt appear as elements in a substantive criminal provision, conspiracy to attempt issues can be avoided by recourse to a conspiracy to defraud charge. For example, the principal federal bribery statute outlaws attempted public corruption.[72] The offense occurs though no tainted official act has been performed or foregone.[73] It is enough that the official has sought or been offered a bribe with the intent of corrupting the performance of his duties.[74] Bribery conspiracy charges appear generally to have been prosecuted, along with bribery, as conspiracy to defraud rather than conspiracy to violate the bribery statute.[75]

Aiding and Abetting

Unlike attempt, aiding and abetting is not a separate offense; it is an alternative basis for liability for the substantive offense. Anyone who aids, abets, counsels, commands, induces, or procures the commission of a federal crime by another is as guilty as if he committed it himself.[76] Aiding and abetting requires proof of intentional assistance in the commission of a crime by another.[77] Federal courts have found convictions for both attempting to aid and abet and for aiding and abetting an attempt permissible under appropriate circumstances.[78]

APPENDIX

State General Attempt Statutes (Citations)

ALA. CODE §§13A-4-2, 13A-4-5; ALASKA STAT. §§11.31.100, 11.31.140, 11.31.1501; ARIZ. REV. STAT. ANN. §§13-1001, 13-1005; ARK. CODE ANN. §§5-3-201 to 5-3-204; CAL. PENAL CODE §664; COLO. REV. STAT. ANN. §18-2-101; CONN. GEN. STAT. ANN. §53a-49; DEL. CODE ANN. tit.11 §§531, 532, 541; FLA. STAT. ANN. §777.04; GA. CODE §§16-4-1 to 16-4-6; HAWAII REV. STAT. §§705-500 to 705-502, 705-530 to 705-531; IDAHO CODE §§18-305 to 18-307; ILL. COMP. STAT. ANN. ch. 720 §§5/8-4, 5/8-5; IND. CODE ANN. §§35-41-5-1, 35-41-5-3; KAN. STAT. ANN. §21-3301; KY. REV. STAT. ANN. §§506.010, 506.020, 506.110; LA. REV. STAT. ANN. §14:27; ME. REV. STAT. ANN. tit. 17-A §§152, 154; Md. Code Ann. Crim. Law §1-201; MASS. GEN. LAWS ANN. ch. 274 §6; MICH. COMP. LAWS ANN. §750.92; MINN. STAT. ANN. §609.17; MISS. CODE ANN. §§97-1-7, 97-1-9; MO. ANN. STAT. §564.011; MONT. CODE ANN. §45-4-103; NEB. REV. STAT. §28-201; NEV. REV. STAT. §193.330; N.H. REV. STAT. ANN. §629.1; N.J. STAT. ANN. §§2C:5-1, 2C:5-4; N.M. CODE ANN. §30-28-1; N.Y. PENAL LAW §§110.00 to 110.10, 40.10; N.C. GEN. STAT. §14-2.5; N.D. CENT. CODE §§12.1-06-01, 12.1-06-05; OHIO REV. CODE ANN. §2923.02; OKLA. STAT. ANN. tit.21§§41 to 44; ORE. REV. STAT. ANN. §§161.405 to 161.430; PA. STAT. ANN. tit. 18, §901;

S.C. Code Ann. §16-1-80; S.D. CODIFIED LAWS §§22-4-1, 22-4-2; TENN. CODE ANN. §§39-12-101, 104 to 109; TEX. PENAL CODE ANN. §§15.01, 15.04, 15.05; UTAH CODE ANN. §§76-4-101, 76-4-102; VT. STAT. ANN. tit. 13 §9; VA. CODE §18.2-26; WASH. REV. CODE ANN. §9A.28.020; W.VA. CODE ANN. §61-11-8; WIS. STAT. ANN. §939.32; WYO. STAT. ANN. §§6-1-301, 6-1-301.

End Notes

[1] Citations to the state general attempt statutes are appended. A few states provide a general statutory penalty provision for attempt and rely on the common law to define the elements of the offense and related matters, e.g., MD. CODE ANN. CRIM. LAW §1-102, United States v. Kelly, 989 F.2d 162, 163 (4th Cir. 1993); S.C. CODE ANN. §16-1-80, State v. Reid, 383 S.C. 285, 292-93, 679 S.E.2d 194, 197-98 (2009). Iowa appears to be the only state in which the general crime of attempt is purely a matter of common law, cf., State v. Spies, 672 N.W.2d 792, 797-98 (Iowa 2003); Fryer v. State, 325 N.W.2d 400, 406 (Iowa 1982).

[2] 18 U.S.C. 474 and 201(b), respectively.

[3] 18 U.S.C. 1113 and 21 U.S.C. 846, respectively.

[4] E.g., H.R. 1823 (112th Cong.); H.R. 1772 (111th Cong.); H.R. 4128 (110th Cong.); S. 735 (107th Cong.); S. 413 (106th Cong.); S. 171 (105th Cong.).

[5] E.g., Sec. 2, P.L. 110-340, 122 Stat. 3735 (2008), 18 U.S.C. 2442 (attempting to recruit or use child soldiers); sec. 201, P.L. 110-177, 121 Stat. 2536 (2008), 18 U.S.C. 1521 (attempting to file a retaliatory false claim against a federal judge or law enforcement officer).

[6] Sayre, Criminal Attempts, 41 HARVARD LAW REVIEW 821, 821 (1928) ("But the present generalized doctrine that attempts to commit crimes are as such and in themselves criminal is of comparatively late origin. Nothing of such a doctrine is to be found in the treatises on criminal law prior to the nineteenth century, in spite of the fact that records of cases going back to early times show occasional convictions where the defendant failed to complete the crime attempted").

[7] See e.g., 1 BISHOP, COMMENTARIES ON THE CRIMINAL LAW 533 (2d ed. 1858)("There is no one title indeed, less understood by the courts, or more obscure in the text-books, than that of attempt"); Hicks v. Commonwealth, 86 Va. 223, 226, 9 S.E. 1024, 1025 (1889)(quotation is unattributed in the original)("It has been truly said by a philosophical writer that 'the subject of criminal attempt, though it presses itself upon the attention wherever we walk through the fields of the criminal law, is very obscure in the books, and apparently not well understood either by the text-writers or the judges'"), quoted in Wagner, A Few Good Laws: Why Federal Criminal Law Needs a General Attempt Provision and How Military Law Can Provide One, 78 UNIVERSITY OF CINCINNATI LAW REVIEW 1043, 1051 n.18 (2010).

[8] The American Law Institute began drafting the Model Penal Code in 1952. Its final draft was approved a decade later in May, 1962. The Institute published revised Commentaries in 1985, American Law Institute, MODEL PENAL CODE AND COMMENTARIES, Pt. 1, i, ii (1985). See generally, Wechsler, Jones & Korn, The Treatment of Inchoate Crimes in the

Model Penal Code of the American Law Institute: Attempt. Solicitation, and Conspiracy, 61COLUMBIA LAW REVIEW 571 (1961).

[9] "Article 5 undertakes to deal systematically with attempt, solicitation and conspiracy. These offenses have in common the fact that they deal with conduct that is designed to culminate in the commission of a substantive offense, but has failed in the discrete case to do so or has not yet achieved its culmination because there is something that the actor or another still must do. The offense are inchoate in this sentence," American Law Institute, MODEL PENAL CODE AND COMMENTARIES (Model Penal Code), Pt. 1, 293 (1985).

[10] For a discussion of some of the diversity of state law see, Cahill, Attempt by Omission, 94 IOWA LAW REVIEW. 1207 (2009).

[11] Public Law 89-801, 80 Stat. 1516 (1966), created the National Commission on Reform of Federal Criminal Laws.

[12] FINAL REPORT OF THE NATIONAL COMMISSION ON REFORM OF FEDERAL CRIMINAL LAWS: A PROPOSED NEW FEDERAL CRIMINAL CODE (TITLE 18, UNITED STATES CODE)(Final Report), Ch. 10 (1971).

[13] Efforts to enact to the National Commission's s recommendations effectively ended on April 27, 1982, when the closure motion on S. 1630 (97th Cong.), which would have enacted an amended version of the Commission's recommendations, failed in the Senate, 128 Cong. Rec. 7777 (1982).

[14] "There must be in the case of robbery ... something feloniously taken, for alto anciently ... an attempt to rob was reputed felony, voluntas reputabatur pro facto [(intent is to be regarded as the act)] yet the law is held otherwise at this day, and for a long time since the time of Edward III [1326-1377]." I HALE'S PLEAS OF THE CROWN 532 (1678) (internal citations omitted and transliteration and translation supplied), quoted in Sayre, Criminal Attempts, 41 HARVARD LAW REVIEW 821, 821 n.1 (1928). The ancient sentiment still lingers, however, see Garvey, Are Attempts Like Treason? 14 NEW CRIMINAL LAW REVIEW 173, (2011)("If the state can legitimately criminalize only wrongs that cause or risk harm, and if it respects the fact that an actor who sets out to commit a crime can always change his mind until he takes the last step, we are apt to end up with a law of attempts in which an attempt is a crime only when the actor has taken the last step, or come very close to taking it. Perhaps it should be that way. My suggestion here, however, is that an actor who chooses to form the intent to commit a crime, and who perhaps in addition resolves to commit it, has violated a duty of loyalty to his fellow citizens, and a state should be permitted to punish him for that breach. Perhaps it can do so while keeping faith with liberalism. Perhaps not").

[15] Model Penal Code §5.01(1)(c). The Model Penal Code's alternative definitions provided: "A person is guilty of an attempt to commit a crime, if acting with the kind of culpability otherwise required for commission of the crime, he: (a) purposely engages in conduct that would constitute the crime if the attendant circumstances were as he believes them to be; or (b) when causing a particular result is an element of the crime, does or omits to do anything with the purpose of causing or with the belief that it will cause such result without further conduct on his part." Id. at §5.01(1)(a), (b).

[16] Id. at §5.01(2).

[17] Final Report §1001(1).

[18] Id.

[19] E.g., ALA. CODE § 13-4-2 ("(a) A person is guilty of an attempt to commit a crime if, with the intent to commit a specific offense, he does any overt act towards the commission of such offense"); ALASKA STAT. §11.31.1001("(a) A person is guilty of an attempt to

commit a crime if, with the intent to commit a crime, the person engages in conduct which constitutes a substantial step toward the commission of that crime"); COLO. REV. STAT. ANN. §18-2-101("(1) A person commits criminal attempt if, acting with the kind of culpability otherwise required for commission of an offense, he engages in conduct constituting a substantial step toward the commission of the offense. A substantial step is any conduct, whether act, omission, or possession, which is strongly corroborative of the firmness of the actor's purpose to complete the commission of the offenses.").

[20] E.g., CONN. GEN. STAT. ANN. §53a-49(b). The states more often include a corroboration definition or requirement comparable to that of the Commission's recommendation, e.g., N.D. Cent. Code Ann. §12.1-06-01 [1] ("A 'substantial step' is any conduct which is strongly corroborative of the firmness of the actor's intent to complete the commission of the crime."); TENN. CODE ANN. §39-12-101(b)("Conduct does not constitute a substantial step under subdivision (a)(3), unless the person's entire course of action is corroborative of the intent to commit the offense"); WYO. STATS. ANN. §6- 1-301(a)(i)("A 'substantial step' is conduct which is strongly corroborative of the firmness of the person's intention to complete the commission of the crime").

[21] United States v. Resendez-Ponce, 549 U.S. 102, 107 (2007); see also, United States v. Pires, 642 F.3d 1, 9 (1st Cir. 2011); United States v. Manzo, 636 F.3d 56, 66 (3d Cir. 2011); United Stats v. Farhane, 634 F.3d 127, 145 (2d Cir. 2011); United States v. Sanchez, 615 F.3d 836, 843 (7th Cir. 2010); United States v. Robertson, 606 F.3d 943, 953 (8th Cir. 2010); United States v. Lee, 603 F.3d 904, 913-14 (11th Cir. 2010); United States v. Mincoff, 574 F.3d 1186, 1195 (9th Cir. 2009); United States v. Barlow, 568 F.3d 215, 219 (5th Cir. 2009); United States v. Vigil, 523 F.3d 1258, 1267 (10th Cir. 2008); United States v. Wesley, 417 F.3d 612, 618 (6th Cir. 2005); United States v. Pratt, 351 F.3d 131, 135 (4th Cir. 2003); United States v. Washington, 106 F.3d 983, 1005 (D.C. Cir. 1997). The crime which is object of the attempt is alternatively referred as the underlying offense, the substantive offense, or the predicate offense.

[22] E.g., United States v. Pires, 642 F.3d 1, 8 (1st Cir. 2011); United States v. Manzo, 636 F.3d 56, 66 (3d Cir. 2011); United States v. Farhane, 634 F.3d 127, 145 (2d Cir. 2011); United States v. Dobbs, 629 F.3d 1199, 1208 (10th Cir. 2011); United States v. Sanchez, 615 F.3d 836, 843 (7th Cir. 2010); United States v. Wahlstrom, 588 F.3d 538, 543 (8th Cir. 2009); United States v. Mincoff, 574 F.3d 1186, 1195 (9th Cir. 2009); in some instances, they will characterize this as "act[ing] with the culpability required to commit the underlying substantive offense," United States v. Barlow, 568 F.3d 215, 219 (5th Cir. 2009); see also, United States v. Tykarsky, 446 F.3d 458, 469 (3d Cir. 2006)("acting with the kind of culpability otherwise required for commission of the crime").

[23] United States v. Dobbs, 629 F.3d 1199, 1208 (10th Cir. 2011)(here and hereafter internal citations and quotation marks hare been omitted)("In some instances, defining conduct which constitutes a substantial step has proved to be a thorny task"); United States v. Pratt, 351 F.3d 131, 136 (4th Cir. 2003), quoting, Chief Judge Learned Hand in United States v. Coplon, 185 F.2d 629, 633 (2d Cir. 1950)("The decisions are to numerous to cite, and would not help much anyway, for there is, and obviously can be, no definite line between preparation and attempt").

[24] United States v. Bauer, 626 F.3d 1004, 1008 (8th Cir. 2010); United States v. Barlow, 568 F.3d 215, 219 (5th Cir. 2009); United States v. Vigil, 523 F.3d 1258, 1267 (10th Cir. 2008).

[25] United States v. Sanchez, 615 F.3d 836, 844 (7th Cir. 2010)("[A] substantial step is an overt act strongly corroborative of the firmness of the defendant's criminal intent"); United States v. Lee, 603 F.3d 904, 914 (11th Cir. 2010)("[A] defendant takes a substantial step toward

completing a crime when his objective acts mark his conduct as criminal and, as a whole, strongly corroborate the required culpability"); United States v. Wesley, 417 F.3d 612, 618-19 (6th Cir. 2005)("Because of the problems of proving intent in attempt cases and the danger of convicting for mere thoughts, desires, or motives, we require that the substantial step consist of objective acts that mark the defendant's conduct as criminal in nature. This objective conduct must unequivocally corroborate the required subjective intent to engage in the criminal conduct").

[26] United States v. Dobbs, 629 F.3d at 1208 ("A substantial step is an appreciable fragment of a crime and an action of such substantiality that, unless frustrated, the crime would have occurred"); United States v. Sanchez, 615 F.3d at 844 ("[A] substantial step must be something that makes it reasonably clear that had the defendant not been interrupted or made a mistake he would have completed the crime"); United States v. Morris, 549 F.3d 548, 550 (7th Cir. 2008)("The substantial step required for conviction of attempt toward completion is the demonstration of dangerousness, and has been usefully described a some overt act adapted to, approximating, and which in the ordinary and likely course of things will result in, the commission the particular crime").

[27] United States v. Farhane, 634 F.3d 127, 147 (2d Cir. 2011)("A substantial step must be something more than mere preparation, yet may be less than the last act necessary before the actual commission of the substantive crime"); United States v. Bauer, 626 F.3d at 1008); United States v. DeMarce, 564 F.3d 989, 998 (8th Cir. 2009).

[28] United States v. Farhane, 634 F.3d at 147, 148 ("While the parameters of the substantial step requirement are simply stated, they do not always provide bright lines for application. This is not surprising; the identification of a substantial step, like the identification of attempt itself, is necessarily a matter of degree, that can vary depending on the particular facts of each case viewed in light of the crime charged. An act that may constitute a substantial step towards the commission of one crime may not constitute such a step with respect to a different crime. Thus, substantial-step analysis necessarily begins with a proper understanding of the crime being attempted.... Further important to a substantial-step assessment is an understanding of the underlying conduct proscribed by the crime being attempted. The conduct here at issue, material support to a foreign terrorist organization, is different from drug trafficking and any number of activities (e.g., murder, robbery, fraud) that are criminally proscribed because they are inherently harmful. The material support statute criminalizes a range of conduct that may not be harmful in itself but that may assist, even indirectly, organizations committed to pursuing acts of devastating harm.... Accordingly, while a substantial step to commit a robbery must be conduct planned clearly to culminate in that particular harm, a substantial step towards the provision of material support need not be planned to culminate in actual terrorist harm, but only in support – even benign support – for an organization committed to such harm"); United States v. Sanchez, 615 F.3d at 844 ("The line between mere preparation and a substantial step is inherently fact specific; conduct that would appear to be mere preparation in one case might qualify as a substantial step in another").

[29] Holmes, THE COMMON LAW, 68 (1938 ed.)(emphasis added)("Eminent judges have been puzzled where to draw the line, or even to state the principle on which it should be drawn, between the two sets of cases. But the principle is believed to be similar to that on which all other lines are drawn by the law. Public policy, that is to say, legislative considerations, are at the bottom of the matter; the considerations being, in this case, the nearness of the danger, the greatness of the harm, and the degree of apprehension felt").

[30] United States v. Pires, 642 F.3d 1, 6 (1st Cir. 2011); United States v. Manzo, 636 F.3d 56, 66 (3d Cir. 2011).

[31] United States v. Manzo, 636 F.3d at 58. Manzo, a candidate for elective office, had been charged with attempted extortion under color of official right based on official actions he would take or omit if elected. The court observed that, "[a] Hobbs Act inchoate offense prohibits a person acting 'under color of official right' from attempting ... to use his or her public office in exchange for payments. It does not prohibit a private person who is a candidate from attempting ... to use a future public office to extort money.... To sustain an 'under color of official right' Hobbs Act charge here would create a 'legal alchemy with the power to transform any gap in the facts into a cohesive extortion charge.'" Id. at 68-9.

[32] United States v. Ballinger, 395 F.3d 1218, 1239 n.8 (11th Cir. 2005); see also, United States v. Tykarsky, 446 F.3d at 465. For a criticism of state law in the area see, Hasnas, Once More unto the Breach: The Inherent Liberalism of the Criminal Law and Liability for Attempting the Impossible, 54 HASTINGS LAW JOURNAL 1 (2002).

[33] United States v. Rehak, 589 F.3d 965, 971 (8th Cir. 2009).

[34] United States v. Bauer, 626 F.3d 1004, 1007 (8th Cir. 2010)("Factual impossibility, however, generally is not a defense to an inchoate offense such as attempt, because a defendant's success in attaining his criminal objective is not necessary for an attempt conviction"); United States v. Cote, 504 F.3d 682, 687 (7th Cir. 2007)("This view is merely an application of the well-established principle that factual impossibility or mistake of act is not a defense to an attempt charge ... Futile attempts because of factual impossibility are attempts still the same. For an attempt conviction, the Government was required to prove [only] that Mr. Cote acted with the specific intent to commit the underlying crime and that he took a substantial step towards completion of the offense"); see also, United States v. Manzo, 636 F.3d 56, 66 (3d Cir. 2011); United States v. Sims, 428 F.3d 945, 959-60 (10th Cir. 2005)(citing cases in accord from the Fifth, Ninth, and Eleventh Circuits).

[35] United States v. Manzo, 636 F.3d at 67.

[36] United States v. Tykarsky, 446 F.3d at 465-66.

[37] Id. at 465.

[38] Model Penal Code §5.01(1)(a).

[39] Final Report §1001(1).

[40] E.g., COLO. REV. STAT. ANN. §18-2-101(1)("Factual or legal impossibility of committing the offense is not a defense if the offense could have been committed had the attendant circumstances been as the actor believed them to be"); GA. CODE §16-4-4; ILL. COMP. STAT. ANN. ch. 720 §5/8-4(b)("It is not a defense to a charge of attempt that because of a misapprehension of the circumstances it would have been impossible for the accused to commit the offense attempted").

[41] United States v. Manzo, 636 F.3d at 67 n.10 ("[L]egal impossibility can sometimes be a defense to a crime"); United States v. Ballinger, 395 F.3d at 1238 ("The traditional view is that legal impossibility is a defense to the charge of attempt"); United States v. Joiner, 418 F.3d 863, 869 (8th Cir. 2005)("Even if we assume arguendo, legal impossibility is a defense."); but see, United States v. Yang, 281 F.3d 534, 542 (6th Cir. 2002)("The court [in United States v. Hsu, 155 F.3d 189 (3d Cir. 1998)] noted that virtually no other circuit continued to recognize the defense of legal impossibility, and that even in the Third Circuit the defense had been severely limited").

[42] United States v. Bauer, 626 F.3d 1004, 1007 (8th Cir. 2010)("Bauer's first contention is one of factual impossibility.... Bauer intended to receive child pornography, but failed only because of circumstances unknown to him [i.e., his solicitation was addressed to an

undercover agent rather than a 14-year old child"); United States v. Rothensberg, 610 F.3d 621, 626 (11th Cir. 2010)("[T]o prove an attempted exploitation offense under 18 U.S.C. §2422(b), the Government does not have to prove the existence or identity of a specific minor victim; a fictitious minor will suffice so long as the defendant understood and believed that a minor was involved"); United States v. Morris, 549 F.3d 548, 550 (7th Cir. 2008)("[T]he fact that a defendant is mistaken in thinking that the person he is trying to entice is underage is not a defense to a charge of attempted illegal sexual contact with a minor"); United States v. Rankin, 487 F.3d 229, 231 (5th Cir. 2007)(The fact that the defendant delivered a bomb to an undercover agent rather a murder-intending spouse did not preclude—on factual impossibility grounds—application of the attempt sentencing guideline); United States v. Sims, 428 F.3d 945, 959-60 (10th Cir. 2005)("[A]s to his Count One conviction for attempting to entice a minor, factual impossibility is generally not a defense to criminal attempt.... We agree with our sister circuits ... it is not a defense to an offense involving enticement and exploitation of minors that the defendant falsely believed a minor to be involved"); United States v. Hamrick, 43 F.3d 877, 884-85 (4th Cir. 1995)("Hamrick's bomb, as constructed, may have been incapable of functioning as a bomb.... Hamrick also claims that the district court erred by refusing to instruct the jury on the theory of legal impossibility as a defense to the charge of attempted murder.... Though not denominated as such, Hamrick appears to have been actually seeking an instruction on factual impossibility.... However, factual impossibility is traditionally not a defense to a charge of attempt").

[43] United States v. Tykarsky, 446 F.3d 458, 466 (3d Cir. 2006)("We, however, find it unnecessary to resolve this thorny semantical questions here ... After examining the text of the statute, its broad purpose and its legislative history, we conclude that Congress did not intend to allow the use of an adult decoy, rather than an actual minor, to be asserted as a defense to §2422(b)"); United States v. Yang, 281 F.3d 534, (6th Cir. 2002)("[T]he Third Circuit ... reviewed its holding in United States v. Everett ... that legal impossibility is not a defense to the charge of attempted distribution of a controlled substance under 21 U.S.C. §846. Consistent with the analysis in Everett, the Hsu Court reviewed the legislative history of the EEA.... Accordingly, the court concluded that legal impossibility is not a defense to a charge of attempted theft of trade secrets.... We find persuasive the logic and reasoning of the Third Circuit").

[44] Model Penal Code §5.01(4)("When an actor's conduct would otherwise constitute an attempt ... it is an affirmative defense that he abandoned his effort to commit the crime or otherwise prevented its commission, under circumstances manifesting a complete and voluntary renunciation of his criminal purpose.").

[45] Id. ("[R]enunciation of criminal purpose is not voluntary if it is motivated, in whole or in part, by circumstances, not present or apparent at the inception of the actor's course of conduct, that increase the probability of detection or apprehension or that make more difficult the accomplishment of the criminal purpose. Renunciation is not complete if it is motivated by a decision to postpone the criminal conduct until a more advantageous time or to transfer the criminal effort to another but similar objective or victim").

[46] Final Report §1005(3)(a), (c).

[47] E.g., MINN. STAT. ANN. §609.17[subd.3]("It is a defense to a charge of attempt that the crime was not committed because the accused desisted voluntarily and in good faith and abandoned the intention to commit the crime"); MONT. CODE ANN. §45-4-103(4)("A person is not liable under this section if, under circumstances manifesting a voluntary and complete renunciation of criminal purpose, the person avoided the commission of the

offense attempted by abandoning the person's criminal effort"); N.H. REV. STAT. ANN. §629.1[III]("(a) It is an affirmative defense to prosecution under this section that the actor voluntarily renounces his criminal purpose by abandoning his effort to commit the crime or otherwise preventing its commission under circumstances manifesting a complete withdrawal of his criminal purpose. (b) A renunciation is not 'voluntary' if it is substantially motivated by circumstances the defendant was not aware of at the inception of his conduct which increase the probability of his detection or which make more difficult the commission of the crime. Renunciation is not complete if the purpose is to postpone the criminal conduct until a more advantageous time or to transfer the criminal effort to another but similar objective or victim").

[48] United States v. Williams, 605 F.3d 556, 569 (8th Cir. 2010); United States v. Gonzalez, 596 F.3d 1228, 1234 (10th Cir. 2010); United States v. Eppolito, 543 F.3d 25, 29 (2d Cir. 2008).

[49] United States v. Young, 613 F.3d 735, 745 (8th Cir. 2010)("We hold today that a defendant cannot abandon an attempt once it has been completed. We emphasize that all of our sister circuits that have faced this issue have either held that a defendant cannot abandon a completed attempt or have alluded to such a determination")(citing cases in accord from the Second, Sixth and Ninth Circuits).

[50] Final Report §1001(3)("Criminal attempt is an offense of the same class as the offense attempted, except that *(a) an attempt to commit a Class A felony shall be a Class B felony, and (b) whenever it is established by a preponderance of the evidence at sentencing that the conduct constituting the attempt did not come dangerously close to commission of the crime, an attempt to commit a Class B felony shall be a Class C Felony and attempt to commit a Class C felony shall be a Class A misdemeanor"); Model Penal Code §5.05.

[51] E.g., ALA. CODE §13A-4-2(d)("An attempt is a: (1) Class A felony if the offense attempted is murder. (2) Class A felony if the offense attempted is a Class A felony. (3) Class C felony if the offense attempted is a Class B felony. (4) Class A misdemeanor if the offense attempted is a Class C felony. (5) Class B misdemeanor if the offense attempted is a Class A misdemeanor. (6) Class C misdemeanor if the offense attempted is a Class B misdemeanor. (7) Violation if the offense attempted is a Class C misdemeanor"); see also, ALASKA STAT. §11.31.100(d); ARIZ. REV. STAT. ANN. §13- 1001[C]; CALF. PENAL CODE §664 ("Every person who attempts to commit any crime ... shall be punished where no provision is made by law for the punishment of those attempts, as follows: (a) If the crime attempted is punishable by imprisonment in the state prison, the person guilty of the attempt shall be punished by imprisonment in the state prison for one-half of the term of imprisonment prescribed upon a conviction of the offense attempted. However, if the crime attempted is ... murder, as defined in Section 189, the person guilty of that attempt shall be punished by imprisonment in the state prison for life with the possibility of parole.").

[52] E.g., DEL. CODE ANN. tit.11 §531("Attempt to commit a crime is an offense of the same grade and degree as the most serious offense which the accused is found guilty of attempting"); IND. CODE ANN. §35-41-5-1(a)("An attempt to commit a crime is a felony or misdemeanor of the same class as the crime attempted. However, at attempt to commit murder is a Class A felony"); N.H. REV. STAT. ANN. §629.1[IV]("The penalty for attempt is the same as that authorized for the crime that was attempted, except that in the case of attempt to commit murder the punishment shall be imprisonment for life or such other term as the court shall order").

[53] E.g., 21 U.S.C. 846(attempted drug offenses); 18 U.S.C. 32(a)(attempted destruction of aircraft or their facilities), 1594(a)(attempts to commit certain human trafficking offenses). In many instances, attempt is interwoven with the elements of the underlying offense, e.g., 18 U.S.C.

984(f)(1)(destruction of U.S. property)("Whoever maliciously damages or destroys, or attempts to damage or destroy, by means of fire or explosives ... shall be imprisoned for not less than 5 years and not more than 20 years, fined under this title, or both"), 1956(a)(1)(money laundering)("Whoever ... conducts or attempts to conduct such a financial transaction ... shall be sentenced to a fine of not more than $500,000 ... or imprisonment for not more than twenty years, or both").

[54] U.S.S.G. §2X1.1(a). When imposing sentence for a violation of federal law, a court must begin by calculating the sentencing range recommended by the Guidelines for a particular case, Gall v. United States, 552 U.S. 38, 49 (2007). The result is advisory, to be considered along with other statutory factors under 18 U.S.C. 3553(a). The resulting sentence will survive appellate scrutiny if it is procedurally and substantively reasonable. A sentence is procedurally reasonable if it is free of procedural error, "such as failing to calculate (or improperly calculating) the Guidelines range, treating the Guidelines as mandatory, failing to consider the §3553(a) factors, selecting a sentence based on clearly erroneous factors, or failing to adequately explain the chosen sentence – including an explanation of any deviation from the Guidelines range," Gall v. United States, 552 U.S. at 51. The Guidelines and subsection 3553(a) factors weigh heavily in the totality of the circumstances assessment of whether a particular sentence is substantively reasonable, Id.

[55] U.S.S.G. §2X1.1(b)(" [D]ecrease by 3 [offense] levels, unless the defendant completed all the acts the defendant believed necessary for successful completion of the substantive offense or the circumstances demonstrate that the defendant was about to complete all such acts but for apprehension or interruption by some similar event beyond the defendant's control"), (c)(exceptions for attempts to commit certain assault, drug, tampering offenses), (d)(exceptions for attempts to commit various terrorism offenses).

[56] United States v. Johnson, 639 F.3d 433, 439 (8th Cir. 2011)("A defendant's success in attaining his criminal objective is not necessary for an attempt conviction"); United States v. Iribe, 564 F.3d 1155, 1161 (9th Cir. 2009); United States v. Dixon, 449 F.3d 194, 202 (1st Cir. 2006); United States v. Sims, 428 F.3d 945, 959-60 (10th Cir. 2005); United States v. Washington, 106 F.3d 983, 1004 (D.C.Cir. 1997).

[57] Sayre, Criminal Attempts, 41 HARVARD LAW REVIEW 821, 838 n. 66 (1928)("Thus, it has been held that there cannot be a conviction for an attempt where the proof shows that the crime attempted was carried through to successful completion. Graham v. People, 181 Ill. 477, 55 N.E. 179 (1899); People v. Stanton, 106 Cal. 139, 39 Pac. 525 (1895); Regina v. Nicholls, 2 Cox C.C. 1847). Contra: State v. Shepard, 7 Conn. 54 (1828)"). States have sometimes crafted explicit rejections in order to escape such precedents, e.g., IDAHO CODE §18-305 ("Any person may be convicted of an attempt to commit a crime, although it appears on the trial that the crime intended or attempted was perpetrated by such person in pursuance of such attempt."); LA. REV. STAT. ANN. §14:27[C]; MONT. CODE ANN. §45-4-103(5)("Proof of the completed offense does not bar conviction for the attempt").

[58] United States v. Malasanos, 472 F.2d 642, 643 (7the Cir. 1973); United States v. York, 578 F.2d 1036, 1040 (5th Cir. 1978)("Proof that a crime had been competed does not absolve the defendants of the attempt"); United States v. Iribe, 564 F.3d 1155, 1161 (9th Cir. 2009).

[59] United States v. Dixon, 509 U.S. 688, 696 (1993); United States v. Pires, 642 F.3d 1, 10 (1st Cir. 2011); United States v. Basciano, 599 F.3d 184, 196 (2d Cir. 2010).

[60] United States v. Mahdi, 598 F.3d 883, 888 (D.C.Cir. 2010); United States v. Robertson, 606 F.3d 943, 950-51 (8th Cir. 2010).

[61] United States v. Pumpkin Seed, 575 F.3d 552, 562 (8th Cir. 2009); United States v. D'Amico, 496 F.3d 95, 99-100 (1st Cir. 2007); United States v. Mitchell, 484 F.3d 762, 773 (5th Cir. 2007).

[62] Other examples include 18 U.S.C. 1594 (human trafficking) and 21 U.S.C. 846 (controlled substances).

[63] 18 U.S.C. 1344 ("Whoever knowingly executes, or attempts to execute, a scheme or artifice – (1) to defraud a financial institution ... shall be fined not more than $1,000,000 or imprisoned not more than 30 years, or both"); see also, 18 U.S.C. 1347 (health care fraud) and 18 U.S.C. 1348 (securities and commodities fraud).

[64] For a general discussion of judicial treatment of "attempt to attempt," "conspiracy to attempt," and "attempt to conspire" cases in both state and federal courts see, Robbins, Double Inchoate Crimes, 26 HARVARD JOURNAL ON LEGISLATION 1 (1989).

[65] Final Report, §1005(1)("An offense defined in sections 1001 to 1004 [(criminal attempt, facilitation, solicitation, and conspiracy)] shall not apply to another offense defined in sections 1001 to 1004"); Model Penal Code §5.04(3)("A person may not be convicted of more than one offense defined by this Article for conduct designed to commit or to culminate in the commission of the same crime").

[66] E.g., ME. REV. STAT. ANN. tit. 17-A §154[1]("It shall not be a crime to conspire to commit, or to attempt, or solicit, any crime set forth in this chapter [relating to the crimes of general application: attempt, conspiracy, and solicitation]"); N.D. CENT. CODE §12.1-06-05; ORE. REV. STAT. ANN. §161.485.

[67] United States v. Iribe, 564 F.3d 1155, 1160-161 (9th Cir. 2009); see also, United States v. Farhane, 634 F.3d 127, 144-45 (2d Cir. 2011)(uphold the defendants convictions for conspiring to provided material support to a foreign terrorist organization and for attempting to do so).

[68] 18 U.S.C. 373.

[69] 18 U.S.C. 2 ("(a) Whoever commits an offense against the United States or aids, abets, counsels, commands, induces or procures its commission, is punishable as a principal. (b) Whoever willfully causes an act to be done which if directly performed by him or another would be an offense against the United States, is punishable as a principal").

[70] 18 U.S.C. 371.

[71] United States v. Mendez, 528 F.3d 811, 815 (11th Cir. 2008); United States v. Douglas, 398 F.3d 407, 412 (6th Cir. 2005); United States v. Jackson, 33 F.3d 866, 871-72 (7th Cir. 1994).

[72] 18 U.S.C. 201(b).

[73] United States v. Peleti, 576 F.3d 377, 382-83 (7th Cir. 2009); United States v. Valle, 538 F.3d 341, 346-47 (5th Cir. 2008); United States v. Quinn, 3598 F.3d 666, 673 (4th Cir. 2004).

[74] 18 U.S.C. 201(b)("Whoever – (1) directly or indirectly, corruptly gives, offers or promises anything of value to any public official ... with intent – (A) to influence any official act; or ... (2) being a public official ... directly or indirectly, corruptly demands, seeks, receives, accepts, or agrees to receive or accept anything of value personally or for any other person or entity, in return for: (A) being influenced in the performance of any official act ... shall be fined under this title ... or imprisoned for not more than fifteen years, or both").

[75] See e.g., United States v. Turner, 548 F.3d 1094, 1096 (D.C.Cir. 2008); United States v. Wantuck, 525 F.3d 505, 510- 11 (7th Cir. 2008); United States v. Coker, 514 F.3d 562, 566 (6th Cir. 2008).

[76] 18 U.S.C. 2(a).

[77] United States v. Pol-Flores, 644 F.3d 1, 4 (1st Cir. 2011)("To be subject to aiding and abetting liability, an individual must have in some way associated himself with the fraudulent scheme and shared the criminal intent of the principal"); United States v. Devries, 630 F.3d 1130, 1133 (8th Cir. 2011);("Liability under that theory [(aiding and abetting)] requires the government to prove that a defendant associated himself with and participated in an unlawful venture in a way that shows he wished to bring it about, and that he acted to make the venture succeed"); United States v. Petersen, 622 F.3d 196, 208 (3d Cir. 2010)("To convict a person of aiding and abetting, the government must prove beyond a reasonable doubt: (1) that the substantive crime has been committed; and (2) that the defendant charged with aiding and abetting knew of the commission of the substantive offense and acted with intent to facilitate it").

[78] United States v. Bristol-Martir, 570 F.3d 29, 45 (1st Cir. 2009)(finding evidence sufficient to conviction on a charge of aiding and abetting an attempt to possess narcotics with the intent to distribute, but vacating on other grounds); United States v. Partida, 385 F.3d 546, 560 (5th Cir. 2004)(evidence sufficient to uphold a conviction for attempting to aid and abet possession of a controlled substance with intent to distribute); United States v. Samuels, 308 F.3d 662, 668 (6th Cir. 2002)(upholding a conviction for aiding and abetting an attempt to possess cocaine with the intent to distribute); United States v. Washington, 106 F.3d 983, 1003 (D.C.Cir. 1997)(same).

INDEX